The Arid Lands

By
JOHN WESLEY POWELL

Edited by Wallace Stegner

With a foreword by John Vernon

UNIVERSITY OF NEBRASKA PRESS
LINCOLN AND LONDON

First Nebraska paperback printing: 2004
Originally published as *Report on the Lands of the Arid Region of the United States: With a More Detailed Account of the Lands of Utah*

Library of Congress Cataloging-in-Publication Data
Powell, John Wesley, 1834–1902.
[Report on the lands of the arid region of the United States]
The arid lands / by John Wesley Powell; edited by Wallace Stegner; with a foreword by John Vernon.
p.   cm.
Originally published: Report on the lands of the arid region of the United States. Cambridge: Belknap Press of Harvard University Press, 1962.
Includes index.
ISBN 0-8032-8781-X (pbk.: alk. paper)
1. Arid regions—United States.   2. Public lands—United States.   3. Arid regions—West (U.S.)   4. Public lands—West (U.S.)   5. Arid regions—Utah.
6. Public lands—Utah.   I. Stegner, Wallace Earle, 1909–   II. Title.
HD1671.U5P68   2004
333.73'0978—dc22   2004015894

FOREWORD

John Vernon

On May 24, 1869, the one-armed Civil War hero John Wesley Powell and his motley crew of nine began what proved to be a lucky and brilliant—as well as foolish and tragic—expedition down the Green and the Colorado rivers and through the Grand Canyon. Their goal was to explore and map the last remaining *terra incognita* of what is today the lower forty-eight states. Powell's scrofulous group consisted of trappers, traders, and greasy mountain men, his own mind-damaged brother, a Scottish bullwhacker, a Denver Sunday School teacher, and an English tourist who appeared just a few days before the boats launched from Green River, Wyoming, and begged to be included.

When looking back at certain events enshrined in history, it can be difficult to imagine just how improvised they were or how they sometimes hung by a thread at any given moment of their unfolding. Powell's successful thousand-mile-long expedition, a mishmash of unanticipated disasters and careful planning based on insufficient knowledge, gave its leader his fifteen minutes of fame and resulted in the death of three crew members. (The trio, discouraged by a leader whom they considered a martinet and by the interminability of what they called a "granite prison"—now known as the Grand Canyon—abandoned the expedition, climbed out of the canyon, and most likely were killed by a band of Paiute Indians. We can't be certain of their fate since their bodies were never recovered. Moreover, when Powell returned to the canyon a year later he seems not to have been especially interested in recovering them. It could have been sour grapes: several of Powell's men blamed him for the loss, accusing him of being a dismissive leader who didn't give a damn about his men.)

Powell's account of the trip, initially published in *Scribner's* magazine and later in book form by the Smithsonian Institution (in 1875), was the first to bring a stunning landscape—the arid canyon country of the Southwest—to the American public's attention. Brutal, monumental, eerily beautiful, and capable of a crushing sameness relieved by a thousand little nuances, this land today is a memorial to a West that once compelled explorers and settlers to adapt to its limitations and harsh conditions. Adaptation is still necessary, of course; every year people lose lives and livelihoods in that country. But in Powell's time adaptation was a way of life, not a weekend's recreation, and it colored the attitudes and ultimately the policies of a man who went on to become a prime mover in the creation of the U.S. Geological Survey and its director for thirteen years.

The career of this remarkable, impetuous, and endlessly curious man can be split right down the chronological middle. In 1872, little more than halfway through his life, he and his wife bought a house in Washington DC, where he spent most of the rest of his sixty-eight years. A pioneering geologist, a member of the National Academy of Sciences, founding director of the Smithsonian's Bureau of Ethnology, head of the U.S. Geological Survey, and an advisor to Congress on land and water policy in the West, for thirty years Powell was the consummate Washington scientist-bureaucrat. In this capacity, he wrote *The Arid Lands* (originally published as *Report on the Lands of the Arid Region of the United States*), which in fact contains two suggested bills for Congress, neither of which made it out of the Public Lands Committee. Powell's failure to convince Congress to adopt his ideas about settling the West has not diminished his reputation, however. Instead, it has made him something of an environmental martyr, the man always quoted when historians and conservationists say, "I told you so."

In contrast to his career as a Washington policy maven, the early John Wesley Powell was a man of action, someone who for the first half of his life never stopped exploring. As a young man living in Wisconsin, he rowed up and down the Mississippi River (once as far as New Orleans) and tramped across the upper Midwest, collecting shells and fossils. He enlisted in the Union army as a private and quickly rose through the ranks. After losing an arm at Shiloh, he stayed on at the urging of General Grant, eventually achieving the rank of major. During the 1869 exploration he repeatedly climbed the steep sides of canyons through which the expedition floated, sometimes scrambling and worming his way up fissures and chimneys with only one arm. He once found himself trapped on the ledge of a cliff until a crew member stripped off his long johns and lowered them as an improvised rope to rescue him. On that same trip the group encountered nearly five hundred rapids, many portaged but most of them run. The expedition was followed two years later by a second journey along the same route, during which Powell sat on a kitchen chair nailed to a platform on the lead boat, to scout the river ahead.

The *Report on the Exploration of the Colorado River* was published in 1875; *The Arid Lands* appeared three years later. Yet the difference between the two reports could not be greater. In them—within the very language used—the two Powells can be seen: the restless adventurer and the sedentary scholar-bureaucrat. The former book is full of stately pines and furs, plunging cataracts, profound chasms, and gloomy solitudes. Its language is that of a sentimental age, a late-romantic rhapsody packed with formulaic phrases and effusions. In the preface Powell himself describes the difficulty of "painting in word colors," which is perhaps why he included in the book a series of etchings that embody a melodramatic romanticism. To be sure, *Report on the Exploration of the Colorado River* contains passages of great descriptive power as well as scientific precision, especially in its discussions of landforms and geology. But the overall effect of this first report is to see the West as repository of aesthetic values. In fact, the canyon became *grand* (to borrow from the title of a recent book about the Grand Canyon) largely through Powell's description of it.

Consequently, fans of Powell may be surprised to discover a very different tone and language in *The Arid Lands*. They may also be dismayed that in this second report Powell treats nature not aesthetically but as a field of data, even as an emporium of resources to be "redeemed." Will the real John Wesley Powell please stand up? Is he the proto-environmentalist, the lover of Western landscapes, the preservationist who advocated limited settlement of the West? Is he, as his biographer Donald Worster asserts, the ethnologist whose attitude to American Indians was unusually sympathetic and humane for its time? Or is he the career administrator who saw the West as a treasure house of mineral, timber, and agricultural resources that could be "recovered" only when the Indians were removed?

John Wesley Powell is all of the above. He may have been ahead of his time but he was also *of* his time. Consequently, most of our twenty-first-century categories don't apply to him. The common thread connecting "early" and "late" Powell is his emphasis upon the harsh and limiting conditions of the West, conditions he experienced firsthand during his 1869 voyage. There are two contradictory ways of approaching issues of land use and development, and most of what we humans do falls somewhere between them. One is to modify the land to suit our particular needs—or wants. The other is to modify our needs and wants to suit the limitations of the land and the environment. Though Powell assumed that science and reason should domesticate nature and force it to submit and become productive—as this book's emphasis on irrigation, dam building, and reservoirs makes clear— he also stressed that there was not enough water to domesticate the arid West. He didn't so much call for limited settlement of the West as warn of the limitations that, as he saw it, would naturally and inevitably be imposed on settlers, and he urged Congress to plan accordingly. Consequently, he insisted on smallness in settling western lands and did so with an intensity augmented by a populist distrust of monopolies and big government. Powell advocated small, self-sustaining farming communities that would adapt themselves to the conditions of their place and control their own water, and called for smaller homesteads (80 acres instead of the sacred 160 acres) for farmers with access to irrigation.

Obviously, Powell did not foresee the huge reclamation schemes that would arise following his death: the massive water diversions like the Colorado–Big Thompson project, whose thirteen-mile tunnel cutting through the Continental Divide emerges from the mountains just up the road from my home, or the "main-stem dams" like the Grand Coulee and Hoover that Wallace Stegner discusses in his footnote to this book (23–24). Nor did Powell anticipate the technology of deep drilling into aquifers, which has transformed the Great Plains west of the hundredth meridian into wheeling rings of green—a bizarre, seemingly Christo-inspired polka dot desert—and given the thirsty suburbs of the West another source of water. Neither could he have envisioned the West's mind-blowing increase in population.

He got the scale wrong, in other words, but not the basic principle of limits. *The Arid Lands* is not a repudiation of development but rather a call for rational planning to minimize development's impact by adapting it to conditions that cannot be changed. Aridity, the key to Powell's understanding of the West's geology, was also the key to his settlement policy and it hasn't gone away. Reservoirs can be depleted and aquifers can be pumped dry. Desperate western cities that purchase water rights from farmers as far as a hundred miles away may soon find there are none left to purchase. Water rights, reservoirs, and diversions can be multiplied but, as Powell might say, if the water isn't there it would be like setting out more buckets in the hope of somehow creating more rain.

For all these reasons *The Arid Lands* has become for many the bible for limited development and, like the Bible itself, it has been taken on authority more often than it has been read. Now a new generation of readers may decide for themselves just how relevant Powell's theories continue to be.

Powell was a man of big ideas about smallness, an ambitious, incisive, curious human being whose mind, though it flew off in all directions, nonetheless kept its focus on fundamental principles. He could be stubborn, though, and his single-mindedness sometimes prevented him from imagining what his clever and equally stubborn countrymen could come up with. All the same, if Powell could see the West today—if he could stand, let's say, on the Glen Canyon Dam and see the waterlines recording the sinking level of the lake named (with oblivious irony) for him, or see with x-ray eyes its bottom silting up—he would point out that all of our mega-dams and aquifers are doomed to give us diminishing returns. And he would surely be appalled at the excavated, drilled, overgrazed, bulldozed, coal-fired, strip-mined, strip-malled, super-highwayed, trophy-homed, casinoed, and dumped-on West—a place we could easily obliterate, like children in backyards playing with Tonka Toys, without something like Powell's reminder of restraint.

CONTENTS

REPORT ON THE LANDS OF THE ARID REGION
OF THE UNITED STATES

EDITOR'S INTRODUCTION

On April 1, 1878, Major John Wesley Powell, Director of the United States Geographical and Geological Survey of the Rocky Mountain Region, handed a manuscript report to Carl Schurz, the Secretary of the Interior. It would ultimately be recognized as one of the most important books ever written about the West, and it was understood at once to be loaded with dynamite. Yet it was by no means a finished piece of work, and by no means a model of scientific method. The data assembled in its substantive chapters were tentative, approximate, sometimes hardly better than educated guesses; its final chapter had only the remotest connection with the body of the report; and the generalizations and recommendations in the first two chapters, considering the imperfections of the statistical data, went considerably beyond the bounds of scientific caution.

The taking of calculated risks was a part of Major Powell's temperament. He had lost an arm at Shiloh while a member of Grant's staff. He had been briefly a national hero following his spectacular exploration of the canyons of the Colorado River in 1869. By sheer capacity he had made himself a place among the fiercely jealous and competitive western surveys, wedging himself between Ferdinand Vandiveer Hayden's Geological and Geographical Survey of the Territories (Interior Department), and Lieutenant Wheeler's Geographical Surveys West of the Hundredth Meridian (War Department), and into a sort of informal alliance with Clarence King's Geological Survey of the Fortieth Parallel (also War Department).[1] He had learned in Washington to make his way while keeping an eye on his flanks and his rear, and his resources in 1878 included eleven years of intimate western experience and the help of able and devoted assistants. The scientific imperfections of the report he handed Schurz on April 1 were imperfections of proof merely, not of general understanding, and

[1] Ferdinand Vandiveer Hayden (1829–1887) had made various surveys of the western territories and in 1879 became a geologist of the U.S. Geological Survey under Clarence King (1842–1901). George Montague Wheeler (1842–1905) published his *Report upon the United States Geographical Surveys* in several volumes (1875–1889).

Powell's willingness to publish before the proofs were all in was the product not of carelessness but of urgency. The nature of the report as he presented it showed that his object was not meticulous scientific demonstration with every *t* crossed and every *i* dotted, but something else. The *Report on the Lands of the Arid Region of the United States, with a More Detailed Account of the Lands of Utah* was less a report than a program — even, some western Congressmen would soon begin to say, a manifesto, a revolution.[2]

It went far beyond the limits of his own survey, which was confined to the plateau country of Utah, western Colorado, and northern Arizona, and it went far beyond any possible definition of his duties as a public servant. Though it was hardly more than some hastily assembled and imperfect fragments of his projected study of the Public Domain, the report was a considered move in a campaign which, while it would serve his immediate bureaucratic ends, would also serve the larger purposes he had been clarifying all during his public career. With the advent of President Hayes and Secretary Schurz in 1877, he had become part of a reform administration, and his notions of reform were not picayune. He wanted to start reforming the West from the grassroots, and by changing land and water laws in advance of further settlement, to change its whole institutional base. If his methods were necessarily political, his long-range aims reflected, as Henry Nash Smith has remarked, a voluntary acceptance of public responsibility rare at any time, and in a time still smelling of two Grant administrations almost unbelievable. And more than an acceptance of public responsibility. Prescience, and a refusal to be swept off his feet by the habitual western optimism. When much of the country, and nearly all of the West, had elected to

[2] Extended accounts of the political maneuvering involving the *Arid Region* report and culminating in the consolidation of the western surveys are to be found in Henry Nash Smith, "Clarence King, John Wesley Powell, and the Establishment of the United States Geological Survey," *Mississippi Valley Historical Review*, XXXIII, 37–58 (June 1947); in William Culp Darrah, *Powell of the Colorado* (Princeton, 1951), pp. 237–254; in Harold H. Dunham, *Government Handout. A Study in the Administration of the Public Lands, 1875–1891* (New York, 1941), pp. 64–87; and in Wallace Stegner, *Beyond the Hundredth Meridian* (Boston, 1954), pp. 212–242. All of these studies take pains to relate the report to the complicated and often confused issues of land-law reform, land classification, and the consolidation of the western surveys, and all take off from the pioneer discussion in Walter Webb, *The Great Plains* (Boston, 1931), pp. 385–425.

overlook the fact, or deny it, he saw that the West was an arid land; and when homesteaders, recovering from the grasshopper plagues and the panic of 1873, had filled up the sub-humid lands and were beginning to invade the dry country beyond the 98th meridian, he foresaw that both sub-humid and arid lands lay under the threat of recurrent drought. When Powell presented his report he was convinced that settlement had already reached as far west as it could go without grave risks to both the settlers and the land.

To do any part of what he wanted to do, he had first to survive as a bureaucrat, and survival meant competing with Hayden and Wheeler for prestige and appropriations. Powell's appropriation for 1877–78 had been cut by a third, and he was working hard behind the scenes to gain scientific and congressional friends. The *Report*, plus the map of Utah Territory that accompanied it, was proof of accomplishment. Yet he risked much in presenting them, too, for embedded in his first two chapters were generalizations and proposals certain to make him enemies. As corollaries to his principal suggestions for revision of the 160-acre homestead and modification of the rectangular surveys in the arid lands, Powell's "general plan" contemplated some other changes: the reform of the notoriously corrupt General Land Office, the transfer of the cadastral surveys to the Coast and Geodetic Survey, the elimination of all contract surveying, and the consolidation of the geological and geographical surveys of the West into one bureau under the Department of the Interior.

There, at one blow, were alienated the War Department, the General Land Office, Hayden, Wheeler, and all their several congressional supporters. Add to those the powerful land, cattle, mining, and timber interests of the West, the speculators and peculators busy under the old land laws gobbling the Public Domain by fraud, grab, appropriation, barbed wire, guns, and the election of political yes-men. And add to those the myth-bound citizens for whom the 160-acre homestead, the sturdy pioneer farmer, the freehold yeoman, the "Garden of the World," [3]

[3] For the best analysis of the conflict between fact and fantasy in the settlement of the West, see Henry Nash Smith, *Virgin Land* (Cambridge, 1950), especially Book Three. I have also been privileged to use, in the preparation of this edition of Powell's report, Mr. Smith's "Man and Climate on the Great Plains, 1867–1880: The Biography of an Erroneous Idea" (MS).

and the other shibboleths had all the force of revealed truth. It is possible that Powell did not yet appreciate how strong the coalition could be, and in particular how potent was the force of myth. But even if he had estimated the political opposition at something like its true strength, he would have had to challenge it, because he could see the lands beyond the 98th meridian going in venal, mistaken, or monopolistic ways to great land and water barons, or being chopped to ruinous bits by the advancing front of the rectangular surveys and the tradition-bound, hopeful, ignorant, and doomed homesteaders.[4]

He risked his own future and the future of his bureau because in the sub-humid and arid lands he saw every successive land law, despite pious platitudes about the independent pioneer farmer, being turned to the advantage of monopolistic and often fraudulent practices, or encouraging a kind of agriculture that would not survive the first period of drought. He knew the traditional grid surveys, very efficient in the humid Midwest, to be entirely unsuited to an agriculture based on irrigation or to a ranching economy dependent on vast open ranges and limited water. Irrigation agriculture called for less than the standard 160 acres, stock-farming called for very much more. Pre-emption Act and Homestead Law had allowed a man to gain title, after appropriate residence and improvements, to 320 acres. The Timber Culture Act of 1873, which by its very nature was inapplicable to the arid lands, allowed farmers in the sub-humid belt another 160. But the Desert Land Act of 1877, linked as it was to the rectangular surveys, and making no allowance for the problems of bringing water to claims, served only to delude the hopeful and to encourage fraud by large landholders, principally cattlemen. The Timber and Stone Act which was in the air when Powell submitted his *Arid Region* report would clearly do the same.[5] If one

[4] The homesteading of the arid lands has produced a voluminous literature, some of it filled with the enthusiasm of town-builders and railroad public relations men, and some of it flavored with the nostalgia of a lost cause. For summary discussions, see especially Webb, *The Great Plains*; Everett Dick, *The Sod-House Frontier, 1854–1890* (Lincoln, 1954); Fred A. Shannon, *The Farmer's Last Frontier* (New York, 1935); and the best first-hand report by a dry-land homesteader, Hamlin Garland, *A Son of the Middle Border* (New York, 1925).

[5] The specifications, implications, and effects of the several land laws have had intensive study. See especially Marion Clawson, *Uncle Sam's Acres* (New York, 1951); Dunham, *Government Handout*; Benjamin Hibbard, *A History of the Public Land Policies* (New York, 1924); Louise Peffer, *The Closing of the Public*

really believed in the small-freehold system, and Powell did, it was time to try saving the freeholder from a body of land law that was doing him in. This was the burden of the second chapter of the report, with its model bills empowering the formation of co-operative irrigation and grazing districts composed of irrigation farms of no more than 80 acres and pasturage farms of four full sections, and altering the survey system so that water rights could be tied to land and so that topography and drainage divides could be made to serve, rather than render hopeless, the small farmer's chances.

Behind Powell's general plan was something absolutely basic: the willingness to look at what was, rather than at what fantasy, hope, or private interest said there should be. He was by no means the first to comprehend that the West beyond the 98th meridian was an arid land — it had been marked "Great American Desert" on most maps since Pike's expedition [6] of 1810, and until after the Civil War it was general opinion that the short-grass Plains would prove to be uncultivable. General W. B. Hazen and others were protesting, in the early 1870's, the misrepresentation of western lands by railroads and land companies,[7] and only the presence in Congress of a substantial number of men, mainly easterners, concerned with the consequences of ill-considered settlement allowed Powell to make his move with any hope of success. What made Powell's formulation of the bearish position significant was that for the first time he stated the problem as a whole, in the context of the entire West, and for the first time pointed out practical solutions for the difficulties of both the arid-lands homesteaders and the farmers in the sub-humid belt, where almost-adequate rainfall tempted men into a kind of farming a period of drought could destroy.

There is no reason to repeat here what the report states with the cogency of an equation. All the proofs that have come in

Domain (Palo Alto, 1951); and Roy M. Robbins, Our Landed Heritage. The Public Domain, 1776–1936 (Princeton, c. 1942).

[6] Zebulon Montgomery Pike (1779–1813) published An Account of Expeditions to the Sources of the Mississippi and through the Western Parts of Louisiana in 1810, the chief source of information about his explorations.

[7] William Babcock Hazen (1830–1877) published Our Barren Lands of the 100th Meridian and East of the Sierra Nevadas (1875). See his article, "The Great Middle Region of the United States, and Its Limited Space of Arable Land," North American Review, CXX, 1–34 (January 1875).

since have done no more than alter by fractions of a per cent the generalizations Powell made about western lands and western water in 1878. On the foundations of the obvious, the report built a program of the logical. But as often happens, the obvious and the logical were not enough to convert and convince.

II

"The need in the Plains," says Karl Frederick Kraenzel, "is for people to make certain adjustments and adaptations to the fact of semiaridity. Otherwise the majority of people must leave the region, and the few who remain will have one of two choices — to live a feast-and-famine type of existence or to have, year in and year out, a standard of living considerably lower than most parts of the nation." [8] He states for the Plains a situation that applies, though with varying degrees of intensity, through much of the arid West. And he states it in our own period, as of 1955. It is even truer — or rather it is more obvious — in 1961, when a new drought of unpredictable duration makes the Dakotas, for the third or fourth time, a drought-disaster area. From 1930 to 1950, when every other state in the union showed substantial gains in population, Oklahoma, Nebraska, and North and South Dakota, all subhumid-to-arid plains states, went down. That is, the adaptation to arid conditions that began for Anglo-Saxon America at least as early as Stephen Austin's 1821 settlement in Texas, is by no means yet completed. The corrections made necessary by ill-considered settlement are still going on. The adaptation may never be fully completed, but only compromised, for it has had to take place within a structure of law often unsuited to the conditions of an arid region; within a political confederation of states and counties, and a survey system of ranges, townships, and sections, arbitrarily indifferent to topographical and climatic dividing lines; against stubborn and incredibly long-lived forces of tradition, inertia, folklore, ignorance, and regional dependency; and in a context of constant quarrel between rival political and bureaucratic authorities, and between public good and private interest.

Some adaptation, it is true, has occurred. The Texans took

[8] *The Great Plains in Transition* (Norman, 1955), p. 283.

over from the Mexicans, who had an experience of many generations in the arid lands, the whole apparatus of cattle ranching, including the institution of the open, unfenced common range and the co-operative roundup, and these were adaptations of an important kind. It is also true that insofar as adaptation involved naturalizing in dry country certain new inventions — the Colt revolver, barbed wire, the windmill, the steel plow, and gang machinery suited to extensive fields [9] — western cowboys and farmers proved themselves as alert to modernization as Americans are supposed to be. But in one thing they did not, for a long time, change: they did not fully acknowledge the fact of aridity, and they did not comprehend its consequences. In this failure of foresight the farmers were worse than the cattlemen.

The history of the West offers plentiful examples of how nearly ineradicable can be the agricultural *expectation* of people reared in a country of adequate rainfall. One of the latest was uncovered by the Harvard Five-Cultures study in New Mexico [10] during the 1950's. There Texas drought refugees on their way to the Coast in the 1930's had stalled and squatted and settled down to grow pinto beans, their habitual Texas crop. Burned out, they struggled through the year and next season planted another crop of pinto beans. Burned out again, they again planted pinto beans, and again, and again, like Cooper Indians leaping after the vanishing Ark; and just about the time when experience was beginning to suggest that pinto beans might be a dubious gamble, the advent of one good year restored all their old optimism and set them off on another spell of planting pinto beans.

Apparently one of the hardest things for a wet-country man to credit is the persistent fact of insufficient rain. That single fact, as Powell told the nation in 1878, and kept telling them until his death in 1902, and has been telling them through converts and

---

[9] See Kraenzel, *op. cit.*, especially ch. VI and VIII; and Webb, *The Great Plains*, especially ch. VI, VII, and VIII. Webb's is the classic study of the failure of adaptation that created so many problems for Plains settlers; Kraenzel brings the discussion down to the present and is particularly valuable for his summary of agricultural and institutional changes since the 1930's.

[10] Described in Evon Vogt, *Modern Homesteaders* (Cambridge, 1955). The persistence of the raiding or gambling attitude in agricultural matters is evidenced even in the humor of the people involved. Thus Vogt quotes a community joke (p. 201) to the effect that a "bean-farmer is a man who is crazy enough to think he is going to make it next year."

disciples ever since, is enough to make impractical and even destructive a whole inherited culture, a whole body of law and custom and political organization.

Essentially, Powell's *Report on the Lands of the Arid Region* was a sober and foresighted warning about the consequences of trying to impose on a dry country the habits that have been formed in a wet one. In the West, which characteristically has not been so much settled as raided — first for its furs, then for its minerals, then for its grass, then in some places for its timber, in some for its wheat, in some for its scenery — consequences have habitually been ignored; and yet the very condition of aridity from which Powell's warning stemmed makes the consequences of mismanagement catastrophic. Moreover, they are seldom simple or single, but almost always multiple and serial. What happens in Big Timber, Montana, concerns Plattesmouth, Nebraska, what gullies my hillside floods your riverbottom, what ruins a farm family may also ruin the land, and hence affect all future farmers in that place.

Much western history is a series of lessons in consequences. That is what the busted homesteaders straggling back from western Kansas in the early 1890's were getting; or the cattlemen counting carcasses and salvaging hides in the corners of the barbed-wire fences after the Big Die-up [11] of 1886–87; or the politicians who looked up one day in Washington, D.C. in 1934 and saw the sky over the Potomac darkened with Plains dust; or the residents of Willard, Utah, who on an afternoon in the summer of 1924 scrambled onto the railroad embankment during a shower and watched a flash flood from the cut-over mountain-side fill their fields and houses with twelve feet of mud and gravel; or the Dustbowl farmer who remarked that the best place to locate a farm in Colorado was over in eastern Kansas; or the lawyers endlessly debating the rights of the several states to the waters of western rivers. What works in a wet country does not necessarily, or even likely, work in a dry one, and when a mistake has been made — when a watershed has been logged off or the range overgrazed or a sloping field gullied by carelessly handled irrigation water — the wounds do not heal naturally as they

[11] See Edward Everett Dale, *The Range Cattle Industry* (Norman, 1930), pp. 108–110, for a brief account of this loss of cattle, and its consequences.

would in a country of ample rain, but grow worse unless they are actively stopped by such rescue operations as total rest of the land, watershed planting, range re-seeding, and the brushing and damming of gullies.

All of this is implicit, and much of it explicit, in Powell's *Report*. Some of it has been learned and applied since, slowly and painfully and with relapses in every wet cycle. Law, habit, folklore, special interests, competing authorities, have bent somewhat because they have had to. The work of the Reclamation Bureau and the Corps of Engineers has dramatized the role of water in the West, though both bureaus have become something like self-perpetuating empires in the process. The Taylor Grazing Act of 1934, fifty-six years after Powell submitted his report to Schurz, finally solved the problem of the dryland homesteader by closing the Public Domain, and it partially solved the problem of the cattleman in need of extensive range by a system of grazing leases administered by the Bureau of Land Management. The Soil Conservation Service, despite political opposition and inadequate budgets, has done something to restore lands that overgrazing and ill-considered cultivation had gullied or turned into dustbowls. The National Park Service and the Forest Service control much of the watershed and timber land, protect it from fire, cutting, and over-grazing, and together with the flood control and reclamation dams, encourage some of the co-operation among the people living on watershed, benchlands, and bottomlands that Powell foresaw to be necessary.[12]

The method, of course, has not been what Powell proposed. Instead of local co-operation, federal ownership and bureaucratic control. Powell's plan assumed the eventual disposal of the better part of the Public Domain, whereas in fact, of the 400,000,000 acres in the states of Montana, Wyoming, Colorado, Utah, Idaho, and Nevada, more than half are still federally owned and managed. The West relies on a degree of federal paternalism that it is not always happy to accept and the benefits of which it is not always willing to acknowledge.

Because Powell failed in that part of his plan which envisaged alteration of the land laws, co-operative settlement of the West

[12] The extent and distribution of the many kinds of federal lands are summarized, as of 1950, in Clawson, *Uncle Sam's Acres*.

could not come about,[13] and individual homesteading on arid lands under the old laws had proved capable of producing mainly failure. Settlement would depend, as Powell said it would, largely on group effort and the massive expenditures and installations that only groups could manage. And if one of the reasons why federal rather than co-operative patterns were established throughout the West was the failure of Congress to make laws favorable to co-operative effort, another was that the federal bureaus have consistently understood western problems better and have been freer from domination by special interests than either local owners or the state governments. It is the federal bureaus which have largely engineered the West's gradual adaptation to aridity. When in 1958 Walter Webb published an article [14] in which he described the West as a semi-desert with a desert heart, he inspired angry resolutions and rebuttals from chambers of commerce all the way from San Angelo to Havre, Montana. Whatever planners, historians, government bureaus, and individuals at large may have learned, a large western public is still myth-bound and reacts to "deficiency terminology" as angrily as did the town-builders and speculators of Kansas in the 1860's.

III

The first edition of the *Report on the Lands of the Arid Region* was printed for the use of Congress in 1878; the second edition, partly for congressional use and partly for the Department of the Interior, was run off the next year. Already, before the second edition was authorized, it had become the blueprint of a reform movement, and as such, fiercely controversial. The devoted advocacy and the angry resistance that it stimulated then were to be continued over many years.

Powell's first limited goal, bureaucratic survival, was won early: his 1878 appropriation was his largest to date. His second, the

[13] But as Louise Peffer points out in *The Closing of the Public Domain* (p. 170), the terms which were found in the Taylor Grazing Act of 1934 derive to some extent from the Mizpah–Pumpkin Creek grazing agreement reached in Montana on March 29, 1928. This was a hopeful experiment in joint leases and involved the co-operation of federal and state governments with the local users of the range. Miss Peffer blames its failure and the need for federal rescue all through the West upon President Hoover's proposal to turn public lands over to the states.

[14] "The American West: Perpetual Mirage," *Harper's Magazine,* CCXIV, 25–31 (May 1957).

reorganization of the scientific bureaus of the federal government, was complex and difficult and was not achieved until 1879, and then only partially. In June 1878 Congress referred the vexed question of the western surveys to the National Academy of Sciences for study and advice. A committee of Powell's friends in the Academy pondered until November and recommended everything that Powell had advocated in his report: consolidation of the four western surveys under Interior; elimination of the office of Surveyor-General and of the practice of contracting land surveys; transfer of the land-parcelling surveys to the Coast and Geodetic Survey, and transfer of that Survey from Treasury to Interior. Before the convening of the next session of Congress Schurz asked Powell to put the Academy recommendations into the form of bills. This Powell did, tying three of the four proposals to appropriations bills so as to by-pass the Public Lands Committee, which with its strong western representation would have buried them. Western Senators and Representatives, opposed almost to a man, fought the reformers bitterly, and only the tenacity of Abraham Hewitt [15] saved the single part that was saved. A clause attached to the Sundry Civil Appropriations Bill consolidated the four western surveys as the United States Geological Survey, under Interior.

It was far from everything, but it was something. At least it eliminated Wheeler and tamed Hayden, who, though he stayed on with the Survey, suffered a steep decline in power and prestige. Clarence King was shortly approved as the first director of the new combined Survey, and Powell, eliminated by his own plans, moved over to the Smithsonian Institution to continue his studies of the Indians in his new Bureau of Ethnology. The scientific functions of government, which Powell conceived to be primarily the provision of accurate information to the people — information that he felt was needed more in the arid West than elsewhere — would be better served, with less waste, less politics, and more science.

And the revolutionary proposals for the classification, survey, and disposal of the western lands? Those got the treatment that unpalatable logic has got before this: The Academy in its recommendations had not dared go so far as Powell and had hedged

[15] Hewitt (1822–1903) was a member of Congress 1874–1886.

by suggesting a Public Lands Commission to study and codify the land laws. Congress authorized the Commission when it consolidated the surveys. It was composed of Clarence King and Commissioner Williamson of the General Land Office, assisted by Alexander Britton, Thomas Donaldson,[16] and Powell. A year later it duly reported, and its report, which elaborated the findings of Powell's *Report on the Lands of the Arid Region*, was quietly received and ignored. Later Donaldson compiled, building on the work of the Commission, the first systematic study of the Public Domain,[17] thus completing what Powell had earlier set himself to. Donaldson's book, though it has been useful to scholars ever since, had no more political effect than Powell's report. The confusing, impracticable, loophole-filled land laws remained as they were, the rectangular surveys went on projecting themselves across drainage divides and out from river and creek valleys, often concentrating all the water within miles in a single section and making it easy for the man who owned the water to engross whole duchies of dry land. Powell's report and its continuations stirred up a flurry of oratory and a stiff congressional battle, but no more. The West went on fumbling its way toward settlement like a man trying to pick a lock with a piece of wet string.

Nevertheless, Powell was not through. He knew too much; he had thought too long on the problems of the West, he took too seriously his position as scientist in the service of the people. A good politician, he kept his peace until another opportunity offered. After he succeeded King as Director of the Geological Survey in 1881, he found himself, as head of two major bureaus, the most powerful scientific man in the capital, and he used his power to get work done. He organized research on the Indian, regularized map symbols, began the nearly endless task of mapping the whole United States, founded the Cosmos Club as a home for

---

[16] James A. Williamson, Commissioner of the General Land Office 1876–1881; Alexander Thompson Britton (1835–1899), specialist in land laws; Thomas Corwin Donaldson (1843–1898) had served previously as registrar of public lands in Idaho.

[17] The Commission's report was published as the *Report of the Public Lands Commission, Created by the Act of March 3, 1879, Relating to Public Lands in the Western Portion of the United States and to the Operation of Existing Land Laws* (Washington, 1880). Donaldson's revision and elaboration appeared as *The Public Domain: Its History, with Statistics* (Washington, 1884).

Washington intellectuals, defended government science against often hostile committees. And he kept his interest in land and water as western resources. Though he did not drop out of the survey's work the *Mineral Resources* annual that had been King's principal preoccupation, he added to mineral-spotting the topographical mapping that was for him basic to much other knowledge, including land classification; and he deepened through his anthropological studies his conviction that the future of the West as a stable community would depend on the storage, diversion, and distribution of water to small irrigated farms and to the supplementary hayfields of ranches. He knew that if the West were to achieve that future without a lot of painful error, somebody would have to do some planning before the West filled up with settlers.

His second opportunity, a greater one, came to him as a result of the decade of drought that began in 1887. Here, with a vengeance, was the recurrent aridity he had warned against, and as he had prophesied, it brought worse hardship to the sub-humid region which had depended on the rains than to the arid lands where settlers had made some provision, however inadequate, for irrigation. Here were some consequences of careless settlement, uncritical optimism, and a reliance on wet-country methods. The consequences blew eastward in great clouds of dust, erupted in demonstrations against the railroads and the banks that made intolerable conditions even more intolerable, reached the legislative halls in gusts of Populist oratory and clamors for government help to farmers. From the arid lands came demands for federal surveys of dam sites and irrigation works, and out of that demand, which was as often as not put forward by those who stood to profit from speculation in adjoining lands, came an unlikely and short-lived alliance between Powell and Senator William Stewart of Nevada.[18] In March 1888 a Joint Resolution of the two houses of Congress called upon the Secretary of the Interior to examine "that portion of the United States where agriculture is carried on by means of irrigation, as to the natural advantages for the storage of water for irrigation purposes with the practicability of constructing reservoirs, together with the

[18] William Morris Stewart (1827–1909), U.S. Senator, 1864–1875 and 1887–1905.

capacity of streams, and the cost of construction and the capacity of reservoirs and such other facts as bear on the question." [19]

The turgid phrasing is probably Stewart's; the opportunity became Powell's. When, on October 2, the Sundry Civil Bill appropriated $100,000 to implement the Joint Resolution, Powell found himself in charge of an Irrigation Survey that had unprecedented, undreamed-of, possibilities.[20] He had not changed his mind about anything in his 1878 report. Now Congress with a fine vague generosity gave him funds, support, a political imperative born of its own sense of urgency. At a stroke he was endowed with enormous power.

How much power certainly Congress did not at first realize; and even Powell, used to accepting all the power the law allowed him, does not seem to have understood what the Joint Resolution really meant. But he did see one thing: he saw this job as something much bigger than what Stewart and the so-called "irrigation clique" wanted — a quick designation of reservoir sites made on existing maps so that speculation and profit would be prompt and easy. What Powell saw was a chance to realize a good part of his general plan for the West. First he would have to complete the topographical mapping of the Public Domain, an enormous task. From those maps he could make a beginning at designating irrigable lands and dam sites, but before that designation could be precise he had to conduct a hydrographic survey, measuring stream flow and plotting catchment basins and canal lines. Finally, on top of the topographic and hydrographic surveys, he would have to make a preliminary engineering survey to determine the feasibility of headworks and other installations. And after all that, he could confidently classify the western lands as irrigable or non-irrigable. He estimated the job at seven years and

[19] The several acts and resolutions bearing upon the initiation of the Irrigation Survey are listed in the United States Geological Survey, *10th Annual Report, 1889*, pp. 1–80. The original and crucial one was the Joint Resolution of March 20, 1888; the appropriation which gave this resolution the force of law was contained in the Sundry Civil Expenses Bill of October 2, 1888 (*24th Stat. L*, 255).

[20] On the Irrigation Survey's short and troubled life and on its potential importance to the West at a critical time, see Everett Stirling, "The Powell Irrigation Survey, 1888–1893," *Mississippi Valley Historical Review*, XXVII, 421–434 (December 1940); *Senate Report No. 1466*, 51st Cong., 1st Sess. (July 2, 1890); the Irrigation Supplements to the 10th, 11th, 12th, and 13th *Annual Reports* of the U.S. Geological Survey; Darrah, *Powell of the Colorado*, pp. 299–314; and Stegner, *Beyond the Hundredth Meridian*, pp. 294–343.

seven million dollars, and he knew that if he were permitted to get it done, the West would have the scientific knowledge that would let it be settled soundly and for keeps.

Cries of impatience began to rise early from Stewart and some others, who objected to the apparently interminable mapmaking. But those cries were as nothing to the uproar which arose when western members of Congress finally comprehended the weapons they had put in Powell's hands. Two amendments had been written into the Joint Resolution authorizing the Irrigation Survey. The first, inserted by Representative Symes of Colorado to forestall land speculation on the basis of the survey, temporarily withdrew from settlement "all lands made susceptible of irrigation" by the reservoirs and canals which the survey would designate. The second amendment, written in as a protection against the effects of the first, said that the President could at his discretion restore for entry under the Homestead Act alone any of the withdrawn lands. But the lands made susceptible of irrigation were not yet known, and would not be until Major Powell's tedious mapmaking was finished and he had certified the irrigable parts to the Secretary of the Interior. Actually, not even the extent of the territory embraced by the survey was known, but on the evidence of the current drought it pretty clearly included the whole Public Domain. There were complaints of speculative entries; the question arose whether or not any lands were open to entry under the terms of the Symes amendment; gradually it dawned on a horror-struck irrigation clique that everything might be locked up. After many backings and fillings and contradictory orders from the General Land Office, the ruling came down from the Attorney General that the General Land Office had been legally out of business since October 2, 1888, when the appropriation of $100,000 had made effective the survey authorized by the Joint Resolution. Any claims filed on any part of the Public Domain after that date were invalid. The President interpreted the situation in the same way in his annual message in 1890, and early in that year the Land Office officially closed to entry 850,000,000 acres of western lands — nearly the entire Public Domain. None of it could legally be restored except by the President, and he would not restore any part of it until it was certified to him by John Wesley Powell.

Accidentally, casually, inadvertently, Powell had been given absolute power over all the lands which had been his lifetime study. The random and wasteful course of settlement could be halted while knowledge was accumulated. Henceforth, if he were lucky, lands could be released for distribution only as they were known to be the raw material for workable farms or ranches, assured of the possibility of water as soon as a corporation, a government agency, or a co-operative group undertook the necessary dams and canals.

He tried. He put his best men from the old Powell Survey, Clarence Dutton [21] and Almon Thompson,[22] back on the hydrographic work they had begun for his *Arid Region* report. He speeded up and greatly extended the topographic mapping. He lectured, he wrote for the magazines. He addressed the constitutional conventions of North Dakota and Montana in 1889 and told the Dakotans that the truest and stablest agriculture had historically been irrigation agriculture, that on the Tigris-Euphrates and the Nile, as well as in the American Southwest, civilizations had built themselves most surely on controlled streams, and that for their young state, intelligent planning in the beginning could save endless trouble later. He urged the Montana delegates to organize their state not according to arbitrary county lines, but by drainage divides, so that watersheds, benchlands, and bottomlands could co-operate without friction, making the maximum use of their water for the common good. In every way he could he drummed his message into heads not yet prepared to receive it, and he came back from his 1889 tour having made a mortal enemy of the impatient and bull-headed and not noticeably far-sighted Senator Stewart. And the moment that Attorney-General Taft and President Cleveland interpreted the situation to mean that all land entries since October 2, 1888, were invalid, Stewart and his friends set out to destroy the Irrigation Survey they had helped create.

If Powell had had another year or two to complete his topo-

---

[21] Clarence Edward Dutton (1841–1912), author, among other works, of *Report on the Geology of the High Plateaus of Utah* (1879–1880); and *Tertiary History of the Grand Canyon District* (1882).

[22] Almon Harris Thompson (1839–1906), Powell's brother-in-law, wrote a *Report upon the Construction of Topographic Maps . . . in Colorado* (1894) and *Report upon the Location and Survey of Reservoir Sites . . .* (1894).

graphical map, he might have beaten them or might have been able to release enough land to pacify them. But he didn't, and because he was far ahead of his time, and they up to their necks in theirs, they cut him down in a few months. The 1890 Sundry Civil Bill reduced the Irrigation Survey budget from the $720,000 that Powell had asked to a mere $162,500 — enough to reduce the whole grand scheme to an aimless mapping of reservoir sites. The believers in the unfailing artesian waters, the walkers in the Garden of the World, the myth-bound men of faith, the speculators and the feudal cattlemen, and the congressmen who were their mouthpieces, had won again. It was no more than a year before the vindictive Stewart got at Powell again, this time by reducing his Geological Survey appropriations. Within three years, unwell and in constant pain from the regenerated nerves in the stump of his arm, Powell retired from the Geological Survey to devote himself to ethnology and philosophy.

But the rod he had cast down before them had turned into a snake, and they could not scotch it. Another decade, and it would be more alive than ever. In the meantime Powell would go on writing and preaching his doctrine of facts, knowledge, science, planning. He would go on linking headwaters and lower waters, watershed and bottomland. He would go on insisting that no more than twenty per cent of the West could ever be reclaimed even with the most economical use of the available water. He would go on patiently throwing himself under the chariot wheels of booster groups and irrigation congresses, insisting on his deficiency terminology. In 1902, the year of his death, he would have the satisfaction of seeing, in the passage of the Newlands Act creating the Bureau of Reclamation, the realization of a part of what he had fought for. He could claim credit for having created the "Wyoming doctrine" tying water rights to land, and partial credit for the repeal of both the Timber Culture Act and the Desert Land Act — a move that he had suggested in 1889 and that came about in 1891.[23] He might even have felt before his death that, by ex-

---

[23] In a letter to Secretary of the Interior John W. Noble, January 2, 1889, Powell enumerated the possible difficulties that could arise from the multiple land laws even after the irrigation surveys were completed, and continued, "With a degree of misgiving the Director begs permission to suggest as his own opinion that the best solution of the problem under the present circumstances is to withdraw all the lands of the arid region from 'sale, entry, settlement, or occupation' except

cruciating but inevitable increments, knowledge slowly gained upon fantasy and error, and adaptation in the West went forward.

IV

It is not a single document that one evaluates in calling the *Report on the Lands of the Arid Region* one of the most significant and seminal books ever written about the West. It is true that it contains, both in its analysis of western conditions and its evaluation of consequences, the classic statement of the terms on which the West could be peopled. It is also true that it forecasts with disconcerting accuracy the droughts, floods, crop failures, land and water monopolies, jurisdictional quarrels, and individual tragedies which have been the consequences of applying wet-country habits in a dry country. Nevertheless, the *Arid Region* would probably not have become the historic document it is if Powell had not supplemented it with two decades of hard missionary effort. It is a campaign, a body of doctrine, a general plan, that one ultimately recognizes as monumentally important; one wishes it were possible to reprint not a single document, but a career.[24]

He was present and fighting all through the critical period when settlers' mistakes were being overtaken by consequences and, finally, by a modified wisdom. He contributed much of the structure of knowledge upon which the wisdom of adaptation has been based, and he formulated some of wisdom's wisest generalizations. As notable as his prescience was his persistence, his disinterested assumption of responsibility. Put down in 1874 during a squabble over the consolidation of the surveys, he regrouped and came back in 1878 with the *Arid Region* report and its ambitious plan for land reform. Defeated in 1878 on everything but consolidation, he came back again in 1888, carried into a position of power

those selected as irrigable lands, and to allow titles to irrigable lands to be acquired only through the operation of the homestead laws and the desert-land laws." United States Geological Survey, *Letters Sent*, 242. This is evidence that at the beginning of 1889 Powell did not comprehend the sweeping nature of the resolution that had put him in the irrigation business, but it indicates his early concern about the manner in which lands should be distributed to settlers and the possible ways of avoiding improper or wasteful settlement.

[24] Three articles which constitute a later restatement of the essential ideas of the *Arid Region* report, are: "The Irrigable Lands of the Arid Region," *Century Illustrated Monthly Magazine*, XXXIX, 766–776 (March 1890); "The Non-Irrigable Lands of the Arid Region," *Century*, XXXIX, 915–922 (April 1890); and "Institutions for the Arid Lands," *Century*, XL, 111–116 (May 1890).

by the period of drought he had predicted, and in the spring of 1890 he had within reach a victory that would have altered the subsequent history of the West. It will still take the West generations to gain, in broken and compromised form, what it might have begun gaining early if its people and its Congressmen and Senators had had the same disinterestedness and somewhat more of the "wise prevision" that Powell knew was needed.

A NOTE ON THE TEXT

The first edition was printed as 45th Congress 2nd Session H.R. Exec. Doc. 73, in 1878. The basis of the present text is the second, published in March 1879. As Powell's Preface indicates, this edition differs from the first only in a few factual and typographical corrections. The present editor has made no further changes except to correct obvious misspellings. Slight modifications of punctuation conform to current usage. The original index has been entirely revised.

CHRONOLOGY OF THE LIFE OF
JOHN WESLEY POWELL, 1834-1902

1834, March 24 — Born in Mount Morris, New York.

1838 — Family moved from western New York to Jackson, Ohio.

1846 — Family moved to South Grove, in Walworth County, Wisconsin.

1846–1850 — Removed from school to work on his father's farm; during these years self-taught, following up the bent for natural history that he had developed in Jackson.

1851 — Family moved to Bonus Prairie, Illinois.

1853–1858 — Attended, for short periods, Illinois Institute (Wheaton), Illinois College (Jacksonville), and Oberlin College, interspersing college terms with spells of country-school teaching in Wisconsin and Illinois and with long collecting expeditions up and down the Mississippi and its tributaries.

1858 — Began teaching in Hennepin, Illinois, and became secretary of the Illinois State Natural History Society.

1861, May 8 — Enlisted as a private in the Twentieth Illinois Volunteer Infantry.

1861, November 28 — Married his cousin, Emma Dean, of Detroit.

1862, April 6 — Lost his right arm at the Battle of Shiloh.

1865, January 4 — Discharged with rank of brevet lieutenant-colonel.

1865 — Accepted a professorship of geology at Illinois Wesleyan University.

1866 — Moved to a professorship at Illinois State Normal University.

1867 — Led his first expedition, under sponsorship of the Illinois State Natural History Society, to the Rocky Mountains.

1868 — Led a second expedition to the Rockies which explored west of the continental divide and wintered at Powell Bottoms, on the White River, in western Colorado.

1869 — Led a party of ten men, in four boats, down the canyons of the Green and Colorado Rivers, from Green River, Wyoming, to the mouth of the Virgin.

1870, July 12 — Congress established the Geographical and Geological Survey of the Rocky Mountain Region, J. W. Powell in charge.

1870–1879 — Directed the survey and mapping of the Plateau Province he had first opened up.

1871 — Led a second boat expedition down the Green and Colorado to the mouth of Kanab Wash.

1879 — Took a leading part in the establishing of the United States Geological Survey, which amalgamated the four surveys of the West under the directorship of Clarence King. Powell himself became the Director of the Bureau of Ethnology within the Smithsonian Institution.

1881 — Succeeded Clarence King as Director of the United States Geological Survey, retaining his position as Director of the Bureau of
Ethnology.

1888–1891 — Conducted, through the Geological Survey, the Irrigation
Surveys whose work later became the basis of the Reclamation Bureau,
which was signed into law by Theodore Roosevelt on June 17, 1902.

1902, September 23 — Died at Haven, Maine.

REPORT ON
THE LANDS OF THE ARID REGION
OF THE UNITED STATES

J. W. POWELL'S REPORT ON SURVEY OF THE ROCKY MOUNTAIN REGION

LETTER FROM

THE SECRETARY OF THE INTERIOR

TRANSMITTING

Report of J. W. Powell, geologist in charge of the United States Geographical and Geological Survey of the Rocky Mountain Region, upon the lands of the Arid Region of the United States.

April 3, 1878. — Referred to the Committee on Appropriations and ordered to be printed.

Department of the Interior,
Washington, D. C., April 3, 1878.

Sir: I have the honor to transmit herewith a report from Maj. J. W. Powell, geologist in charge of the United States Geographical and Geological Survey of the Rocky Mountain Region, upon the lands of the Arid Region of the United States, setting forth the extent of said region, and making suggestions as to the conditions under which the lands embraced within its limit may be rendered available for agricultural and grazing purposes. With the report is transmitted a statement of the rainfall of the western portion of the United States, with reports upon the subject of irrigation by Capt. C. E. Dutton, U. S. A., Prof. A. H. Thompson, and Mr. G. K. Gilbert.[1]

Herewith are also transmitted draughts of two bills, one entitled "A bill to authorize the organization of pasturage districts by homestead settlements on the public lands which are of value for pasturage purposes only," and the other "A bill to authorize the organization of irrigation districts by homestead settlements upon

[1] Grove Karl Gilbert (1843–1918) joined Powell in 1874 on surveys and was chief geologist of the United States Geological Survey 1889–1892.

the public lands requiring irrigation for agricultural purposes,"
intended to carry into effect a new system for the disposal of the
public lands of said region, and to promote the settlement and
development of that portion of the country.

In view of the importance of rendering the vast extent of
country referred to available for agricultural and grazing purposes,
I have the honor to commend the views set forth by Major Powell
and the bills submitted herewith to the consideration of Congress.

Very respectfully,

C. SCHURZ,
Secretary.

Hon. Samuel J. Randall,
Speaker of the House of Representatives.

Department of the Interior, General Land Office,
Washington, D. C., April 1, 1878.

Sir: I have the honor to submit herewith a report from Maj.
J. W. Powell, in charge of the Geographical and Geological Survey of the Rocky Mountains, in regard to the Arid Region of the
United States, and draughts of two bills, one entitled "A bill to
authorize the organization of pasturage districts by homestead
settlements on the public lands which are of value for pasturage
purposes only," and the other "A bill to authorize the organization
of irrigation districts by homestead settlements upon the public
lands requiring irrigation for agricultural purposes."

Major Powell reviews at length the features of, and furnishes
statistics relative to, the Arid Region of the United States, which
is substantially the territory west of the one hundredth meridian
and east of the Cascade Range, and the bills named are intended,
if passed, to carry into effect the views expressed in his report for
the settlement and development of this region.

He has, in the performance of his duties in conducting the geological and geographical survey, been over much of the country
referred to, and is qualified by observation, research, and study
to speak of the topography, characteristics, and adaptability of
the same.

I have not been able, on account of more urgent official duties,
to give Major Powell's report and proposed bills the careful inves-

tigation necessary, in view of their great importance, to enable me to express a decided opinion as to their merits. Some change is necessary in the survey and disposal of the lands, and I think his views are entitled to great weight, and would respectfully recommend that such action be taken as will bring his report and bills before Congress for consideration by that body.

Very respectfully,

J. A. WILLIAMSON,
Commissioner.

Hon. C. Schurz,
Secretary of the Interior.

Department of the Interior,
U. S. Geographical and Geological Survey
of the Rocky Mountain Region,
Washington, D. C., April 1, 1878.

Sir: I have the honor to transmit herewith a report on the lands of the Arid Region of the United States. After setting forth the general facts relating to the conditions under which these lands must be utilized, I have taken the liberty to suggest a system for their disposal which I believe would be adapted to the wants of the country.

I wish to express my sincere thanks for the assistance you have given me in the collection of many of the facts necessary to the discussion, and especially for the aid you have rendered in the preparation of the maps.

Permit me to express the hope that the great interest you take in the public domain will be rewarded by the consciousness that you have assisted many citizens in the establishment of farm homes thereon.

I am, with great respect, your obedient servant,

J. W. POWELL,
In charge U. S. G. and G. Survey Rocky Mountain Region.

Hon. J. A. Williamson,
Commissioner General Land Office, Washington, D. C.

PREFACE

It was my intention to write a work on the Public Domain. The object of the volume was to give the extent and character of the lands yet belonging to the Government of the United States. Compared with the whole extent of these lands, but a very small fraction is immediately available for agriculture; in general, they require drainage or irrigation for their redemption.

It is true that in the Southern States there are some millions of acres, chiefly timber lands, which at no remote time will be occupied for agricultural purposes. Westward toward the Great Plains, the lands in what I have, in the body of this volume, termed the Humid Region have passed from the hands of the General Government. To this statement there are some small exceptions here and there — fractional tracts, which, for special reasons, have not been considered desirable by persons in search of lands for purposes of investment or occupation.

In the Sub-humid Region settlements are rapidly extending westward to the verge of the country where agriculture is possible without irrigation.

In the Humid Region of the Columbia the agricultural lands are largely covered by great forests, and for this reason settlements will progress slowly, as the lands must be cleared of their timber.

The redemption of the Arid Region involves engineering problems requiring for their solution the greatest skill. In the present volume only these lands are considered. Had I been able to execute the original plan to my satisfaction, I should have treated of the coast swamps of the South Atlantic and the Gulf slopes, the Everglade lands of the Floridian Peninsula, the flood plain lands of the great rivers of the south, which have heretofore been made available only to a limited extent by a system of levees, and the lake swamp lands found about the headwaters of the Mississippi and the region of the upper Great Lakes. All of these lands require either drainage or protection from overflow, and the engineering problems involved are of diverse nature. These lands are to be redeemed from excessive humidity, while the former are to be redeemed from excessive aridity. When the excessively humid lands are redeemed, their fertility is almost inexhaustible, and the agricultural capacity of the United States will eventually be largely increased by the rescue of these lands from their present valueless condition. In like manner, on the other hand, the arid lands, so far as they can be redeemed by irrigation, will perennially yield bountiful crops, as the means for their redemption involves their constant fertilization.

To a great extent, the redemption of all these lands will require extensive and comprehensive plans, for the execution of which aggregated capital or coöperative labor will be necessary. Here, individual farmers, being poor men, cannot undertake the task. For its accomplishment a wise prevision, embodied in carefully considered legislation, is necessary. It was my purpose not only to consider the character of the lands themselves, but also the engineering problems involved in their redemption, and further to make suggestions for the legislative action necessary to inaugurate the enterprises by which these lands may eventually be rescued from their present worthless state. When I addressed myself to the broader task as indicated above, I found that my facts in relation to some of the classes of lands mentioned, especially the coast swamps of the Gulf and some of the flood plain lands of the southern rivers, were too meager for anything more than general statements. There seemed to be no immediate necessity for the discussion of these subjects; but to the Arid Region of the West thousands of persons are annually repairing, and the questions relating to the utilization of these lands are of present importance. Under these considerations I have decided to publish that portion of the volume relating to the arid lands, and to postpone to some future time that part relating to the excessively humid lands.

In the preparation of the contemplated volume I desired to give a historical sketch of the legislation relating to swamp lands and executive action thereunder; another chapter on bounty lands and land grants for agricultural schools, and still another on land grants in aid of internal improvements — chiefly railroads. The latter chapter has already been prepared by Mr. Willis Drummond, Jr.,[1] and as the necessary map is ready I have concluded to

[1] Willis Drummond, Jr., a clerk in the General Land office, should not be

publish it now, more especially as the granted lands largely lie in the Arid Region. Mr. Drummond's chapter has been carefully prepared and finely written, and contains much valuable information.

To the late Prof. Joseph Henry, secretary of the Smithsonian Institution, I am greatly indebted for access to the records of the Institution relating to rainfall. Since beginning my explorations and surveys in the far west, I have received the counsel and assistance of the venerable professor on all important matters relating to my investigations; and whatever of value has been accomplished is due in no small part to his wisdom and advice. I cannot but express profound sorrow at the loss of a counselor so wise, so patient, and so courteous.

I am also indebted to Mr. Charles A. Schott,[2] of the United States Coast Survey, to whom the discussion of the rain gauge records has been intrusted by the Smithsonian Institution, for furnishing to me the required data in advance of publication by himself.

Unfortunately, the chapters written by Messrs. Gilbert, Dutton, Thompson, and Drummond have not been proof-read by themselves, by reason of their absence during the time when the volume was going through the press; but this is the less to be regretted from the fact that the whole volume has been proof-read by Mr. J. C. Pilling, whose critical skill is all that could be desired.

J. W. P.

August, 1878.

---

confused with his father, commissioner of that office from 1871 to 1876. Apparently the son retained his place after the father resigned.

[2] Charles Anthony Schott (1826–1901), geodesist, chief of the computer division of the United States Coast Survey, 1855.

PREFACE TO THE SECOND EDITION

The first edition of this report having been exhausted in a few months and without satisfying the demand which the importance of the subject created, a second was ordered by Congress in March, 1879. The authors were thus given an opportunity to revise their text and eliminate a few formal errors which had crept in by reason of their absence while the first edition was passing through the press. The substance of the report is unchanged.

J. W. P.

July, 1879.

CHAPTER I

PHYSICAL CHARACTERISTICS
OF THE ARID REGION

The eastern portion of the United States is supplied with abundant rainfall for agricultural purposes, receiving the necessary amount from the evaporation of the Atlantic Ocean and the Gulf of Mexico; but westward the amount of aqueous precipitation diminishes in a general way until at last a region is reached where the climate is so arid that agriculture is not successful without irrigation. This Arid Region begins about midway in the Great Plains and extends across the Rocky Mountains to the Pacific Ocean. But on the northwest coast there is a region of greater precipitation, embracing western Washington and Oregon and the northwest corner of California. The winds impinging on this region are freighted with moisture derived from the great Pacific currents; and where this waterladen atmosphere strikes the western coast in full force, the precipitation is excessive, reaching a maximum north of the Columbia River of 80 inches annually. But the rainfall rapidly decreases from the Pacific Ocean eastward to the summit of the Cascade Mountains. It will be convenient to designate this humid area as the Lower Columbia Region. Rain gauge records have not been made to such an extent as to enable us to define its eastern and southern boundaries, but as they are chiefly along high mountains, definite boundary lines are unimportant in the consideration of agricultural resources and the questions relating thereto. In like manner on the east the rain gauge records, though more full, do not give all the facts necessary to a thorough discussion of the subject; yet the records are such as to indicate approximately the boundary between the Arid Region, where irrigation is necessary to agriculture, and the Humid Region, where the lands receive enough moisture from the clouds for the maturing of crops. Experience teaches that it is not wise to depend upon rainfall where the amount is less than 20 inches annually, if this amount is somewhat evenly distributed throughout the year; but if the rainfall is unevenly distributed, so that "rainy seasons" are produced, the question whether agriculture is possible without irrigation depends upon the time of the "rainy season" and the amount of its rainfall. Any unequal distribution of rain through the year, though the inequality be so slight as not to produce "rainy seasons," affects agriculture either favorably or unfavorably. If the spring and summer precipitation exceeds that of the fall and winter, a smaller amount of annual rain may be sufficient; but if the rainfall during the season of growing crops is less than the average of the same length of time during the remainder of the year, a greater amount of annual precipitation is necessary. In some localities in the western portion of the United States this unequal distribution of rainfall through the seasons affects agriculture favorably, and this is true immediately west of the northern portion of the line of 20 inches of rainfall, which extends along the plains from our northern to our southern boundary.

The isohyetal or mean annual rainfall line of 20 inches, as indicated on the rain chart accompanying this report, begins on the southern boundary of the United States, about 60 miles west of Brownsville, on the Rio Grande del Norte, and intersects the northern boundary about 50 miles east of Pembina. Between these two points the line is very irregular, but in middle latitudes makes a general curve to the westward. On the southern portion of the line the rainfall is somewhat evenly distributed through the seasons, but along the northern portion the rainfall of spring and summer is greater than that of fall and winter, and hence the boundary of what has been called the Arid Region runs farther to the west. Again, there is another modifying condition, namely, that of temperature. Where the temperature is greater, more rainfall is needed; where the temperature is less, agriculture is successful with a smaller amount of precipitation. But geographically this temperature is dependent upon two conditions — altitude and latitude. Along the northern portion of the line latitude is an important factor, and the line of possible agriculture without irrigation is carried still farther westward. This conclusion, based upon the consideration of rainfall and latitude, accords with the experience of the farmers of the region, for it is a well known fact that agriculture without irrigation is successfully carried on in the valley of the Red River of the North, and also in the southeastern portion of Dakota Territory. A much more extended series of rain-gauge records than we now have is necessary before this line constituting the eastern boundary of the Arid Region can be well defined. It is doubtless more or less meandering in its course throughout its whole extent from south to north, being affected by local conditions of rainfall, as well as by the general conditions above mentioned; but in a general way it may be represented by the one hundredth meridian, in some places passing to the east, in others to the west, but in the main to the east.

The limit of successful agriculture without irrigation has been set at 20 inches, that the extent of the Arid Region should by no means be exaggerated; but at 20 inches agriculture will not be uniformly successful from season to season. Many droughts will occur; many seasons in a long series will be fruitless; and it may be doubted whether, on the whole, agriculture will prove remunerative. On this point it is impossible to speak with certainty. A larger experience than the history of agriculture in the western portion of the United States affords is necessary to a final determination of the question.

In fact, a broad belt separates the Arid Region of the west from the Humid Region of the east. Extending from the one hundredth meridian eastward to about the isohyetal line of 28 inches, the district of country thus embraced will be subject more or less to disastrous droughts, the frequency of which will diminish from west to east. For convenience let this be called the Sub-humid Region. Its western boundary is the line already defined as running irregularly along the one hundredth meridian. Its eastern boundary passes west of the isohyetal line of 28 inches of rainfall in Minnesota, running approximately parallel to the western boundary line above described. Nearly one-tenth of the whole area of the United States, exclusive of Alaska, is embraced in this Sub-humid Region. In the western portion disastrous droughts will be frequent; in the eastern portion infrequent. In the western portion agriculturists will early resort to irrigation to secure immunity from such disasters, and this event will be hastened because irrigation when properly conducted is a perennial source of fertilization, and is even remunerative for this purpose alone; and for the same reason the inhabitants of the eastern part will gradually develop irrigating methods. It may be confidently expected that at a time not far distant irrigation will be practiced to a greater or less extent throughout this Sub-humid Region. Its settlement presents problems differing materially from those pertaining to the region to the westward. Irrigation is not immediately necessary, and hence agriculture does not immediately depend upon capital. The region may be settled and its agricultural capacities more or less developed, and the question of the construction of irrigating canals may be a matter of time and convenience. For many reasons, much of the sub-humid belt is attractive to settlers: it is almost destitute of forests, and for this reason is more readily subdued, as the land is ready for the plow. But because of the lack of forests the country is more dependent upon railroads for the transportation of building and fencing materials and for fuel. To a large extent it is a region where timber may be successfully cultivated. As the rainfall is on a general average nearly sufficient for continuous successful agriculture, the amount of water to be supplied by irrigating canals will be comparatively small, so that its streams can serve proportionally larger areas than the streams of the Arid Region. In its first settlement the people will be favored by having lands easily subdued, but they will have to contend against a lack of timber. Eventually this will be a region of great agricultural wealth, as in general the soils are good. From our northern to our southern boundary no swamp lands are found, except to some slight extent in the northeastern portion, and it has no excessively hilly or mountainous districts. It is a beautiful prairie country throughout, lacking somewhat in rainfall; but this want can be easily supplied by utilizing the living streams; and, further, these streams will afford fertilizing materials of great value.

The Humid Region of the lower Columbia and the Sub-humid Region of the Great Plains have been thus briefly indicated in order that the great Arid Region, which is the subject of this paper, may be more clearly defined.

THE ARID REGION

The Arid Region is the great Rocky Mountain Region of the United States, and it embraces something more than four-tenths of the whole country, excluding Alaska. In all this region the mean annual rainfall is insufficient for agriculture, but in certain seasons some localities, now here, now there, receive more than their average supply. Under such conditions crops will mature without irrigation. As such seasons are more or less infrequent even in the more favored localities, and as the agriculturist cannot determine in advance when such seasons may occur, the opportunities afforded by excessive rainfall cannot be improved.

In central and northern California an unequal distribution of rainfall through the seasons affects agricultural interests favorably. A "rainy season" is here found, and the chief precipitation occurs in the months of December–April. The climate, tempered by mild winds from the broad expanse of Pacific waters, is genial, and certain crops are raised by sowing the seeds immediately before or during the "rainy season," and the watering which they receive causes the grains to mature so that fairly remunerative crops are produced. But here again the lands are subject to the droughts of abnormal seasons. As many of these lands can be irrigated, the farmers of the country are resorting more and more to the streams, and soon all the living waters of this region will be brought into requisition.

In the tables of a subsequent chapter this will be called the San Francisco Region.

Again in eastern Washington and Oregon, and perhaps in northern Idaho, agriculture is practiced to a limited extent without irrigation. The conditions of climate by which this is rendered possible are not yet fully understood. The precipitation of moisture on the mountains is greater than on the lowlands, but the hills and mesas adjacent to the great masses of mountains receive a little of the supply condensed by the mountains themselves, and it will probably be found that limited localities in Montana, and even in Wyoming, will be favored by this condition to an extent sufficient to warrant agricultural operations independent of irrigation. These lands, however, are usually supplied with living streams, and their irrigation can be readily effected, and to secure greater certainty and greater yield of crops irrigation will be practiced in such places.

Within the Arid Region only a small portion of the country is irrigable. These irrigable tracts are lowlands lying along the streams. On the mountains and high plateaus forests are found at elevations so great that frequent summer frosts forbid the cultivation of the soil. Here are the natural timber lands of the Arid Region — an upper region set apart by nature for the growth of timber necessary to the mining, manufacturing, and agricultural industries of the country. Between the low irrigable lands and the elevated forest lands there are valleys, mesas, hills, and mountain slopes bearing grasses of greater or less value for pasturage purposes.

Then, in discussing the lands of the Arid Region, three great classes are recognized — the irrigable lands below, the forest lands above, and the pasturage lands between. In order to set forth the characteristics of these lands and the conditions under which they can be most profitably utilized, it is deemed best to discuss first a somewhat limited region in detail as a fair type of the whole. The survey under the direction of the writer has been extended over the greater part of Utah, a small part of Wyoming and Colorado, the northern portion of Arizona, and a small part of Nevada, but it is proposed to take up for this discussion only the area embraced in Utah Territory.

In Utah Territory agriculture is dependent upon irrigation. To this statement there are some small exceptions. In the more elevated regions there are tracts of meadow land from which small crops of hay can be taken: such lands being at higher altitudes need less moisture, and at the same time receive a greater amount of rainfall because of the altitude; but these meadows have been, often are, and in future will be, still more improved by irrigation. Again, on the belt of country lying between Great Salt Lake and the Wasatch Mountains the local rainfall is much greater than the general rainfall of the region. The water evaporated from the lake is carried by the westerly winds to the adjacent moun-

tains on the east and again condensed, and the rainfall thus produced extends somewhat beyond the area occupied by the
mountains, so that the foot hills and contiguous bench lands
receive a modicum of this special supply.[1] In some seasons this
additional supply is enough to water the lands for remunerative
agriculture, but the crops grown will usually be very small, and
they will be subject to seasons of extreme drought when all agriculture will result in failure. Most of these lands can be irrigated,
and doubtless will be, from a consideration of the facts already
stated, namely, that crops will thereby be greatly increased and
immunity from drought secured. Perhaps other small tracts, on
account of their subsoils, can be profitably cultivated in favorable
seasons, but all of these exceptions are small, and the fact remains
that agriculture is there dependent upon irrigation. Only a small
part of the territory, however, can be redeemed, as high, rugged
mountains and elevated plateaus occupy much of its area, and
these regions are so elevated that summer frosts forbid their
occupation by the farmer. Thus thermic conditions limit agriculture to the lowlands, and here another limit is found in the supply
of water. Some of the large streams run in deep gorges so far
below the general surface of the country that they cannot be used;
for example, the Colorado River runs through the southeastern
portion of the Territory and carries a great volume of water, but
no portion of it can be utilized within the Territory from the fact
that its channel is so much below the adjacent lands. The Bear
River, in the northern part of the Territory, runs in a somewhat
narrow valley, so that only a portion of its waters can be utilized.
Generally the smaller streams can be wholly employed in agriculture, but the lands which might thus be reclaimed are of greater
extent than the amount which the streams can serve; hence in
all such regions the extent of irrigable land is dependent upon the
volume of water carried by the streams.

In order to determine the amount of irrigable land in Utah it was
necessary to determine the areas to which the larger streams can
be taken by proper engineering skill, and the amount which the

---

[1] The 1950 census indicated that more than two-thirds of Utah's population
was concentrated in a dense, narrow band of settlement in the six counties along
the foot of the Wasatch, where greater rainfall plus the availability of irrigation
water made agriculture most feasible. The remaining third was scattered in oasis
valleys through twenty-three counties.

smaller streams can serve. In the latter case it was necessary to determine first the amount of land which a given amount or unit of water would supply, and then the volume of water running in the streams; the product of these factors giving the extent of the irrigable lands. A continuous flow of one cubic foot of water per second was taken as the unit, and after careful consideration it was assumed that this unit of water will serve from 80 to 100 acres of land. Usually the computations have been made on the basis of 100 acres. This unit was determined in the most practical way — from the experience of the farmers of Utah who have been practicing agriculture for the past thirty years. Many of the farmers will not admit that so great a tract can be cultivated by this unit. In the early history of irrigation in this country the lands were oversupplied with water, but experience has shown that irrigation is most successful when the least amount of water is used necessary to a vigorous growth of the crops; that is, a greater yield is obtained by avoiding both scanty and excessive watering; but the tendency to overwater the lands is corrected only by extended experience. A great many of the waterways are so rudely constructed that much waste ensues. As irrigating methods are improved this wastage will be avoided; so in assuming that a cubic foot of water will irrigate from 80 to 100 acres of land it is at the same time assumed that only the necessary amount of water will be used, and that the waterways will eventually be so constructed that the waste now almost universal will be prevented.

In determining the volume of water flowing in the streams great accuracy has not been attained. For this purpose it would be necessary to make continuous daily, or even hourly, observations for a series of years on each stream, but by the methods described in the following chapters it will be seen that a fair approximation to a correct amount has been made. For the degree of accuracy reached much is due to the fact that many of the smaller streams are already used to their fullest capacity, and thus experience has solved the problem.

Having determined from the operations of irrigation that one cubic foot per second of water will irrigate from 80 to 100 acres of land when the greatest economy is used, and having determined the volume of water or number of cubic feet per second flowing in the several streams of Utah by the most thorough methods available under the circumstances, it appears that within the territory, excluding a small portion in the southeastern corner where the survey has not yet been completed, the amount of land which it is possible to redeem by this method is about 2,262 square miles, or 1,447,920 acres.[2] Of course this amount does not lie in a continuous body, but is scattered in small tracts along the water courses. For the purpose of exhibiting their situations a map of the territory has been prepared, and will be found accompanying this report, on which the several tracts of irrigable lands have been colored. A glance at this map will show how they are distributed. Excluding that small portion of the territory in the southeast corner not embraced in the map, Utah has an area of 80,000 square miles, of which 2,262 square miles are irrigable. That is, 2.8 per cent of the lands under consideration can be cultivated by utilizing all the available streams during the irrigating season.

In addition to the streams considered in this statement there are numerous small springs on the mountain sides scattered throughout the territory — springs which do not feed permanent streams; and if their waters were used for irrigation the extent of irrigable land would be slightly increased; to what exact amount cannot be stated, but the difference would be so small as not to materially affect the general statement, and doubtless these springs can be used in another way and to a better purpose, as will hereafter appear.

This statement of the facts relating to the irrigable lands of Utah will serve to give a clearer conception of the extent and condition of the irrigable lands throughout the Arid Region. Such as can be redeemed are scattered along the water courses, and are in general the lowest lands of the several districts to which they belong. In some of the states and territories the percentage of irrigable land is less than in Utah, in others greater, and it is probable that the percentage in the entire region is somewhat greater than in the territory which we have considered.

The Arid Region is somewhat more than four-tenths of the

[2] In 1955, 2.1% of Utah's lands was irrigated; another 1.1% was in dry farms, made possible by techniques developed since Powell's time. The crop land harvested, plus irrigated pastures, totaled about 2,000,000 acres. Since the dry farms even with summer-fallowing and dust-mulch techniques are marginal and subject to periodic crop failure, Powell's "educated guess" of 1878 is revealed as over-optimistic rather than the reverse. ElRoy Nelson, *Utah's Economic Patterns* (Salt Lake City, 1956), p. 24.

total area of the United States, and as the agricultural interests of so great an area are dependent upon irrigation it will be interesting to consider certain questions relating to the economy and practicability of distributing the waters over the lands to be redeemed.

Advantages of Irrigation

There are two considerations that make irrigation attractive to the agriculturist. Crops thus cultivated are not subject to the vicissitudes of rainfall; the farmer fears no droughts; his labors are seldom interrupted and his crops rarely injured by storms. This immunity from drought and storm renders agricultural operations much more certain than in regions of greater humidity. Again, the water comes down from the mountains and plateaus freighted with fertilizing materials derived from the decaying vegetation and soils of the upper regions, which are spread by the flowing water over the cultivated lands. It is probable that the benefits derived from this source alone will be full compensation for the cost of the process. Hitherto these benefits have not been fully realized, from the fact that the methods employed have been more or less crude. When the flow of water over the land is too great or too rapid the fertilizing elements borne in the waters are carried past the fields, and a washing is produced which deprives the lands irrigated of their most valuable elements, and little streams cut the fields with channels injurious in diverse ways. Experience corrects these errors, and the irrigator soon learns to flood his lands gently, evenly, and economically. It may be anticipated that all the lands redeemed by irrigation in the Arid Region will be highly cultivated and abundantly productive, and agriculture will be but slightly subject to the vicissitudes of scant and excessive rainfall.

A stranger entering this Arid Region is apt to conclude that the soils are sterile, because of their chemical composition, but experience demonstrates the fact that all the soils are suitable for agricultural purposes when properly supplied with water. It is true that some of the soils are overcharged with alkaline materials, but these can in time be "washed out." Altogether the fact suggests that far too much attention has heretofore been paid to the chemical constitution of soils and too little to those physical conditions by which moisture and air are supplied to the roots of the growing plants.

Coöperative Labor or Capital Necessary for the Development of Irrigation

Small streams can be taken out and distributed by individual enterprise, but coöperative labor or aggregated capital must be employed in taking out the larger streams.

The diversion of a large stream from its channel into a system of canals demands a large outlay of labor and material. To repay this all the waters so taken out must be used, and large tracts of land thus become dependent upon a single canal. It is manifest that a farmer depending upon his own labor cannot undertake this task. To a great extent the small streams are already employed, and but a comparatively small portion of the irrigable lands can be thus redeemed; hence the chief future development of irrigation must come from the use of the larger streams. Usually the confluence of the brooks and creeks which form a large river takes place within the mountain district which furnishes its source before the stream enters the lowlands where the waters are to be used. The volume of water carried by the small streams that reach the lowlands before uniting with the great rivers, or before they are lost in the sands, is very small when compared with the volume of the streams which emerge from the mountains as rivers. This fact is important. If the streams could be used along their upper ramifications while the several branches are yet small, poor men could occupy the lands, and by their individual enterprise the agriculture of the country would be gradually extended to the limit of the capacity of the region; but when farming is dependent upon larger streams such men are barred from these enterprises until coöperative labor can be organized or capital induced to assist. Before many years all the available smaller streams throughout the entire region will be occupied in serving the lands, and then all future development will depend on the conditions above described.

In Utah Territory coöperative labor, under ecclesiastical organization, has been very successful. Outside of Utah there are but few instances where it has been tried; but at Greeley, in the State of Colorado, this system has been eminently successful.

The Use of Smaller Streams Sometimes Interferes With the Use
of the Larger

A river emerging from a mountain region and meandering through a valley may receive small tributaries along its valley course. These small streams will usually be taken out first, and the lands which they will be made to serve will often lie low down in the valley, because the waters can be more easily controlled here and because the lands are better; and this will be done without regard to the subsequent use of the larger stream to which the smaller ones are tributary. But when the time comes to take out the larger stream, it is found that the lands which it can be made to serve lying adjacent on either hand are already in part served by the smaller streams, and as it will not pay to take out the larger stream without using all of its water, and as the people who use the smaller streams have already vested rights in these lands, a practical prohibition is placed upon the use of the larger river. In Utah, church authority, to some extent at least, adjusts these conflicting interests by causing the smaller streams to be taken out higher up in their course. Such adjustment is not so easily attained by the great body of people settling in the Rocky Mountain Region, and some provision against this difficulty is an immediate necessity. It is a difficulty just appearing, but in the future it will be one of great magnitude.

Increase of Irrigable Area by the Storage of Water

Within the Arid Region great deposits of gold, silver, iron, coal, and many other minerals are found, and the rapid development of these mining industries will demand *pari passu* a rapid development of agriculture. Thus all the lands that can be irrigated will be required for agricultural products necessary to supply the local market created by the mines. For this purpose the waters of the non-growing season will be stored, that they may be used in the growing season.

There are two methods of storing the waste waters. Reservoirs may be constructed near the sources of the streams and the waters held in the upper valleys, or the water may be run from the canals into ponds within or adjacent to the district where irrigation is practiced. This latter method will be employed first. It is already employed to some extent where local interests demand and favorable opportunities are afforded. In general, the opportunities for ponding water in this way are infrequent, as the depressions where ponds can easily be made are liable to be so low that the waters cannot be taken from them to the adjacent lands, but occasionally very favorable sites for such ponds may be found. This is especially true near the mountains where alluvial cones have been formed at the debouchure of the streams from the mountain cañons. Just at the foot of the mountains are many places where ancient glaciation has left the general surface with many depressions favorable to ponding.

Ponding in the lower region is somewhat wasteful of water, as the evaporation is greater than above, and the pond being more or less shallow a greater proportional surface for evaporation is presented. This wastage is apparent when it is remembered that the evaporation in an arid climate may be from 60 to 80 inches annually, or even greater.

Much of the waste water comes down in the spring when the streams are high and before the growing crops demand a great supply. When this water is stored the loss by evaporation will be small.

The greater storage of water must come from the construction of great reservoirs in the highlands where lateral valleys may be dammed and the main streams conducted into them by canals. On most streams favorable sites for such water works can be found. This subject cannot be discussed at any length in a general way, from the fact that each stream presents problems peculiar to itself.³

³ The "main-stem dams" of the Hoover-Grand Coulee-Glen Canyon kind are a modern development that Powell evidently did not foresee. Hydroelectric power rather than irrigation has often been their principal justification and the means of meeting their very large costs. With the multi-purpose aims — irrigation, flood control, power, recreation, and industrial and culinary water, Powell would certainly have been in sympathy. With the bureaucratic management he would almost certainly have disagreed, though he himself set the essential pattern for scientific government bureaus and was, through the Irrigation Survey, the spiritual father of the Bureau of Reclamation. In "Institutions for the Arid Lands," his latest and most considered statement on the subject of reclamation, he says, "A thousand millions of money must be used; who shall furnish it? Great and many industries are to be established; who shall control them? Millions of men are to labor; who shall employ them? This is a great nation, the Government is powerful; shall it engage in this work? So dreamers may dream, and so ambition may dictate, but in the name of the men who labor I demand that the laborers shall employ them-

It cannot be very definitely stated to what extent irrigation can be increased by the storage of water. The rainfall is much greater in the mountain than in the valley districts. Much of this precipitation in the mountain districts falls as snow. The great snow banks are the reservoirs which hold the water for the growing seasons. Then the streams are at flood tide; many go dry after the snows have been melted by the midsummer sun; hence they supply during the irrigating time much more water than during the remainder of the year. During the fall and winter the streams are small; in late spring and early summer they are very large. A day's flow at flood time is greater than a month's flow at low water time. During the first part of the irrigating season less water is needed, but during that same time the supply is greatest. The chief increase will come from the storage of this excess of water in the early part of the irrigating season. The amount to be stored will then be great, and the time of this storage will be so short that it will be but little diminished by evaporation. The waters of the fall and winter are so small in amount that they will not furnish a great supply, and the time for their storage will be so great that much will be lost by evaporation. The increase by storage will eventually be important, and it would be wise to anticipate the time when it will be needed by reserving sites for principal reservoirs and larger ponds.

TIMBER LANDS

Throughout the Arid Region timber of value is found growing spontaneously on the higher plateaus and mountains. These timber regions are bounded above and below by lines which are very irregular, due to local conditions. Above the upper line no timber grows because of the rigor of the climate, and below no timber grows because of aridity. Both the upper and lower lines descend in passing from south to north; that is, the timber districts are found at a lower altitude in the northern portion of the Arid

selves; that the enterprise shall be controlled by the men who have the genius to organize, and whose homes are in the lands developed, and that the money shall be furnished by the people; and I say to the Government: Hands off! Furnish the people with institutions of justice, and let them do the work for themselves." There was the making of at least half a Populist in Major Powell; one finds it hard to guess which way he would have leaned when the era of Big Business presented him with the alternatives of industrial monopolies or government control.

Region than in the southern. The forests are chiefly of pine, spruce, and fir, but the pines are qf principal value. Below these timber regions, on the lower slopes of mountains, on the mesas and hills, low, scattered forests are often found, composed mainly of dwarfed piñon pines and cedars. These stunted forests have some slight value for fuel, and even for fencing, but the forests of principal value are found in the Timber Region as above described.

Primarily the growth of timber depends on climatic conditions — humidity and temperature. Where the temperature is higher, humidity must be greater, and where the temperature is lower, humidity may be less. These two conditions restrict the forests to the highlands, as above stated. Of the two factors involved in the growth of timber, that of the degree of humidity is of the first importance; the degree of temperature affects the problem comparatively little, and for most of the purposes of this discussion may be neglected. For convenience, all these upper regions where conditions of temperature and humidity are favorable to the growth of timber may be called the *timber regions*.

Not all these highlands are alike covered with forests. The timber regions are only in part *areas of standing timber*. This limitation is caused by fire. Throughout the timber regions of all the arid land fires annually destroy larger or smaller districts of timber, now here, now there, and this destruction is on a scale so vast that the amount taken from the lands for industrial purposes sinks by comparison into insignificance. The cause of this great destruction is worthy of careful attention. The conditions under which these fires rage are climatic. Where the rainfall is great and extreme droughts are infrequent, forests grow without much interruption from fires; but between that degree of humidity necessary for their protection, and that smaller degree necessary to growth, all lands are swept bare by fire to an extent which steadily increases from the more humid to the more arid districts, until at last all forests are destroyed, though the humidity is still sufficient for their growth if immunity from fire were secured. The amount of mean annual rainfall necessary to the growth of forests if protected from fire is probably about the same as the amount necessary for agriculture without irrigation; at any rate it is somewhere from 20 to 24 inches. All timber growth below that amount is so slow that, when once the timber has been taken from the country, the time necessary for a new forest growth is so great that no practical purpose is subserved.

The evidence that the growth of timber, if protected from fires, might be extended to the limits here given is abundant. It is a matter of experience that planted forests thus protected will thrive throughout the prairie region and far westward on the Great Plains. In the mountain region it may be frequently observed that forest trees grow low down on the mountain slopes and in the higher valleys wherever local circumstances protect them from fires, as in the case of rocky lands that give insufficient footing to the grass and shrubs in which fires generally spread. These cases must not be confounded with those patches of forest that grow on alluvial cones where rivers leave mountain cañons and enter valleys or plains. Here the streams, clogged by the material washed from the adjacent mountains by storms, are frequently turned from their courses and divided into many channels running near the surface. Thus a subterranean watering is effected favorable to the growth of trees, as their roots penetrate to sufficient depth. Usually this watering is too deep for agriculture, so that forests grow on lands that cannot be cultivated without irrigation.

Fire is the immediate cause of the lack of timber on the prairies, the eastern portion of the Great Plains, and on some portions of the highlands of the Arid Region; but fires obtain their destructive force through climatic conditions, so that directly and remotely climate determines the growth of all forests. Within the region where prairies, groves, and forests appear, the local distribution of timber growth is chiefly dependent upon drainage and soil, a subject which needs not be here discussed. Only a small portion of the Rocky Mountain Region is protected by climatic conditions from the invasion of fires, and a sufficiency of forests for the country depends upon the control which can be obtained over that destructive agent. A glance at the map of Utah will exhibit the extent and distribution of the forest region throughout that territory, and also show what portions of it are in fact occupied by standing timber. The *area of standing timber*, as exhibited on the map, is but a part of the Timber Region as there shown, and includes all of the timber, whether dense or scattered.

Necessarily the area of standing timber has been generalized. It was not found practicable to indicate the growth of timber in any refined way by grading it, and by rejecting from the general area the innumerable small open spaces. If the area of standing timber were considered by acres, and all acres not having timber valuable for milling purposes rejected, the extent would be reduced at least to one-fourth of that colored. Within the territory represented on the map the Timber Region has an extent of 18,500 square miles; that is, 23 per cent belongs to the Timber Region. The general area of standing timber is about 10,000 square miles, or 12.5 per cent of the entire area. The area of milling timber, determined in the more refined way indicated above, is about 2,500 square miles, or $3\frac{1}{8}$ per cent of the area embraced on the map. In many portions of the Arid Region these percentages are much smaller. This is true of southern California, Nevada, southern Arizona, and Idaho. In other regions the percentages are larger. Utah gives about a fair average. In general it may be stated that the timber regions are fully adequate to the growth of all the forests which the industrial interests of the country will require if they can be protected from desolation by fire. No limitation to the use of the forests need be made.[4] The amount which the citizens of the country will require will bear but a small proportion to the amount which the fires will destroy; and if the fires are prevented, the renewal by annual growth will more than replace that taken by man. The protection of the forests of the entire Arid Region of the United States is reduced to one single problem — Can these forests be saved from fire? The writer has witnessed two fires in Colorado, each of which destroyed more timber than all that used by the citizens of that State from its settlement to the present day; and at least three

---

[4] With all his prescience about western problems, Powell never seems to have understood the need of protecting the forests; that was reserved for Gifford Pinchot, who as a rival bureaucrat at times found himself in somewhat tart conflict with the Major. Gifford Pinchot, *Breaking New Ground* (New York, 1947), p. 24. It was precisely because he feared a federal forest service might become corrupt, and because of his distaste for big-government management in general, that Powell spoke against Pinchot's dream of the United States Forest Service. Considering his own record as a notably non-corrupt bureaucrat, his opposition is hard to understand. Certainly his feeling that "no limitation to the use of the forests need be made" reflects a limitedly regional view of the future of the West, and a failure to foresee the extent to which western resources would be gutted by eastern corporations.

in Utah, each of which has destroyed more timber than that taken by the people of the territory since its occupation. Similar fires have been witnessed by other members of the surveying corps. Everywhere throughout the Rocky Mountain Region the explorer away from the beaten paths of civilization meets with great areas of dead forests; pines with naked arms and charred trunks attesting to the former presence of this great destroyer. The younger forests are everywhere beset with fallen timber, attesting to the rigor of the flames, and in seasons of great drought the mountaineer sees the heavens filled with clouds of smoke.

In the main these fires are set by Indians. Driven from the lowlands by advancing civilization, they resort to the higher regions until they are forced back by the deep snows of winter. Want, caused by the restricted area to which they resort for food; the desire for luxuries to which they were strangers in their primitive condition, and especially the desire for personal adornment, together with a supply of more effective instruments for hunting and trapping, have in late years, during the rapid settlement of the country since the discovery of gold and the building of railroads, greatly stimulated the pursuit of animals for their furs — the wealth and currency of the savage. On their hunting excursions they systematically set fire to forests for the purpose of driving the game. This is a fact well known to all mountaineers. Only the white hunters of the region properly understand why these fires are set, it being usually attributed to a wanton desire on the part of the Indians to destroy that which is of value to the white man. The fires can, then, be very greatly curtailed by the removal of the Indians.

These forest regions are made such by inexorable climatic conditions. They are high among the summer frosts. The plateaus are scored by deep cañons, and the mountains are broken with crags and peaks. Perhaps at some distant day a hardy people will occupy little glens and mountain valleys, and wrest from an unwilling soil a scanty subsistence among the rigors of a sub-arctic climate. Herdsmen having homes below may in the summer time drive their flocks to the higher lands to crop the scanty herbage. Where mines are found mills will be erected and little towns spring up, but in general habitations will be remote. The forests will be dense here or scattered there, as the trees may with ease or difficulty gain a foothold, but the forest regions will remain such, to be stripped of timber here and there from time to time to supply the wants of the people who live below; but once protected from fires, the forests will increase in extent and value. The first step to be taken for their protection must be by prohibiting the Indians from resorting thereto for hunting purposes, and then slowly, as the lower country is settled, the grasses and herbage of the highlands, in which fires generally spread, will be kept down by summer pasturage, and the dead and fallen timber will be removed to supply the wants of people below. This protection, though sure to come at last, will be tardy, for it depends upon the gradual settlement of the country; and this again depends upon the development of the agricultural and mineral resources and the establishment of manufactories, and to a very important extent on the building of railroads, for the whole region is so arid that its streams are small, and so elevated above the level of the sea that its few large streams descend too rapidly for navigation.

Agriculture and Timber Industries Differentiated

It is apparent that the irrigable lands are more or less remote from the timber lands; and as the larger streams are employed for irrigation, in the future the extended settlements will be still farther away. The pasturage lands that in a general way intervene between the irrigable and timber lands have a scanty supply of dwarfed forests, as already described, and the people in occupying these lands will not resort, to any great extent, to the mountains for timber; hence timber and agricultural enterprises will be more or less differentiated; lumbermen and woodmen will furnish to the people below their supply of building and fencing material and fuel. In some cases it will be practicable for the farmers to own their timber lands, but in general the timber will be too remote, and from necessity such a division of labor will ensue.

Cultivation of Timber

In the irrigable districts much timber will be cultivated along the canals and minor waterways. It is probable that in time a sufficient amount will thus be raised to supply the people of the irrigable districts with fuel wherever such fuel is needed, but often such a want will not exist, for in the Rocky Mountain Region there is a great abundance of lignitic coals that may be cheaply mined. All these coals are valuable for domestic purposes, and many superior grades are found. These coals are not uniformly distributed, but generally this source of fuel is ample.

PASTURAGE LANDS

The irrigable lands and timber lands constitute but a small fraction of the Arid Region. Between the lowlands on the one hand and the highlands on the other is found a great body of valley, mesa, hill, and low mountain lands. To what extent, and under what conditions can they be utilized? Usually they bear a scanty growth of grasses. These grasses are nutritious and valuable both for summer and winter pasturage. Their value depends upon peculiar climatic conditions; the grasses grow to a great extent in scattered bunches, and mature seeds in larger proportion perhaps than the grasses of the more humid regions. In general the winter aridity is so great that the grasses when touched by the frosts are not washed down by the rains and snows to decay on the moist soil, but stand firmly on the ground all winter long and "cure," forming a *quasi* uncut hay. Thus the grass lands are of value both in summer and winter. In a broad way, the greater or lesser abundance of the grasses is dependent on latitude and altitude; the higher the latitude the better are the grasses, and they improve as the altitude increases. In very low altitudes and latitudes the grasses are so scant as to be of no value; here the true deserts are found. These conditions obtain in southern California, southern Nevada, southern Arizona, and southern New Mexico, where broad reaches of land are naked of vegetation, but in ascending to the higher lands the grass steadily improves. Northward the deserts soon disappear, and the grass becomes more and more luxuriant to our northern boundary. In addition to the desert lands mentioned, other large deductions must be made from the area of the pasturage lands. There are many districts in which the "country rock" is composed of incoherent sands and clays; sometimes sediments of ancient Tertiary lakes; elsewhere sediments of more ancient Cretaceous seas. In these districts perennial or intermittent streams have carved deep waterways, and the steep hills are ever washed naked by fierce but infrequent storms, as the incoherent rocks are unable to withstand the beating of the rain. These districts are known as the *mauvaises terres* or bad lands of the Rocky Mountain Region. In other areas the streams have carved labyrinths of deep gorges and the waters flow at great depths below the general surface. The lands between the streams are beset with towering cliffs, and the landscape is an expanse of naked rock. These are the alcove lands and cañon lands of the Rocky Mountain Region. Still other districts have been the theater of late volcanic activity, and broad sheets of naked lava are found; cinder cones are frequent, and scoria and ashes are scattered over the land. These are the lava-beds of the Rocky Mountain Region. In yet other districts, low broken mountains are found with rugged spurs and craggy crests. Grasses and chaparral grow among the rocks, but such mountains are of little value for pasturage purposes.

After making all the deductions, there yet remain vast areas of valuable pasturage land bearing nutritious but scanty grass. The lands along the creeks and rivers have been relegated to that class which has been described as irrigable, hence the lands under consideration are away from the permanent streams. No rivers sweep over them and no creeks meander among their hills.

Though living water is not abundant, the country is partially supplied by scattered springs, that often feed little brooks whose waters never join the great rivers on their way to the sea, being able to run but a short distance from their fountains, when they spread among the sands to be reëvaporated. These isolated springs and brooks will in many cases furnish the water necessary for the herds that feed on the grasses. When springs are not found wells may be sometimes dug, and where both springs and wells fail reservoirs may be constructed. Wherever grass grows water may be found or saved from the rains in sufficient quantities for all the herds that can live on the pasturage.

Pasturage Farms Need Small Tracts of Irrigable Land

The men engaged in stock raising need small areas of irrigable lands for gardens and fields where agricultural products can be raised for their own consumption, and where a store of grain and hay may be raised for their herds when pressed by the severe storms by which the country is sometimes visited.[5] In many places the lone springs and streams are sufficient for these purposes. Another and larger source of water for the fertilization of the gardens and fields of the pasturage farms is found in the smaller branches and upper ramifications of the larger irrigating streams. These brooks can be used to better advantage for the pasturage farms as a supply of water for stock gardens and small fields than for farms where agriculture by irrigation is the only industry. The springs and brooks of the permanent drainage can be employed in making farms attractive and profitable where large herds may be raised in many great districts throughout the Rocky Mountain Region.

The conditions under which these pasturage lands can be employed are worthy of consideration.

The Farm Unit for Pasturage Lands

The grass is so scanty that the herdsman must have a large area for the support of his stock. In general a quarter section of land alone is of no value to him; the pasturage it affords is entirely inadequate to the wants of a herd that the poorest man needs for his support.

Four square miles may be considered as the minimum amount necessary for a pasturage farm, and a still greater amount is necessary for the larger part of the lands; that is, pasturage farms, to be of any practicable value, must be of at least 2,560 acres, and in many districts they must be much larger.[*] [6]

[5] In contrast with his limited understanding of the problems of the forests, Powell saw those of the Plains with great clarity. The Big Die-Up of 1886–87 would demonstrate the rightness of his feeling that pasturage lands should not be fenced, for in the great storms of that winter cattle all through the Plains drifted into fences and died by the thousands. It would also demonstrate the need of a winter feeding program for range stock. The Big Die-Up taught that lesson to most of the ranchers who survived on the American Plains; it took another terrible winter, that of 1906, to teach the lesson to the last open-range ranchers on the Saskatchewan-Montana border, between the Milk River and the Cypress Hills. And it took the winter of 1948–49 to clinch the lesson, for without the feeding program, which in many places had to be put into effect by planes, the range might have seen another disaster comparable to that of 1887.

[*] For the determination of the proper unit for pasturage farms the writer has conferred with many persons living in the Rocky Mountain Region who have had experience. His own observations have been extensive, and for many years while conducting surveys and making long journeys through the Arid Region this question has been uppermost in his mind. He fears that this estimate will disappoint

Regular Division Lines for Pasturage Farms Not Practicable

Many a brook which runs but a short distance will afford sufficient water for a number of pasturage farms; but if the lands are surveyed in regular tracts as square miles or townships, all the water sufficient for a number of pasturage farms may fall entirely within one division. If the lands are thus surveyed, only the divisions having water will be taken, and the farmer obtaining title to such a division or farm could practically occupy all the country adjacent by owning the water necessary to its use. For this reason divisional surveys should conform to the topography, and be so made as to give the greatest number of water fronts. For example, a brook carrying water sufficient for the irrigation of 200 acres of land might be made to serve for the irrigation of 20 acres to each of ten farms, and also supply the water for all the stock that could live on ten pasturage farms, and ten small farmers could have homes. But if the water was owned by one man, nine would be excluded from its benefits and nine-tenths of the land remain in the hands of the government.

Farm Residences Should Be Grouped

These lands will maintain but a scanty population. The homes must necessarily be widely scattered from the fact that the farm unit must be large. That the inhabitants of these districts may

---

many of his western friends, who will think he has placed the minimum too low, but after making the most thorough examination of the subject possible he believes the amount to be sufficient for the best pasturage lands, especially such as are adjacent to the minor streams of the general drainage, and when these have been taken by actual settlers the size of the pasturage farms may be increased as experience proves necessary. [Powell's note]

⁶ In his proposals for pasturage farms Powell was moving in the direction already indicated in the land laws of Texas, which on admission to the Union had retained its public domain, and which had learned from the Mexicans certain truths about arid-land ranching. Powell did not suggest the system of purchase, rather than homesteading, which had enabled Texas to prevent much random and unconsidered settlement; but he comprehended the need for very large units of range. Mexican and early Texas law had provided a homestead unit of 4,470 acres. In 1880 the unsold public domain of Texas was divided into agricultural land, grazing land, and forest land, and in subsequent acts the state land board ruled that purchasers might take as a homestead one section of agricultural or two of grazing land. In 1887 the legitimate amount of grazing land purchasable was raised to four sections, the amount Powell proposed in 1878, and in 1906 the homestead-purchase unit was raised to eight sections, or 5,120 acres. For its humid eastern section, Texas had to revise its land laws *downward*, thus reversing the trend in the rest of the Public Domain. See Webb, *The Great Plains*, pp. 426–427.

have the benefits of the local social organizations of civilization — as schools, churches, etc., and the benefits of coöperation in the construction of roads, bridges, and other local improvements, it is essential that the residences should be grouped to the greatest possible extent. This may be practically accomplished by making the pasturage farms conform to topographic features in such manner as to give the greatest possible number of water fronts.[7]

Pasturage Lands Cannot Be Fenced

The great areas over which stock must roam to obtain subsistence usually prevents the practicability of fencing the lands. It will not pay to fence the pasturage fields, hence in many cases the lands must be occupied by herds roaming in common; for poor men coöperative pasturage is necessary, or communal regulations for the occupancy of the ground and for the division of the increase of the herds. Such communal regulations have already been devised in many parts of the country.

RECAPITULATION

The Arid Region of the United States is more than four-tenths of the area of the entire country excluding Alaska.

In the Arid Region there are three classes of lands, namely, irrigable lands, timber lands, and pasturage lands.

Irrigable Lands

Within the Arid Region agriculture is dependent upon irrigation.

The amount of irrigable land is but a small percentage of the whole area.

[7] It is interesting to note that on the Red River in 1869–70 and on the Saskatchewan in 1885 Louis Riel led *métis* rebellions brought on in part by the insistence of the Dominion Government that surveys should follow the American grid pattern. The *métis* system of settlement, borrowed from Quebec and chosen in the first instance because of the need of water transportation, divided the land into long narrow strips reaching back from a river frontage and merging with large common pastures. It proved to be a system better adapted to the arid Saskatchewan and Manitoba plains than the rectangular system ever was, and if it had been allowed to continue, it would have established on the northern Plains a pattern of irrigated farms and open pastures very like Powell's plan. See Joseph Kinsey Howard, *Strange Empire* (New York, 1952), pp. 94–96, 372.

The chief development of irrigation depends upon the use of the large streams.

For the use of large streams coöperative labor or capital is necessary.

The small streams should not be made to serve lands so as to interfere with the use of the large streams.

Sites for reservoirs should be set apart, in order that no hindrance may be placed upon the increase of irrigation by the storage of water.

Timber Lands

The timber regions are on the elevated plateaus and mountains.

The timber regions constitute from 20 to 25 per cent of the Arid Region.

The area of standing timber is much less than the timber region, as the forests have been partially destroyed by fire.

The timber regions cannot be used as farming lands; they are valuable for forests only.

To preserve the forests they must be protected from fire. This will be largely accomplished by removing the Indians.

The amount of timber used for economic purposes will be more than replaced by the natural growth.

In general the timber is too far from the agricultural lands to be owned and utilized directly by those who carry on farming by irrigation.

A division of labor is necessary, and special timber industries will be developed, and hence the timber lands must be controlled by lumbermen and woodmen.

Pasturage Lands

The grasses of the pasturage lands are scant, and the lands are of value only in large quantities.

The farm unit should not be less than 2,560 acres.

Pasturage farms need small tracts of irrigable land; hence the small streams of the general drainage system and the lone springs and streams should be reserved for such pasturage farms.

The division of these lands should be controlled by topographic features in such manner as to give the greatest number of water fronts to the pasturage farms.

Residences of the pasturage farms should be grouped, in order to secure the benefits of local social organizations, and coöperation in public improvements.

The pasturage lands will not usually be fenced, and hence herds must roam in common.

As the pasturage lands should have water fronts and irrigable tracts, and as the residences should be grouped, and as the lands cannot be economically fenced and must be kept in common, local communal regulations or coöperation is necessary.

CHAPTER II

THE LAND SYSTEM NEEDED FOR
THE ARID REGION

THE growth and prosperity of the Arid Region will depend largely upon a land system which will comply with the requirements of the conditions and facts briefly set forth in the former chapter.

Any citizen of the United States may acquire title to public lands by purchase at public sale or by ordinary "private entry," and in virtue of preëmption, homestead, timber culture, and desert land laws.

Purchase at public sale may be effected when the lands are offered at public auction to the highest bidder, either pursuant to proclamation by the President or public notice given in accordance with instructions from the General Land Office. If the land is thus offered and purchasers are not found, they are then subject to "private entry" at the rate of $1.25 or $2.50 per acre. For a number of years it has not been the practice of the Government to dispose of the public lands by these methods; but the public lands of the southern states are now, or soon will be, thus offered for sale.

Any citizen may preëmpt 160 acres of land, and by settling thereon, erecting a dwelling, and making other improvements, and by paying $1.25 per acre in some districts, without the boundaries of railroad grants, and $2.50 within the boundaries of railroad grants in others, may acquire title thereto. The preëmption right can be exercised but once. No person can exercise the preëmption right who is already the owner of 320 acres of land.

Any citizen may, under the homestead privilege, obtain title to 160 acres of land valued at $1.25 per acre, or 80 acres valued at the rate of $2.50, by payment of $5 in the first case and $10 in the last, and by residing on the land for the term of five years and by making certain improvements.

The time of residence is shortened for persons who have served in the army or navy of the United States, and any such person may homestead 160 acres of land valued at $2.50 per acre.

Any citizen may take advantage of both the homestead and preëmption privileges.

Under the timber culture act, any citizen who is the head of a family may acquire title to 160 acres of land in the prairie region by cultivating timber thereon in certain specific quantities; the title can be acquired at the expiration of eight years from the date of entry.

Any citizen may acquire title to one section of desert land (irrigable lands as described in this paper) by the payment at the time of entry of 25 cents per acre, and by redeeming the same by irrigation within a period of three years and by the payment of $1 per acre at the expiration of that time, and a patent will then issue.

Provision is also made for the disposal of public lands as town sites.

From time to time land warrants have been issued by the Government as bounties to soldiers and sailors, and for other purposes. These land warrants have found their way into the market, and the owners thereof are entitled to enter Government lands in the quantities specified in the warrants.

Agricultural scrip has been issued for the purpose of establishing and endowing agricultural schools. A part of this scrip has been used by the schools in locating lands for investment. Much of the scrip has found its way into the market and is used by private individuals. Warrants and scrip can be used when lands have been offered for sale, and preëmptors can use them in lieu of money.

Grants of lands have been made to railroad and other companies, and as these railroads have been completed in whole or in part, the companies have obtained titles to the whole or proportional parts of the lands thus granted.

Where the railroads are unfinished the titles are inchoate to an extent proportional to the incomplete parts.

With small exceptions, the lands of the Arid Region have not been offered for sale at auction or by private entry.

The methods, then, by which the lands under consideration can be obtained from the Government are by taking advantage of the preëmption, homestead, timber culture, or desert land privileges.

IRRIGABLE LANDS

By these methods adequate provision is made for actual settlers on all irrigable lands that are dependent on the waters of minor streams; but these methods are insufficient for the settlement of the irrigable lands that depend on the larger streams, and also for the pasturage lands and timber lands, and in this are included nearly all the lands of the Arid Region. If the irrigable lands are to be sold, it should be in quantities to suit purchasers, and but one condition should be imposed, namely, that the lands should be actually irrigated before the title is transferred to the purchaser. This method would provide for the redemption of these lands by irrigation through the employment of capital. If these lands are to be reserved for actual settlers, in small quantities, to provide homes for poor men, on the principle involved in the homestead laws, a general law should be enacted under which a number of persons would be able to organize and settle on irrigable districts, and establish their own rules and regulations for the use of the water and subdivision of the lands, but in obedience to the general provisions of the law.

TIMBER LANDS

The timber lands cannot be acquired by any of the methods provided in the preëmption, homestead, timber culture, and desert land laws, from the fact that they are not agricultural lands. Climatic conditions make these methods inoperative. Under these laws "dummy entries" are sometimes made. A man wishing to obtain the timber from a tract of land will make homestead or preëmption entries by himself or through his employés without intending to complete the titles, being able thus to hold these lands for a time sufficient to strip them of their timber.

This is thought to be excusable by the people of the country, as timber is necessary for their industries, and the timber lands cannot honestly be acquired by those who wish to engage in timber enterprises. Provision should be made by which the timber can be purchased by persons or companies desiring to engage in the lumber or wood business, and in such quantities as may be necessary to encourage the construction of mills, the erection of flumes, the making of roads, and other improvements necessary to the utilization of the timber for the industries of the country.

PASTURAGE LANDS

If divisional surveys were extended over the pasturage lands, favorable sites at springs and along small streams would be rapidly taken under the homestead and preëmption privileges for the nuclei of pasturage farms.

Unentered lands contiguous to such pasturage farms could be controlled to a greater or less extent by those holding the water, and in this manner the pasturage of the country would be rendered practicable. But the great body of land would remain in the possession of the Government; the farmers owning the favorable spots could not obtain possession of the adjacent lands by homestead or preëmption methods, and if such adjacent lands were offered for sale, they could not afford to pay the Government price.

Certain important facts relating to the pasturage farms may be advantageously restated.

The farm unit should not be less than 2,560 acres; the pasturage farms need small bodies of irrigable land; the division of these lands should be controlled by topographic features to give water fronts; residences of the pasturage lands should be grouped; the pasturage farms cannot be fenced — they must be occupied in common.

The homestead and preëmption methods are inadequate to meet these conditions. A general law should be enacted to provide for the organization of pasturage districts, in which the residents should have the right to make their own regulations for the division of the lands, the use of the water for irrigation and for watering stock, and for the pasturage of the lands in common or in severalty. But each division or pasturage farm of the district should be owned by an individual; that is, these lands could be settled and improved by the "colony" plan better than by any other.[1] It should not be understood that the colony system applies

[1] The Canadian Pacific Railway's system of "assisted settlement" offers the best chance to study the effects of colonizing as opposed to individual pioneering on the Plains. After the railroad's initial policy of selling land to colonizing speculators (who in turn sold it to individuals as if it were humid-country farmland)

only to such persons as migrate from the east in a body; any number of persons already in this region could thus organize. In fact very large bodies of these lands would be taken by people who are already in the country and who have herds with which they roam about seeking water and grass, and making no permanent residences and no valuable improvements. Such a plan would give immediate relief to all these people.

This district or colony system is not untried in this country. It is essentially the basis of all the mining district organizations of the west. Under it the local rules and regulations for the division of mining lands, the use of water, timber, etc., are managed better than they could possibly be under specific statutes of the United States. The association of a number of people prevents single individuals from having undue control of natural privileges, and secures an equitable division of mineral lands; and all this is secured in obedience to statutes of the United States providing general regulations.

Customs are forming and regulations are being made by common consent among the people in some districts already; but these provide no means for the acquirement of titles to land, no incentive is given to the improvement of the country, and no legal security to pasturage rights.

If, then, the irrigable lands can be taken in quantities to suit purchasers, and the colony system provided for poor men who wish to coöperate in this industry; if the timber lands are opened to timber enterprises, and the pasturage lands offered to settlement under a colony plan like that indicated above, a land system would be provided for the Arid Region adapted to the wants of all persons desiring to become actual settlers therein. Thousands of men who now own herds and live a semi-nomadic life; thousands

---

had proved disastrous in ways that Powell would have forecast, the company eventually decided upon "colony" settlements, both irrigated and non-irrigated, in which it built the houses and barns, plowed and seeded the land, and had control both of crops and of agricultural methods. There is little doubt that this benevolent supervision, as well as the experience of the Ruthenian and other ethnic colonies, helped to create the whole complex of co-operative institutions that in the 20th century have made Alberta and Saskatchewan virtually socialist provinces. Cooperation and group planning of some sort, whether under the guidance of the railroad or spontaneous, proved in the northern Plains to be almost essential, for "the least successful farmer usually occupied the isolated farm." See James B. Hedges, *Building the Canadian West: The Land and Colonization Policies of the Canadian Pacific Railway* (New York, 1939), especially pp. viii, x, xii, and xiii.

of persons who now roam from mountain range to mountain range prospecting for gold, silver, and other minerals; thousands of men who repair to that country and return disappointed from the fact that they are practically debarred from the public lands; and thousands of persons in the eastern states without employment, or discontented with the rewards of labor, would speedily find homes in the great Rocky Mountain Region.

In making these recommendations, the wisdom and beneficence of the homestead system have been recognized and the principles involved have been considered paramount.

To give more definite form to some of the recommendations for legislation made above, two bills have been drawn, one relating to the organization of irrigation districts, the other to pasturage districts. These bills are presented here. It is not supposed that these forms are the best that could be adopted; perhaps they could be greatly improved; but they have been carefully considered, and it is believed they embody the recommendations made above.

A BILL to authorize the organization of irrigation districts by homestead settlements upon the public lands requiring irrigation for agricultural purposes

Be it enacted by the Senate and House of Representatives of the United States of America in Congress assembled, That it shall be lawful for any nine or more persons who may be entitled to acquire a homestead from the public lands, as provided for in sections twenty-two hundred and eighty-nine to twenty-three hundred and seventeen, inclusive, of the Revised Statutes of the United States, to settle an irrigation district and to acquire titles to irrigable lands under the limitations and conditions hereinafter provided.

Sec. 2. That it shall be lawful for the persons mentioned in section one of this act to organize an irrigation district in accordance with a form and general regulations to be prescribed by the Commissioner of the General Land Office, which shall provide for a recorder; and said persons may make such by-laws, not in conflict with said regulations, as they may deem wise for the use of waters in such district for irrigation or other purposes, and for the division of the lands into such parcels as they may deem most convenient for irrigating purposes; but the same must accord with the provisions of this act.

SEC. 3. That all lands in those portions of the United States where irrigation is necessary to agriculture, which can be redeemed by irrigation and for which there is accessible water for such purpose, not otherwise utilized or lawfully claimed, sufficient for the irrigation of three hundred and twenty acres of land, shall, for the purposes set forth in this act, be classed as irrigable lands.

SEC. 4. That it shall be lawful for the requisite number of persons, as designated in section one of this act, to select from the public lands designated as irrigable lands in section three of this act, for the purpose of settling thereon, an amount of land not exceeding eighty acres to each person; but the lands thus selected by the persons desiring to organize an irrigation district shall be in one continuous tract, and the same shall be subdivided as the regulations and by-laws of the irrigation district shall prescribe: *Provided*, That no one person shall be entitled to more than eighty acres.

SEC. 5. That whenever such irrigation district shall be organized the recorder of such district shall notify the register and receiver of the land district in which such irrigation district is situate, and also the Surveyor-General of the United States, that such irrigation district has been organized; and each member of the organization of said district shall file a declaration with the register and receiver of said district that he has settled upon a tract of land within such irrigation district, not exceeding the prescribed amount, with the intention of residing thereon and obtaining a title thereto under the provisions of this act.

SEC. 6. That if within three years after the organization of the irrigation district the claimants therein, in their organized capacity, shall apply for a survey of said district to the Surveyor-General of the United States, he shall cause a proper survey to be made, together with a plat of the same; and on this plat each tract or parcel of land into which the district is divided, such tract or parcel being the entire claim of one person, shall be numbered, and the measure of every angle, the length of every line in the boundaries thereof, and the number of acres in each tract or parcel shall be inscribed thereon, and the name of the district shall appear on the plat in full; and this plat and the field-notes of such survey shall be submitted to the Surveyor-General of the United States; and it shall be the duty of that officer to examine the plat and notes therewith and prove the accuracy of the survey in such manner as the Commissioner of the General Land Office may prescribe; and if it shall appear after such examination and proving that correct surveys have been made, and that the several tracts claimed are within the provisions of this act, he shall certify the same to the register of the land district, and shall thereupon furnish to the said register of the land district, and to the recorder of the irrigation district, and to the recorder or clerk of the county in which the irrigation district is situate, and to the Commissioner of the General Land Office, a copy thereof to each, and the original shall be retained in the office of the Surveyor-General of the United States for preservation.

SEC. 7. That each person applying for the benefits of this act shall, in addition to compliance therewith, conform to the methods provided for the acquirement of a homestead in sections twenty-two hundred and eighty-nine to twenty-three hundred and seventeen, inclusive, of the Revised Statutes of the United States, so far as they are applicable and consistent with this act, and shall also furnish such evidence as the Commissioner of the General Land Office may require that such land has actually been redeemed by irrigation, and may thereupon obtain a patent: *Provided*, That no person shall obtain a patent under this act to any coal lands, town sites, or tracts of public lands on which towns may have been built, or to any mine of gold, silver, cinnabar, copper, or other mineral for the sale or disposal of which provision has been made by law.

SEC. 8. That the lands patented under the provisions of this act shall be described as irrigation farms, and designated by the number of the tract or parcel and the name of the irrigation district.

SEC. 9. That the right to the water necessary to the redemption of an irrigation farm shall inhere in the land from the time of the organization of the irrigation district, and in all subsequent conveyances the right to the water shall pass with the title to the land. But if after the lapse of five years from the date of the organization of the district the owner of any irrigation farm shall have failed to irrigate the whole or any part of the same, the right to the use of the necessary water to irrigate the unreclaimed lands shall thereupon lapse, and any subsequent right to water necessary for the cultivation of said unreclaimed land shall be acquired only by priority of utilization.

SEC. 10. That it shall be lawful for any person entitled to acquire a homestead from the public lands as designated in section one of this act to settle on an irrigation farm contiguous to any irrigation district after such district has been organized by making the notifications and declaration provided for in section five of this act, and by notifying the recorder of such irrigation district, and also by complying with the rules and regulations of such district; and such person may thereupon become a member of the district and entitled to the same privileges as the other members thereof; and it shall be the duty of the recorder of the irrigation district to notify the register and receiver of the land district, and also the Surveyor-General of the United States, that such claim has been made; and such person may obtain a patent to the same under the conditions and by conforming to the methods prescribed in this act: *Provided*, That the water necessary for the irrigation of such farm can be taken without injury to the rights of any person who shall have entered an irrigation farm in such district: *And provided further*, That the right to the water necessary to the redemption of such irrigation farm shall inhere in the land from the time when said person becomes a member of said district, and in all subsequent conveyances the right to the water shall pass with the title to the land; but if, after the lapse of five years from the date of said notifications and declaration, the owner of said irrigation farm shall have failed to irrigate the whole or any part of the same, the right to the use of the necessary water to irrigate the unreclaimed lands shall thereupon lapse, and any subsequent right to the water necessary for the cultivation of the said unreclaimed land shall be acquired only by priority of utilization.

A BILL to authorize the organization of pasturage districts by homestead settlements on the public lands which are of value for pasturage purposes only

Be it enacted by the Senate and House of Representatives of the United States of America in Congress assembled, That it shall be lawful for any nine or more persons who may be entitled to acquire a homestead from the public lands, as provided for in section twenty-two hundred and eighty-nine to twenty-three hundred and seventeen, inclusive, of the Revised Statutes of the United States, to settle a pasturage district and to acquire titles to pasturage lands under the limitations and conditions hereinafter provided.

SEC. 2. That it shall be lawful for the persons mentioned in section one of this act to organize a pasturage district in accordance with a form and general regulations to be prescribed by the Commissioner of the General Land Office, which shall provide for a recorder; and said persons may make such by-laws, not in conflict with said regulations, as they may deem wise for the use of waters in such district for irrigation or other purposes, and for the pasturage of the lands severally or conjointly; but the same must accord with the provisions of this act.

SEC. 3. That all lands in those portions of the United States where irrigation is necessary to agriculture shall be, for the purposes set forth in this act, classed as pasturage lands, excepting all tracts of land of not less than three hundred and twenty acres which can be redeemed by irrigation, and where there is sufficient accessible water for such purpose not otherwise utilized or lawfully claimed, and all lands bearing timber of commercial value.

SEC. 4. That it shall be lawful for the requisite number of persons, as designated in section one of this act, to select from the public lands designated as pasturage lands in section three of this act, for the purpose of settling thereon, an amount of land not exceeding two thousand five hundred and sixty acres to each person; but the lands thus selected by the persons desiring to organize a pasturage district shall be in one continuous tract, and the same shall be subdivided as the regulations and by-laws of the pasturage district shall prescribe: *Provided,* That no one person shall be entitled to more than two thousand five hundred and sixty acres, and this may be in one continuous body, or it may be in two parcels, one for irrigation, the other for pasturage purposes; but the parcel for irrigation shall not exceed twenty acres: *And provided further,* That no tract or tracts of land selected for any one person shall be entitled to a greater amount of water for irrigating purposes than that sufficient for the reclamation and cultivation of twenty acres of land; nor shall the tract be selected in such a manner along a stream as to monopolize a greater amount.

Sec. 5. That whenever such pasturage district shall be organized, the recorder of such district shall notify the register and receiver of the land district in which such pasturage district is situate, and also the Surveyor-General of the United States, that such pasturage district has been organized; and each member of the organization of said district shall file a declaration with the register and receiver of said land district that he has settled upon a tract of land within such pasturage district, not exceeding the prescribed amount, with the intention of residing thereon and obtaining a title thereto under the provisions of this act.

Sec. 6. That if within three years after the organization of the pasturage district the claimants therein, in their organized capacity, shall apply for a survey of said district to the Surveyor-General of the United States, he shall cause a proper survey to be made, together with a plat of the same; and on this plat each tract or parcel of land into which the district is divided shall be numbered, and the measure of every angle, the length of every line in the boundaries thereof, and the number of acres in each tract or parcel, shall be inscribed thereon, and the name of the district shall appear on the plat in full; and this plat and the field-notes of such survey shall be submitted to the Surveyor-General of the United States; and it shall be the duty of that officer to examine the plat and notes therewith and prove the accuracy of the survey in such manner as the Commissioner of the General Land Office may prescribe; and if it shall appear after such examination and proving that correct surveys have been made, and that the several tracts claimed are within the provisions of this act, he shall certify the same to the register of the land district, and shall furnish to the said register of the land district, and to the recorder of the pasturage district, and to the recorder or clerk of the county in which the pasturage district is situate, and to the Commissioner of the General Land Office, a copy thereof to each; and the original shall be retained in the office of the Surveyor-General of the United States for preservation.

Sec. 7. That each person applying for the benefits of this act shall, in addition to compliance therewith, conform to the methods provided for the acquirement of a homestead in sections twenty-two hundred and eighty-nine to twenty-three hundred and seventeen, inclusive, of the Revised Statutes of the United States, so far as they are applicable and consistent with this act, and may thereupon obtain a patent: *Provided,* That no person shall obtain a patent under this act to any coal lands, town sites, or tracts of public lands on which towns may have been built, or to any mine of gold, silver, cinnabar, copper, or other mineral for the sale or disposal of which provision has been made by law.

SEC. 8. That the lands patented under the provisions of this act shall be described as pasturage farms, and designated by the number of the tract or pracel and the name of the pasturage district.

SEC. 9. That the right to the water necessary to the redemption of an irrigation tract of a pasturage farm shall inhere in the land from the time of the organization of the pasturage district, and in all subsequent conveyances the right to the water shall pass with the title to the tract; but if after a lapse of five years from the date of the organization of the pasturage district the owner of any pasturage farm shall have failed to irrigate the whole or any part of the irrigable tract the right to the use of the necessary water to irrigate the unreclaimed land shall thereupon lapse, and any subsequent right to water necessary for the cultivation of such unreclaimed land shall be acquired only by priority of utilization.

SEC. 10. That it shall be lawful for any person entitled to acquire a homestead from the public lands designated in section one of this act to settle on a pasturage farm contiguous to any pasturage district after such district has been organized, by making the notifications and declaration provided for in section five of this act, and by notifying the recorder of such pasturage district, and also by complying with the rules and regulations of such district; and such person may thereupon become a member of the district and entitled to the same privileges as the other members thereof; and it shall be the duty of the recorder of the pasturage district to notify the register and receiver of the land district, and also the Surveyor-General of the United States, that such claim has been made; and such person may obtain a patent to the same under the conditions and by conforming to the methods prescribed in this act: *Provided*, That the water necessary for such farm can be taken without injury to the rights of any person who shall have entered a pasturage farm in such district: *And provided further*, That the right to the water necessary to the redemption of the irrigable tract of such pasturage farm shall inhere in the land from the time when said person becomes a member of said district, and in all subsequent conveyances the right to the water shall pass with the title to the land; but if, after the lapse of five years from the date of such notifications and declaration, the owner of said irrigable tract shall have failed to irrigate the whole or any part of the same, the right to the use of the necessary water to irrigate the unreclaimed land shall thereupon lapse, and any subsequent right to the water necessary to the cultivation of the said unreclaimed land shall be acquired only by priority of utilization.

The provisions in the submitted bills by which the settlers themselves may parcel their lands may need further comment and elucidation. If the whole of the Arid Region was yet unsettled, it might be wise for the Government to undertake the parceling of the lands and employ skilled engineers to do the work, whose duties could then be performed in advance of settlement. It is manifest that this work cannot be properly performed under the contract system; it would be necessary to employ persons of skill and judgment under a salary system. The mining industries which have sprung up in the country since the discovery of gold on the Pacific coast, in 1849, have stimulated immigration, so that settlements are scattered throughout the Arid Region; mining towns have sprung up on the flanks of almost every great range of mountains, and adjacent valleys have been occupied by persons desiring to engage in agriculture. Many of the lands surveyed along the minor streams have been entered, and the titles to these lands are in the hands of actual settlers. Many pasturage farms, or ranches, as they are called locally, have been established throughout the country. These remarks are true of every state and territory in the Arid Region. In the main these ranches or pasturage farms are on Government land, and the settlers are squatters, and some are not expecting to make permanent homes. Many other persons have engaged in pasturage enterprises without having made fixed residences, but move about from place to place with their herds. It is now too late for the Government to parcel the pasturage lands in advance of the wants of settlers in the most available way, so as to closely group residences and give water privileges to the several farms. Many of the settlers are actually on the ground, and are clamoring for some means by which they can obtain titles to pasturage farms of an extent adequate to their wants, and the tens of thousands of individual interests would make the problem a difficult one for the officers of the Government to solve. A system less arbitrary than that of the rectangular surveys now in vogue, and requiring unbiased judgment, overlooking the interests of single individuals and considering only the interests of the greatest number, would meet with local opposition. The surveyors themselves would be placed under many temptations, and would be accused — sometimes rightfully perhaps, sometimes unjustly — of favoritism and corruption, and the service would be subject to the false charges of disappointed men on the one hand, and to truthful charges against corrupt men on the other. In many ways it would be surrounded with difficulties and fall into disrepute.

Under these circumstances it is believed that it is best to permit the people to divide their lands for themselves — not in a way by which each man may take what he pleases for himself, but by providing methods by which these settlers may organize and mutually protect each other from the rapacity of individuals. The lands, as lands, are of but slight value, as they cannot be used for ordinary agricultural purposes, i. e., the cultivation of crops; but their value consists in the scant grasses which they spontaneously produce, and these values can be made available only by the use of the waters necessary for the subsistence of stock, and that necessary for the small amount of irrigable land which should be attached to the several pasturage farms. Thus, practically, all values inhere in the water, and an equitable division of the waters can be made only by a wise system of parceling the lands; and the people in organized bodies can well be trusted with this right, while individuals could not thus be trusted. These considerations have led to the plan suggested in the bill submitted for the organization of pasturage districts.

In like manner, in the bill designed for the purpose of suggesting a plan for the organization of irrigation districts, the same principle is involved, viz, that of permitting the settlers themselves to subdivide the lands into such tracts as they may desire.

The lands along the streams are not valuable for agricultural purposes in continuous bodies or squares, but only in irrigable tracts governed by the levels of the meandering canals which carry the water for irrigation, and it would be greatly to the advantage of every such district if the lands could be divided into parcels, governed solely by the conditions under which the water could be distributed over them; and such parceling cannot be properly done prior to the occupancy of the lands, but can only be made *pari passu* with the adoption of a system of canals; and the people settling on these lands should be allowed the privilege of dividing the lands into such tracts as may be most available for such purposes, and they should not be hampered with the present arbitrary system of dividing the lands into rectangular tracts.[2]

Those who are acquainted with the history of the land system of the eastern states, and know the difficulty of properly identifying or determining the boundaries of many of the parcels or tracts of land into which the country is divided, and who appreciate the cumbrous method of describing such lands by metes and bounds in conveyances, may at first thought object to the plan of parceling lands into irregular tracts. They may fear that if the system of parceling the lands into townships and sections, and describing the same in conveyances by reference to certain great initial points in the surveys of the lands, is abandoned, it will lead to the uncertainties and difficulties that belonged to the old system. But the evils of that system did not belong to the shape into which the lands were divided. The lands were often not definitely and accurately parceled; actual boundary lines were not fixed on the ground and accurate plats were not made, and the description of the boundary lines was usually vague and uncertain. It matters not what the shape of tracts or parcels may be; if these parcels are

[2] The flatness of the Plains encouraged the system of rectangular surveys; aridity, and the consequent need of access to irrigation water, negated it. In practice, what has happened is that those areas where water is available have been settled from an early date; the rest, which might legitimately have been attached to watered home-ranches as grazing land, has remained in the hands of the federal government and is leased as range. But first the rectangular system encouraged land-steals by cattlemen, and since 1934 the grazing lands, some of them restored to productivity by the Soil Conservation Service, have stirred both local stock interests and the local governments they influence to agitate for a "return" of the public lands to the states. They cannot be returned, since the states never owned them, but there is no doubt that a system such as Powell proposed would have promoted a greater, and probably more equitable, distribution of the grasslands to individuals.

accurately defined by surveys on the ground and plotted for record, none of these uncertainties will arise, and if these tracts or parcels are lettered or numbered on the plats, they may be very easily described in conveyances without entering into a long and tedious description of metes and bounds.

In most of our western towns and cities lots are accurately surveyed and plotted and described by number of lot, number of block, etc., etc., and such a simple method should be used in conveying the pasturage lands. While the system of parceling and conveying by section, township, range, etc., was a very great improvement on the system which previously existed, the much more simple method used in most of our cities and towns would be a still further improvement.

The title to no tract of land should be conveyed from the Government to the individual until the proper survey of the same is made and the plat prepared for record. With this precaution, which the Government already invariably takes in disposing of its lands, no fear of uncertainty of identification need be entertained.

Water Rights

In each of the suggested bills there is a clause providing that, with certain restrictions, the right to the water necessary to irrigate any tract of land shall inhere in the land itself from the date of the organization of the district. The object of this is to give settlers on pasturage or irrigation farms the assurance that their lands shall not be made worthless by taking away the water to other lands by persons settling subsequently in adjacent portions of the country. The men of small means who under the theory of the bill are to receive its benefits will need a few years in which to construct the necessary waterways and bring their lands under cultivation. On the other hand, they should not be permitted to acquire rights to water without using the same. The construction of the waterways necessary to actual irrigation by the land owners may be considered as a sufficient guarantee that the waters will subsequently be used.

The general subject of water rights is one of great importance. In many places in the Arid Region irrigation companies are organized who obtain vested rights in the waters they control, and consequently the rights to such waters do not inhere in any particular tracts of land.

When the area to which it is possible to take the water of any given stream is much greater than the stream is competent to serve, if the land titles and water rights are severed, the owner of any tract of land is at the mercy of the owner of the water right. In general, the lands greatly exceed the capacities of the streams. Thus the lands have no value without water. If the water rights fall into the hands of irrigating companies and the lands into the hands of individual farmers, the farmers then will be dependent upon the stock companies, and eventually the monopoly of water rights will be an intolerable burden to the people.

The magnitude of the interests involved must not be over-looked. All the present and future agriculture of more than four-tenths of the area of the United States is dependent upon irrigation, and practically all values for agricultural industries inhere, not in the lands but in the water. Monopoly of land need not be feared. The question for legislators to solve is to devise some practical means by which water rights may be distributed among individual farmers and water monopolies prevented.

The pioneers in the "new countries" in the United States have invariably been characterized by enterprise and industry and an intense desire for the speedy development of their new homes. These characteristics are no whit less prominent in the Rocky Mountain Region than in the earlier "new countries"; but they are even more apparent. The hardy pioneers engage in a multiplicity of industrial enterprises surprising to the people of long established habits and institutions. Under the impetus of this spirit irrigation companies are organized and capital invested in irrigating canals, and but little heed is given to philosophic considerations of political economy or to the ultimate condition of affairs in which their present enterprises will result. The pioneer is fully engaged in the present with its hopes of immediate remuneration for labor. The present development of the country fully occupies him. For this reason every effort put forth to increase the area of the agricultural land by irrigation is welcomed. Every man who turns his attention to this department of industry is considered a public benefactor. But if in the eagerness for present development a land and water system shall grow up in which the practical control of agriculture shall fall into the hands of water companies, evils will result therefrom that generations may not be able to correct, and the very men who are now lauded as benefactors to the country will, in the ungovernable reaction which is sure to come, be denounced as oppressors of the people.

The right to use water should inhere in the land to be irrigated, and water rights should go with land titles.

Those unacquainted with the industrial institutions of the far west, involving the use of lands and waters, may without careful thought suppose that the long recognized principles of the common law are sufficient to prevent the severance of land and water rights; but other practices are obtaining which have, or eventually will have, all the force of common law, because the necessities of the country require the change, and these practices are obtaining the color of right from state and territorial legislation, and to some extent by national legislation. In all that country the natural channels of the streams cannot be made to govern water rights without great injury to its agricultural and mining industries. For the great purposes of irrigation and hydraulic mining the water has no value in its natural channel. In general the water cannot be used for irrigation on the lands immediately contiguous to the streams — i. e., the flood plains or bottom valleys — for reasons more fully explained in a subsequent chapter. The waters must be taken to a greater or less extent on the bench lands to be used in irrigation. All the waters of all the arid lands will eventually be taken from their natural channels, and they can be utilized only to the extent to which they are thus removed, and water rights must of necessity be severed from the natural channels. There is another important factor to be considered. The water when used in irrigation is absorbed by the soil and re-ëvaporated to the heavens. It cannot be taken from its natural channel, used, and returned. Again, the water cannot in general be properly utilized in irrigation by requiring it to be taken from its natural channel within the limits ordinarily included in a single ownership. In order to conduct the water on the higher bench lands where it is to be used in irrigation, it is necessary to go up the stream until a level is reached from which the waters will flow to the lands to be redeemed. The exceptions to this are so small that the statement scarcely needs qualification. Thus, to use the water it must be diverted from its natural course often miles or scores of miles from where it is to be used.

The ancient principles of common law applying to the use of natural streams, so wise and equitable in a humid region, would, if applied to the Arid Region, practically prohibit the growth of its most important industries. Thus it is that a custom is springing up in the Arid Region which may or may not have color of authority in statutory or common law; on this I do not wish to express an opinion; but certain it is that water rights are practically being severed from the natural channels of the streams; and this must be done. In the change, it is to be feared that water rights will in many cases be separated from all land rights as the system is now forming. If this fear is not groundless, to the extent that such a separation is secured, water will become a property independent of the land, and this property will be gradually absorbed by a few. Monopolies of water will be secured, and the whole agriculture of the country will be tributary thereto — a condition of affairs which an American citizen having in view the interests of the largest number of people cannot contemplate with favor.

Practically, in that country the right to water is acquired by priority of utilization, and this is as it should be from the necessities of the country. But two important qualifications are needed. The *user right* should attach to the *land* where used, not to the individual or company constructing the canals by which it is used. The right to the water should inhere in the land where it is used; the priority of usage should secure the right. But this needs some slight modification. A farmer settling on a small tract, to be redeemed by irrigation, should be given a reasonable length of time in which to secure his water right by utilization, that he may secure it by his own labor, either directly by constructing the waterways himself, or indirectly by coöperating with his neighbors in constructing systems of waterways. Without this provision there is little inducement for poor men to commence farming operations, and men of ready capital only will engage in such enterprises.

The tentative bills submitted have been drawn on the theory thus briefly enunciated.

If there be any doubt of the ultimate legality of the practices of the people in the arid country relating to water and land rights, all such doubts should be speedily quieted through the enactment of appropriate laws by the national legislature. Perhaps an amplification by the courts of what has been designated as the *natural right* to the use of water may be made to cover the practices now obtaining; but it hardly seems wise to imperil interests so great by intrusting them to the possibility of some future court made law.

The Lands Should Be Classified

Such a system of disposing of the public lands in the Arid Region will necessitate an authoritative classification of the same. The largest amount of land that it is possible to redeem by irrigation, excepting those tracts watered by lone springs, brooks, and the small branches, should be classed as irrigable lands, to give the greatest possible development to this industry. The limit of the timber lands should be clearly defined, to prevent the fraudulent acquirement of these lands as pasturage lands. The irrigable and timber lands are of small extent, and their boundaries can easily be fixed. All of the lands falling without these boundaries would be relegated to the greater class designated as pasturage lands. It is true that all such lands will not be of value for pasturage purposes, but in general it would be difficult to draw a line between absolutely desert lands and pasturage lands, and no practical purposes would be subserved thereby. Fix the boundaries of the timber lands that they may be acquired by proper methods; fix the boundaries of the irrigable lands that they may also be acquired by proper methods, and then permit the remaining lands to be acquired by settlers as pasturage lands, to the extent that they may be made available, and there will be no fear of settlers encroaching on the desert or valueless lands.

Heretofore we have been considering only three great classes of lands — namely, irrigable, timber, and pasturage lands, although practically and under the laws there are two other classes of lands to be recognized — namely, mineral lands, *i. e.*, lands bearing lodes or placers of gold, silver, cinnabar, etc., and coal lands. Under the law these lands are made special. Mineral lands are withheld from general sale, and titles to the mines are acquired by the investment of labor and capital to an amount specified in the law. Coal lands are sold for $20 per acre. The mineral lands proper, though widely scattered, are of small extent. Where the mines are lodes, the lands lie along the mountains, and are to a greater or less extent valueless for all other purposes. Where the mines are placers, they may also be agricultural lands, but their extent is very limited. To withhold these lands from purchase and settlement as irrigable, timber, and pasturage lands will in no material way affect the interests of the industries connected with the last mentioned lands. The General Government cannot reasonably engage in the research necessary to determine the mineral lands, but this is practically done by the miners themselves. Thousands of hardy, skilful men are vigorously engaged in this work, and as mines are discovered mining districts are organized, and on the proper representation of these interested parties the mineral lands are withheld from general sale by the Land Department. Thus, proper provision is already made for this branch of the work of classification.

In many parts of the Arid Region there are extensive deposits of coal. These coal fields are inexhaustible by any population which the country can support for any length of time that human prevision can contemplate. To withhold from general settlement the entire area of the workable coal fields would be absurd. Only a small fraction will be needed for the next century. Only those lands should be classed as coal lands that contain beds of coal easily accessible, and where there is a possibility of their being used as such within the next generation or two. To designate or set apart these lands will require the highest geological skill; a thorough geological survey is necessary.

In providing for a general classification of the lands of the Arid Region, it will, then, be necessary to recognize the following classes, namely: mineral lands, coal lands, irrigable lands, timber lands, and pasturage lands. The mineral lands are practically classified by the miners themselves, and for this no further legal provision is necessary. The coal lands must be determined by geological survey. The work of determining the areas which should be relegated to the other classes — namely, irrigable, timber, and pasturage lands — will be comparatively inexpensive.

CHAPTER III

THE RAINFALL OF THE WESTERN PORTION OF THE UNITED STATES

T HE Smithsonian Institution conducted for a number of years an extensive system of measurements of rainfall in the United States, and at the same time diligently collected pluvial records from every possible source. The accumulated data thus collected were placed in the hands of Mr. Charles A. Schott for reduction and discussion, and he prepared the "Smithsonian Tables of Precipitation in Rain and Snow," which appeared in 1868. Since that time much additional material has been acquired by the continuation of the work to the present time, and also by a great increase in the number of observation stations, and so valuable is this new material that it has been determined to recompile the tables and issue a second edition. By the time the present report was called for, the preliminary computations for the tables had developed an important body of facts bearing on the climate of the Arid Region, and through the courtesy of Prof. Joseph Henry, Secretary of the Smithsonian Institution, and of Mr. Schott, they were placed at my disposal. Mr. Schott also made such a change in the order of computation as to give precedence to the states and territories which form the subject of this investigation, and by this timely favor made it possible to base the following discussion on the very latest determinations of rainfall.

The results thus made available exhibit the mean precipitation at each station of observation west of the Mississippi River for each month, for each season, and for the year. A number of other data are also tabulated, including the latitude, longitude, and altitude of each station, and the extent of each series of observations in years and months. In selecting material for the present purpose the shorter records were ignored. The variations from year to year are so great that an isolated record of a single year is of no value as an indication of the average rainfall. The mean of two or three years is almost equally liable to mislead, and only a long series of observations can afford accurate results. In the following tables no stations are included (with one exception) which show records of less than five years' extent.

Table I shows the precipitation of the Sub-humid Region; Table II, of the Arid Region; Table III, of the San Francisco Region; and Table IV, of the Region of the Lower Columbia. The limits of each region have been given in a former chapter, and need not be repeated. In each table the first column contains the names of the stations of observation; the second, their latitudes; the third, their longitudes (west from Greenwich); and the fourth, their altitudes in feet above the level of the sea. The next four columns show for each season of the year the mean observed rainfall in inches, and their sum appears in the following column as the mean yearly rainfall. In the last column the extent of each series of observations is given in years and months. In Table I the stations are arranged by latitudes, in Tables II, III, and IV, alphabetically.

TABLE I. — *Precipitation of the Sub-humid Region*

Station	Latitude	Longitude	Height	Mean precipitation, in inches					Extent of record
				Spring	Summer	Autumn	Winter	Year	
	° ′	° ′	Feet						Y. M.
Pembina, Dak.	48 57	97 03	768	4.02	7.24	2.71	1.53	15.50	4 8
Fort Totten, Dak.	47 56	99 16	1,480	5.18	7.17	2.50	1.59	16.44	5 5
Fort Abercrombie, Dak.	46 27	96 21	. . .	4.80	8.67	3.46	1.85	18.78	13 6
Fort Wadsworth, Dak.	45 43	97 10	1,650	7.00	10.25	3.98	2.92	24.15	6 5
Omaha Agency, Nebr.	42 07	96 22	. . .	8.21	8.70	5.77	2.90	25.58	5 2
Fort Kearney, Nebr.	40 38	98 57	2,360	7.81	11.13	4.83	1.45	25.22	14 4
Fort Riley, Kans.	39 03	96 35	1,300	5.49	10.48	5.92	2.63	24.52	20 10
Fort Hays, Kans.	38 59	99 20	2,107	6.93	6.23	5.77	3.77	22.70	6 11
Fort Larned, Kans.	38 10	98 57	1,932	5.17	9.63	4.95	1.67	21.42	10 9
Fort Belknap, Tex.	33 08	98 46	1,600	6.41	9.44	8.34	3.86	28.05	5 10
Fort Griffin, Tex.	32 54	99 14	. . .	4.95	6.25	6.15	4.17	21.51	5 3
Fort Chadbourne, Tex.	31 58	100 15	2,020	5.77	6.53	7.06	3.52	22.88	8 7
Fort McKavett, Tex.	30 48	100 08	2,060	5.21	6.71	7.81	4.22	23.95	9 7
New Braunfels, Tex.	29 42	98 15	720	7.60	7.60	8.83	4.25	27.58	5 1
Fort Clark, Tex.	29 17	100 25	1,000	4.14	7.57	6.55	4.35	22.61	12 5
Fort Inge, Tex.	29 10	99 50	845	5.38	9.67	6.88	3.53	25.46	7 4
Fort Duncan, Tex.	28 39	100 30	1,460	3.56	8.60	6.54	2.63	21.33	11 7
Fort Brown, Tex.	25 50	97 37	50	3.18	7.64	13.02	4.04	27.88	15 0

TABLE II. — *Precipitation of the Arid Region*

Station	Latitude	Longitude	Height	Mean precipitation, in inches — Spring	Summer	Autumn	Winter	Year	Extent of record
	° '	° '	Feet						Y. M.
Albuquerque, N. Mex.	35 06	106 38	5,032	0.83	4.35	2.04	0.89	8.11	12 2
Camp Bowie, Ariz.	32 10	109 30	4,872	1.29	7.35	2.03	4.50	15.26	6 8
Camp Douglas, Utah	40 46	111 50	5,024	7.20	2.18	3.24	6.20	18.82	10 3
Camp Grant, Ariz.	32 54	110 40	4,833	2.08	6.25	3.27	3.48	15.08	6 10
Camp Halleck, Nev.	40 49	115 20	5,790	3.66	1.19	2.31	3.82	10.98	5 8
Camp Harney, Oreg.	43 00	119 00	. . .	2.29	1.09	1.59	3.79	8.76	6 0
Camp Independence, Cal.	36 50	118 11	4,800	1.09	0.35	0.62	4.54	6.60	8 2
Camp McDermitt, Nev.	41 58	117 40	4,700	3.02	0.72	1.13	3.66	8.53	6 4
Camp McDowell, Ariz.	33 46	111 36	. . .	1.11	4.79	1.73	3.82	11.45	8 2
Camp Mohave, Ariz.	35 02	114 36	604	0.81	1.27	0.93	1.64	4.65	9 1
Camp Verde, Ariz.	34 34	111 54	3,160	1.25	4.65	2.41	2.54	10.85	6 1
Camp Warner, Oreg.	42 28	119 42	. . .	4.31	1.10	2.53	6.47	14.41	5 3
Camp Whipple, Ariz.	34 27	112 20	5,700	3.88	8.07	2.15	5.18	19.28	7 5
Cantonment Burgwin, N. Mex.	36 26	105 30	7,900	1.57	2.92	2.42	1.74	8.65	5 9
Drum Barracks, Cal.	33 47	118 17	32	2.26	0.26	0.35	5.87	8.74	5 5
Denver, Colo.	39 45	105 01	5,250	5.02	3.69	3.16	1.90	13.77	5 1
Fort Bayard, N. Mex.	32 46	108 30	4,450	1.54	7.22	2.28	3.28	14.32	7 6
Fort Benton, Mont.	47 50	110 39	2,730	5.34	4.48	1.65	1.79	13.26	7 1
Fort Bidwell, Cal.	41 50	120 10	4,680	4.95	1.54	3.03	10.71	20.23	8 3
Fort Bliss (El Paso), Tex.	31 47	106 30	3,830	0.43	3.49	3.38	1.23	8.53	14 3
Fort Boisé, Idaho	43 40	116 00	1,998	5.16	1.15	2.50	6.67	15.48	9 5
Fort Bridger, Wyo.	41 20	110 23	6,656	2.99	2.05	1.68	1.71	8.43	12 10
Fort Buford, Dak.	48 01	103 58	1,900	3.76	4.06	2.01	2.01	11.84	7 10
Fort Colville, Wash.	48 42	118 02	1,963	3.63	3.04	2.56	4.83	14.06	11 0
Fort Craig, N. Mex.	33 38	107 00	4,619	0.70	5.87	3.43	1.06	11.06	15 9
Fort D. A. Russell, Wyo.	41 12	104 50	. . .	4.76	4.56	3.27	1.50	14.09	5 1
Fort Davis, Tex.	30 40	104 07	4,700	1.84	8.76	4.72	1.80	17.12	8 11
Fort Defiance, Ariz.	35 43	109 10	6,500	2.03	5.91	3.72	2.55	14.21	8 5
Fort Fetterman, Wyo.	42 50	105 29	4,973	4.48	4.12	2.99	3.51	15.10	5 7
Fort Fillmore, N. Mex.	32 14	106 42	3,937	0.48	4.16	3.02	0.76	8.42	8 3
Fort F. Steele, Wyo.	41 47	106 57	6,841	4.57	3.48	3.05	4.28	15.38	5 5
Fort Garland, Colo.	37 25	105 40	7,864	3.28	6.70	2.37	2.51	14.86	13 1
Fort Lapwai, Idaho	46 18	116 54	2,000	4.11	2.41	3.38	4.99	14.89	9 8
Fort Laramie, Wyo.	42 12	104 31	4,472	5.35	4.40	2.73	1.97	14.45	17 8
Fort Lyon, Colo.	38 08	102 50	4,000	4.33	5.44	2.30	0.49	12.56	7 9
Fort Massachusetts, Colo.	37 32	105 23	8,365	3.12	5.56	6.28	2.27	17.23	5 1
Fort McPherson, Nebr.	41 00	100 30	3,726	6.90	7.56	3.25	1.25	18.96	6 9
Fort McIntosh, Tex.	27 35	99 48	806	3.22	6.56	5.38	2.35	17.51	14 7
Fort McRae, N. Mex.	33 18	107 03	4,500	2.43	6.15	2.32	0.69	11.59	5 0
Fort Randall, Dak.	43 01	98 37	1,245	4.72	6.22	3.40	1.18	15.52	15 6
Fort Rice, Dak.	46 32	100 33	. . .	3.63	4.87	1.54	1.35	11.39	6 1
Fort Sanders, Wyo.	41 17	105 36	7,161	3.55	4.15	2.33	1.43	11.46	6 10
Fort Selden, N. Mex.	32 23	106 55	. . .	0.58	4.83	1.86	1.22	8.49	8 5
Fort Shaw, Mont.	47 30	111 42	6,000	2.18	2.30	1.34	1.13	6.95	7 3
Fort Stanton, N. Mex.	33 29	105 38	5,000	3.03	10.61	4.86	2.44	20.94	7 9
Fort Stevenson, Dak.	47 36	101 10	. . .	3.41	4.97	2.15	1.31	11.84	6 2
Fort Stockton, Tex.	30 20	102 30	4,950	1.24	5.66	3.31	1.29	11.50	5 8
Fort Sully, Dak.	44 50	100 35	1,672	6.52	7.18	1.70	1.14	16.54	7 8
Fort Union, N. Mex.	35 54	104 57	6,670	2.12	11.92	3.79	1.32	19.15	17 5
Fort Walla Walla, Wash.	46 03	118 20	800	4.69	2.07	4.98	7.62	19.36	8 8
Fort Wingate, N. Mex.	35 29	107 45	6,982	1.96	6.50	3.42	5.44	17.32	9 1
Fort Yuma, Cal.	32 44	114 36	200	0.27	1.30	1.36	0.98	3.91	16 6
Ringgold Barracks, Tex.	26 23	99 00	521	3.71	7.00	6.31	2.58	19.60	14 2
Salt Lake City, Utah	40 46	111 54	4,534	6.25	6.28	4.71	7.57	24.81	9 2
San Diego, Cal.	32 42	117 14	150	1.89	0.36	1.89	5.17	9.31	24 2
Santa Fé, N. Mex.	35 41	106 02	6,846	2.17	6.82	3.45	2.47	14.91	19 10

TABLE III. — *Precipitation of the San Francisco Region*

Station	Latitude		Longitude		Height	Mean precipitation, in inches					Extent of record	
						Spring	Summer	Autumn	Winter	Year		
	°	′	°	′	Feet						Y.	M.
Alcatraz Island	37	49	122	25	...	2.59	0.01	1.85	12.04	16.49	9	5
Angel Island	37	51	122	26	30	3.52	0.02	2.75	12.29	18.58	5	11
Benicia Barracks	38	03	122	09	64	4.10	0.13	2.28	8.39	14.90	18	3
Fort Miller	37	00	119	40	402	7.25	0.00	2.94	8.81	19.00	6	9
Fort Point	37	48	122	29	27	3.66	0.03	2.28	11.39	17.36	14	11
Monterey	36	37	121	52	40	4.43	0.26	2.24	8.78	15.71	12	3
Sacramento	38	34	121	26	81	5.55	0.09	2.76	10.84	19.24	18	3
San Francisco; Presidio	37	47	122	28	150	4.80	0.49	2.68	12.32	20.29	20	2
San Francisco	37	48	122	25	130	5.03	0.22	3.05	13.19	21.49	24	4

TABLE IV. — *Precipitation of the Region of the Lower Columbia*

Station	Latitude		Longitude		Height	Mean precipitation, in inches					Extent of record	
						Spring	Summer	Autumn	Winter	Year		
	°	′	°	′	Feet						Y.	M.
Astoria, Oreg.	46	11	123	48	52	18.90	5.72	18.19	34.80	77.61	22	4
Cape Disappointment, Wash.	46	17	124	03	30	14.97	5.97	20.46	29.84	71.24	5	9
Fort Dalles, Oreg.	45	33	120	50	350	3.91	1.16	5.78	11.27	22.12	12	8
Camp Gaston, Cal.	41	01	123	34	...	14.76	1.15	9.92	31.56	57.39	12	0
Camp Wright, Cal.	39	48	123	17	...	8.26	0.27	8.17	27.27	43.97	9	8
Fort Crook, Cal.	41	07	121	29	3,390	6.37	0.97	4.55	11.29	23.18	9	0
Fort Hoskins, Oreg.	45	06	123	26	...	14.69	2.65	14.88	34.48	66.70	6	9
Fort Humboldt, Cal.	40	45	124	10	50	9.36	0.73	6.49	18.73	35.31	11	2
Fort Jones, Cal.	41	36	122	52	2,570	5.23	0.91	4.19	11.37	21.70	5	0
Fort Steilacoom, Wash.	47	11	122	34	300	8.98	2.81	10.12	17.01	38.92	12	9
Fort Stevens, Oreg.	46	12	123	57	...	17.67	7.88	18.21	34.81	78.57	6	5
Fort Umpqua, Oreg.	43	42	124	10	8	16.83	2.86	15.64	32.08	67.41	5	10
Fort Vancouver, Wash.	45	40	122	30	50	8.70	3.78	9.17	16.72	38.37	16	11
Fort Yamhill, Oreg.	45	21	123	15	...	13.10	2.39	13.20	26.90	55.59	9	3
Portland, Oreg.	45	30	122	36	45	13.75	2.50	11.31	19.64	47.20	7	0
Port Townsend, Wash.	48	07	122	45	8	5.45	4.22	2.31	4.07	16.05	5	6
San Juan Island, Wash.	48	28	123	01	150	5.01	4.60	7.89	10.84	28.34	9	4

DISTRIBUTION OF RAIN THROUGH THE YEAR

In a general way the limit of agriculture without irrigation, or "dry farming," is indicated by the curve of 20 inches rainfall, and where the rainfall is equally distributed through the year this limitation is without exception. But in certain districts the rainfall is concentrated in certain months so as to produce a "rainy season," and wherever the temperature of the rainy season is adapted to the raising of crops it is found that "dry farming" can be carried on with less than 20 inches of annual rain. There are two such districts upon the borders of the Arid Region, and within its limits there may be a third.

First District — Along the eastern border of the Arid Region a contrast has been observed between the results obtained at the north and at the south. In Texas 20 inches of rain are not sufficient for agriculture, while in Dakota and Minnesota a less amount is sufficient. The explanation is clearly developed by a comparison of the tables of rainfall with reference to the distribution of rain in different seasons.

TABLE V. — *Precipitation of Texas*

Station	Latitude	Longitude	Height	Mean precipitation, in inches					Extent of record
				Spring	Summer	Autumn	Winter	Year	
	o ′	o ′	Feet						Y. M.
Austin	30 17	97 44	650	8.61	7.94	10.74	6.23	33.52	18 8
Camp Verde	30 00	99 10	1,400	6.11	9.81	8.30	5.05	29.27	5 9
Fort Belknap	33 08	98 46	1,600	6.41	9.44	8.34	3.86	28.05	5 10
Fort Bliss (El Paso)	31 47	106 30	3,830	0.43	3.49	3.38	1.23	8.53	14 3
Fort Brown	25 50	97 37	50	3.18	7.64	13.02	4.04	27.88	15 0
Fort Chadbourne	31 58	100 15	2,020	5.77	6.53	7.06	3.52	22.88	8 7
Fort Clark	29 17	100 25	1,000	4.14	7.57	6.55	4.35	22.61	12 5
Fort Davis	30 40	104 07	4,700	1.84	8.76	4.72	1.80	17.12	8 11
Fort Duncan	28 39	100 30	1,460	3.56	8.60	6.54	2.63	21.33	11 7
Fort Griffin	32 54	99 14	...	4.95	6.25	6.14	4.17	21.51	5 3
Fort Inge	29 10	99 50	845	5.38	9.67	6.88	3.53	25.46	7 4
Fort Mason	30 40	99 15	1,200	6.36	10.44	8.22	3.96	28.98	5 1
Fort McIntosh	27 35	99 48	806	3.22	6.56	5.38	2.35	17.51	14 7
Fort McKavett	30 48	100 08	2,060	5.21	6.71	7.81	4.22	23.95	9 7
Fort Stockton	30 20	102 30	4,950	1.24	5.66	3.31	1.29	11.50	5 8
Galveston	29 18	94 47	30	13.15	14.90	16.83	12.19	57.07	6 1
Gilmer (near)	32 40	94 59	950	13.36	9.93	11.77	10.93	45.99	7 9
New Braunfels	29 42	98 15	720	7.60	6.90	8.83	4.25	27.58	5 1
Ringgold Barracks	26 23	99 00	521	3.71	7.00	6.31	2.58	19.60	14 2
San Antonio	29 25	98 25	600	6.77	8.91	9.30	6.32	31.30	10 2
Means				4.62	6.78	6.64	3.69	21.73	...

Table V includes every station in Texas that has a record of five years or more, in all twenty stations. If the means of rainfall for the state be compared with the means for single stations, it will be seen that there is a general correspondence in the ratios pertaining to the different seasons, so that the former can fairly be considered to represent for the state the distribution through the year. Table VI presents the data for Dakota in the same way, and the correspondence between the general mean and the station

TABLE VI. — *Precipitation of Dakota*

Station	Latitude	Longitude	Height	Mean precipitation, in inches					Extent of record
				Spring	Summer	Autumn	Winter	Year	
	° ′	° ′	*Feet*						*Y. M.*
Fort Abercrombie	46 27	96 21	...	4.80	8.67	3.46	1.85	18.78	13 6
Fort Buford	48 01	103 58	1,900	3.76	4.06	2.01	2.01	11.84	7 10
Fort Randall	43 01	98 37	1,245	4.72	6.22	3.40	1.18	15.52	15 6
Fort Rice	46 32	100 33	...	3.63	4.87	1.54	1.35	11.39	6 1
Fort Stevenson	47 36	101 10	...	3.41	4.97	2.15	1.31	11.84	6 2
Fort Sully	44 50	100 35	1,672	6.52	7.18	1.70	1.14	16.54	7 8
Fort Totten	47 56	99 16	1,480	5.18	7.17	2.50	1.59	16.44	5 5
Fort Wadsworth	45 43	97 10	1,650	7.00	10.25	3.98	2.92	24.15	6 5
Pembina	48 57	97 03	768	4.02	7.24	2.71	1.53	15.50	4 8
Means				4.78	6.74	2.61	1.65	15.78	...

mean is here exceedingly close. At each of the nine stations, the greatest rainfall is recorded in summer, the next greatest in spring, and the least in winter. Placing the two series of results in the form of percentages, they show a decided contrast:

	Spring	Summer	Autumn	Winter	Year
Dakota	30	43	17	10	100
Texas	21	31	31	17	100

In Dakota a rainy season is well marked, and 73 per cent. of the rain falls in spring and summer, or at the time when it is most needed by the farmer. In Texas only 52 per cent. of the rain falls in the season of agriculture. The availability of rain in the two regions is therefore in the ratio of 73 to 52, and for agricultural purposes 20 inches of rainfall in Texas is equivalent to about 15 inches in Dakota.

For the further exhibition of the subject, Table VII has been prepared, comprising stations in the Region of the Plains all the way from our northern to our southern boundary. By way of restricting attention to the practical problem of the limit of "dry farming," only those stations are admitted which exhibit a mean annual rainfall of more than 15 and less than 25 inches. The order of arrangement is by latitudes, and in the columns at the right the seasonal rainfalls are expressed in percentages of the yearly. The column at the extreme right gives the sum of the spring and summer quotas, and is taken to express the availability of the rainfall.

TABLE VII. — *Seasonal precipitation in the Region of the Plains*

Station	Latitude	Extent of record	Mean yearly rainfall	Percentages of annual rainfall				
				Spring	Summer	Autumn	Winter	Spring and summer
	° ′	Y. M.	Inches					
Pembina, Dak.	48 57	4 8	15.50	26	47	17	10	73
Fort Totten, Dak.	47 56	5 5	16.44	31	44	15	10	75
Fort Abercrombie, Dak.	46 27	13 6	18.78	26	46	18	10	72
Fort Wadsworth, Dak.	45 43	6 5	24.15	29	42	17	12	71
Fort Sully, Dak.	44 50	7 8	16.54	39	44	10	7	83
Sibley, Minn.	44 30	7 11	24.74	21	40	29	10	61
Fort Randall, Dak.	43 01	15 6	15.52	30	40	22	8	70
Fort McPherson, Nebr.	41 00	6 9	18.96	36	40	17	7	76
Fort Riley, Kans.	39 03	20 10	24.52	22	43	24	11	65
Fort Hays, Kans.	38 59	6 11	22.70	31	27	25	17	58
Fort Larned, Kans.	38 10	10 9	21.42	24	45	23	8	69
Fort Griffin, Tex.	32 54	5 3	21.51	23	29	29	19	52
Fort Chadbourne, Tex.	31 58	8 7	22.88	25	29	31	15	54
Fort McKavett, Tex.	30 48	9 7	23.95	22	28	32	18	50
Fort Davis, Tex.	30 40	8 11	17.12	11	51	28	10	62
Fort Clark, Tex.	29 17	12 5	22.61	18	34	29	19	52
Fort Duncan, Tex.	28 39	11 7	21.33	17	40	31	12	57
Fort McIntosh, Tex.	27 35	14 7	17.51	18	38	31	13	56
Ringgold Barracks, Tex.	26 23	14 2	19.60	19	36	32	13	55

The graduation of the ratios from north to south is apparent to inspection, but is somewhat irregular. The irregularity, however, is not greater than should be anticipated from the shortness of the terms of observation at the several stations, and it disappears when the stations are combined in natural groups. Dividing the whole series into three groups, as indicated by the cross lines in Table VII, and computing weighted means of the seasonal ratios, we have —

TABLE VII (a) *

Groups of stations	Mean latitude of group	Total years of record	Percentage of annual rainfall				
			Spring	Summer	Autumn	Winter	Spring and summer
	° ′						
Eight stations in Dakota, Minnesota, and Nebraska	45 20	67	29	43	19	9	72
Three stations in Kansas	38 45	38	24	41	24	11	65
Eight stations in Texas	29 45	85	19	36	31	14	55

* In computing the several means of Table VII (a) from the seasonal means of Table VII, the latter were weighted according to the lengths of the records by which they had been obtained.

A moment's inspection will show that the middle group is intermediate between the northern and southern in all its characters. The spring quota of rainfall progressively diminishes from north to south, and so does the summer, while the fall and winter quotas increase. What is lost in summer is gained in winter, and thereby the inequality of rainfall from season to season is diminished, so that a rainy season is not so well defined in Texas as in Dakota. What is lost in spring is gained in autumn, and thereby the place of the rainy season in the year is shifted. In Dakota the maximum of rain is earlier than in Texas, and corresponds more nearly with the maximum of temperature.

TABLE VIII. — *Seasonal precipitation in the San Francisco Region*

Station	Extent of record	Mean annual rainfall	Percentage of annual rainfall				
			Spring	Summer	Autumn	Winter	Winter and spring
	Y. M.	Inches					
Alcatraz Island	9 5	16.49	16	0	11	73	89
Angel Island	5 11	18.58	19	0	15	66	85
Benicia Barracks	18 3	14.90	28	1	15	56	84
Fort Miller	6 9	19.00	38	0	16	46	84
Fort Point	14 11	17.36	21	0	13	66	87
Monterey	12 3	15.71	28	2	14	56	84
Sacramento	18 3	19.24	29	1	14	56	85
San Francisco; Presidio	20 2	20.29	24	2	13	61	85
San Francisco	24 4	21.49	24	1	14	61	85
Weighted means	. . .	. . .	25	1	14	60	85

Total extent of record = 130 years   Mean of yearly rainfalls = 15.90

Second District — In the San Francisco Region a rainy season is still more definitely marked, but occurs at a different time of year. It will be seen by Tables III and VIII that no rain falls in summer, while the winter months receive 60 per cent. of the annual precipitation, and the spring 25 per cent. The general yearly rainfall of the district is only about 16 inches, but by this remarkable concentration a period of five months is made to receive 13 inches. The winter temperature of the district is no less remarkable, and supplies the remaining condition essential to agriculture. Frosts are rare, and in the valleys all the precipitation has the form of rain. The nine stations which afford the rainfall records given above show a mean spring temperature of 57° (see Table IX).

Thirteen inches of rain coming in a frostless winter and spring have been found sufficient for remunerative agriculture.

TABLE IX. — *Mean temperatures, by seasons, for the San Francisco Region*

Station	Extent of record	Mean temperatures, in degrees Fahr.				
		Spring	Summer	Autumn	Winter	Year
	Y. M.					
Alcatraz Island	8 6	55	57	60	54	57
Angel Island	3 1	58	63	61	52	58
Benicia Barracks	15 7	58	67	62	49	59
Fort Miller	7 6	64	86	67	49	67
Fort Point	10 11	55	59	58	52	56
Monterey	12 5	55	60	57	50	55
Sacramento	14 0	59	71	62	48	60
San Francisco; Presidio	19 0	54	57	57	50	55
San Francisco	11 2	55	58	58	50	55
Means	. . .	57	64	60	50	58

The same winter maximum of rainfall is characteristic of the whole Pacific coast. The Region of the Lower Columbia, with an average rainfall of 46 inches, receives 47 per cent of it in winter and 24 per cent in spring. Southward on the coast, Drum Barracks (near Los Angeles) and San Diego receive more than half their rain in winter, but as the whole amount is only 9 inches agriculture is not benefited. The eastern bases of the Sierra Nevada and Cascade Range exhibit the winter maximum of rainfall, and this feature can be traced eastward in Idaho and Nevada, but in these districts it is accompanied by no amelioration of winter temperature. (See Table X.)

Third District — In Arizona and New Mexico there is a general maximum of rainfall in summer, and a restricted maximum in winter. The principal minimum is in spring. In Table XI the stations are arranged according to longitudes, a disposition well suited to exhibit their relations. In eastern New Mexico the distribution of rainfall has the same character as in adjacent Texas, but with a more decided maximum. Half of the total rainfall is in summer and half of the remainder in autumn. Westward the maximum diminishes slightly, but it appears in every station of the two territories. In western Arizona the winter maximum of the Pacific coast asserts itself, and it can be traced eastward as far as Fort Wingate, New Mexico. Except at Camp Mohave, on the western border of Arizona, it is inferior in amount to the summer maximum.

TABLE X. — *Seasonal precipitation and temperatures on the Pacific coast, etc.*

Station	Mean annual rainfall	Percentages of rainfall				Mean temperature	
		Spring	Summer	Autumn	Winter	Spring	Winter
	Inches						
San Francisco Region	15.90	25	1	14	60	57	50
Region of Lower Columbia	46.45	24	6	23	47	51	40
Drum Barracks, Cal.	8.74	26	3	4	67	60	56
San Diego, Cal.	9.31	20	4	20	56	60	54
Camp Independence, Cal.	6.60	17	5	9	69	57	39
Fort Bidwell, Cal.	20.23	24	8	15	53	48	32
Camp Warner, Oreg.	14.41	30	8	17	45	42	29
Camp Harney, Oreg.	8.76	26	13	18	43	47	27
Fort Colville, Wash.	14.06	26	22	18	34	45	24
Fort Walla Walla, Wash.	19.36	24	11	26	39	52	34
Camp McDermitt, Nev.	8.53	35	9	13	43	46	29
Camp Halleck, Nev.	10.98	33	11	21	35	45	28
Fort Lapwai, Idaho	14.89	28	16	23	33	53	33
Fort Boisé, Idaho	15.48	33	8	16	43	52	30

TABLE XI. — *Seasonal precipitation in Arizona and New Mexico*

Station	Longitude	Mean annual rainfall	Percentage of annual rainfall			
			Spring	Summer	Autumn	Winter
	° ′	*Inches*				
Western Texas	....	...	19	36	31	14
Fort Union, N. Mex.	104 57	19.15	11	62	20	7
Cantonment Burgwin, N. Mex.	105 30	8.65	18	34	28	20
Fort Stanton, N. Mex.	105 38	20.94	14	51	23	12
Santa Fé, N. Mex.	106 02	14.91	14	46	23	17
Albuquerque, N. Mex.	106 38	8.11	10	54	25	11
Fort Fillmore, N. Mex.	106 42	8.42	5	50	36	9
Fort Selden, N. Mex.	106 55	8.49	7	57	22	14
Fort Craig, N. Mex.	107 00	11.06	6	53	31	10
Fort McRae, N. Mex.	107 03	11.59	21	53	20	6
Fort Wingate, N. Mex.	107 45	17.32	11	38	20	31
Fort Bayard, N. Mex.	108 30	14.32	11	50	16	23
Fort Defiance, Ariz.	109 10	14.21	14	42	26	18
Camp Bowie, Ariz.	109 30	15.26	9	48	13	30
Camp Grant, Ariz.	110 40	15.08	14	41	22	23
Camp McDowell, Ariz.	111 36	11.45	10	42	45	33
Camp Verde, Ariz.	111 54	10.85	12	43	22	23
Camp Whipple, Ariz.	112 20	19.28	20	42	11	27
Camp Mohave, Ariz.	114 36	4.65	18	27	20	35
San Francisco Region	....	...	25	1	14	60

In all this region the daily range of temperature is great, and frosts occur so early in autumn that no use can be made of the autumnal rainfall. The yearly precipitation is very small, and the summer quota rarely exceeds seven or eight inches. Nevertheless the Pueblo Indians have succeeded, in a few localities, and by a unique method, in raising maize without irrigation. The yield is too meagre to tempt the white man to follow their example, and for his use the region is agricultural only where it can be watered artificially.

CHAPTER IV

WATER SUPPLY

By G. K. GILBERT

The following discussion is based upon a special study of the drainage-basin of Great Salt Lake.

INCREASE OF STREAMS

The residents of Utah who practice irrigation have observed that many of the streams have increased in volume since the settlement of the country. Of the actuality of this increase there can be no question. A popular impression in regard to the fluctuations of an unmeasured element of climate may be very erroneous, as, for example, the impression that the rainfall of the timbered states has been diminished by the clearing of the land, but in the case of these streams relative measurements have practically been made. Some of them were so fully in use twenty years ago that all of their water was diverted from its channels at the "critical period," and yet the dependent fields suffered from drought in the drier years. Afterward, it was found that in all years there was enough water and to spare, and operations were extended. Additional canals were dug and new lands were added to the fields; and this was repeated from time to time, until in many places the service of a stream was doubled, and in a few it was increased tenfold, or even fiftyfold. It is a matter of great importance to the agricultural interests, not only of Utah but of the whole district dependent on irrigation, that the cause or causes of this change shall be understood. Until they are known we cannot tell whether the present gain is an omen of future gain or of future loss, nor whether the future changes are within or beyond our control. I shall therefore take the liberty to examine somewhat at length the considerations which are supposed by myself or others to bear upon the problem.

Fortunately we are not compelled to depend on the incidental observations of the farming community for the amount of the increase of the streams, but merely for the fact of their increase. The amount is recorded in an independent and most thorough manner, by the accumulation of the water in Great Salt Lake.

RISE OF GREAT SALT LAKE

A lake with an outlet has its level determined by the height of the outlet. Great Salt Lake, having no outlet, has its level determined by the relation of evaporation to inflow. On one hand the drainage of a great basin pours into it a continuous though variable tribute; on the other, there is a continuous absorption of its water by the atmosphere above it. The inflow is greatest in the spring time, while the snows are melting in the mountains, and least in the autumn after the melting has ceased, but before the cooling of the air has greatly checked evaporation on the uplands. The lake evaporation is greatest in summer, while the air is warm, and least in winter. Through the winter and spring the inflow exceeds the evaporation, and the lake rises. In the latter part of the summer and in autumn the loss is greater than the gain, and the lake falls. The maximum occurs in June or July, and the minimum probably in November. The difference between the two, or the height of the annual tide, is about 20 inches.

But it rarely happens that the annual evaporation is precisely equal to the annual inflow, and each year the lake gains or loses an amount which depends upon the climate of the year. If the air which crosses the drainage basin of the lake in any year is unusually moist, there is a twofold tendency to raise the mean level. On one hand there is a greater precipitation, whereby the inflow is increased, and on the other hand there is a less evaporation. So, too, if the air is unusually dry, the inflow is correspondingly small, the loss by evaporation is correspondingly great, and the contents of the lake diminish. This annual gain or loss is an expression, and a very delicate expression, of the mean annual humidity of a large district of country, and as such is more trustworthy than any result which might be derived from local observations with psychrometer and rain gauge. A succession of relatively dry years causes a progressive fall of the lake, and a succession of moist years a progressive rise. As the water falls it retires from its shore, and the slopes being exceedingly gentle the area of the lake is rapidly contracted. The surface for evaporation diminishes and its ratio to the inflow becomes less. As the water rises the surface of the lake rapidly increases, and the ratio of evaporation to inflow becomes greater. In this way a limit is set to the oscillation of the lake as dependent on the ordinary fluctuations of climate, and the cumulation of results is prevented. Whenever the variation of the water level from its mean position becomes great, the resistance to its further advance in that direction becomes proportionally great. For the convenience of a name, I shall speak of this oscillation of the lake as the *limited oscillation.* It depends on an oscillation of climate which is universally experienced, but which has not been found to exhibit either periodicity, or synchrony over large areas, or other features of regularity.

Besides the annual tide and the limited oscillation, the lake has been found to exhibit a third change, and this third or *abnormal* change seems to be connected with the increase of the tributary streams. In order to exhibit it, it will be necessary to discuss somewhat fully the history of the rise and fall of the lake, and I shall take occasion at the same time to call attention to the preparations that have recently been made for future observations.

Previous to the year 1875 no definite record was made. In 1874 Prof. Joseph Henry, secretary of the Smithsonian Institution, began a correspondence with Dr. John R. Park, of Salt Lake City, in regard to the fluctuations and other peculiarities of the lake, and as a chief result a systematic record was begun. With the coöperation of Mr. J. L. Barfoot and other citizens of Utah, Dr. Park erected a graduated pillar at Black Rock, a point on the southern shore which was then a popular summer resort. It consisted of a granite block cut in the form of an obelisk and engraved on one side with a scale of feet and inches. It was set in gravel beneath shallow water, with the zero of its scale near the surface. The water level was read on the pillar by Mr. John T. Mitchell at frequent intervals from September 14, 1875, to October 9, 1876, when the locality ceased to be used as a watering place, and the systematic record was discontinued. Two observations were made by the writer in 1877, and it was found in making the second that the shifting gravel of the beach had buried the column so deeply as to conceal half the graduation.

Dr. Park has kindly furnished me a copy of Mr. Mitchell's record. The observer was instructed to choose such times of observation that the influence of wind storms upon the level of the lake would be eliminated, and the work appears to have been faithfully performed.

Record of the height of Great Salt Lake above the zero of the granite pillar at Black Rock

Date			Reading		Wind		Date			Reading		Wind	
Year	Month	Day	Feet	Inches	Direction	Force	Year	Month	Day	Feet	Inches	Direction	Force
1875	September	14	0	6	N.	Gentle.	1876	April	17	1	2	...	Calm.
		22	0	5½	N. E.	Quiet.			25	1	3	N. E.	Quiet.
		25	0	5	N. E.	Quiet.		May	2	1	4	N. E.	Quiet.
	October	6	0	4½	N.	Quiet.			22	1	9	N.	Quiet.
		12	0	4	N. E.	Quiet.		June	2	1	11	W.	Quiet.
		18	0	3½	N. E.	Quiet.			8	2	0	...	Calm.
		26	0	3	N. E.	Quiet.			13	2	2	N. E.	Quiet.
	November	9	0	2	W.	Quiet.			23	2	4	N. E.	Quiet.
		16	0	1½	N.	Quiet.			30	2	6	S.	Quiet.
		23	0	4	N. E.	Quiet.		July	18	2	3	N. E.	Quiet.
		29	0	5½	E.	Quiet.			25	2	4	N. E.	Quiet.
	December	7	0	5	E.	Quiet.		August	1	2	3	N. E.	Quiet.
		14	0	5½	E.	Quiet.			10	2	2	N. E.	Quiet.
		21	0	6	N. E.	Quiet.			22	1	9	N. E.	Quiet.
1876	January	5	0	8	N. E.	Quiet.			29	1	8	S. E.	Strong.
		11	0	8½	N. E.	Quiet.			30	1	8	N.	Quiet.
		29	0	9	E.	Quiet.		September	14	1	7	...	Calm.
	February	1	0	9	S.E.	Quiet.			19	1	6½	N.	Quiet.
		15	0	9½	...	Calm.			26	1	6	...	Quiet.
		22	0	9½	N. E.	Quiet.		October	9	1	5½	N. E.	Quiet.
	March	15	0	11	N. E.	Quiet.	1877	July	12	2	0	...	Calm.
		22	1	0	N. E.	Quiet.		October	19	0	10	...	Calm.
		28	1	½	N. E.	Quiet.							

Comparing the October observations for three years, it appears that the lake rose 13 inches from 1875 to 1876, and fell in the next year 6½ inches.

The Black Rock pillar has not the permanence that is desirable. Although it has thus far been only the more firmly established by the action of the waves, it is still true that the lake is encroaching on the land in this part of the coast, and a storm may at any time undermine and overthrow the pillar. To provide for such a contingency it was determined to establish a bench mark out of reach of the waves, and connect it with the pillar by leveling, so that if the existing standard should be destroyed its record would still have a definite meaning, and the relative height of a new standard could be ascertained with precision. In this undertaking I was joined by Mr. Jesse W. Fox, a gentleman who has long held the office of territorial surveyor of Utah. A suitable stone was furnished by the Hon. Brigham Young, and was carried to

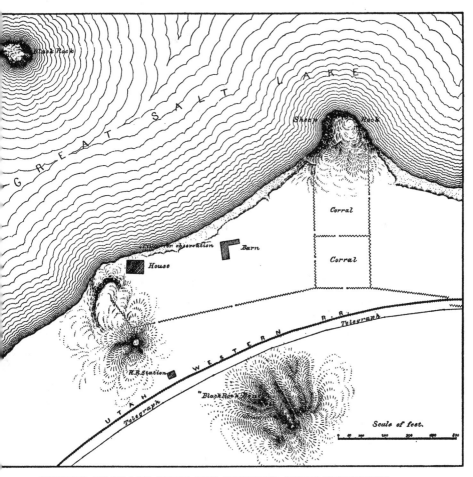

SKETCH OF BLACK ROCK AND VICINITY, UTAH TERRITORY.

Prepared to show the position of the graduated pillar erected by Dr. John Park for observations on the water-level of Great Salt Lake, and the position of the granite bench-mark.

Black Rock without charge through the courtesy of Mr. Heber P. Kimball, superintendent of the Utah Western Railroad. The block is of granite, and is three feet in length. It was sunk in the earth, all but a few inches, on the northern slope of a small limestone knoll just south of the railroad track at Black Rock. Its top is dressed square, about 10 × 10 inches, and is marked with a +. It will be convenient to speak of the top of this monument as the *Black Rock bench.* On the 11th of July, 1877, the surface of the lake was 34.5 feet below the bench, and it then marked 2.0 feet on the pillar erected by Dr. Park. The zero of the observation pillar is therefore 36.5 feet below the bench.

The accompanying topographic sketch will serve at any time to identify the position of the bench.

After consultation with Dr. Park, I concluded that it would be better not to depend on the Black Rock station for observations in the future — at least in the immediate future — and other points were discussed. Eventually it was determined to establish a new station near Farmington, on the eastern shore of the lake. The point selected is in an inlet so sheltered that a heavy swell in the lake will not interfere with accurate observation. At the present stage of water the spot is well adapted to the purpose, and it can be used with the water 2 feet lower or 5 feet higher. I was not able to attend personally to the erection of the pillar, but left the matter in the hands of Mr. Jacob Miller, of Farmington, who writes me that it was placed in position and the record begun on the 24th of November, 1877. The pillar is of wood, and is graduated to inches for 9 feet of its length.

On the day of its establishment the reading of the water surface was 2 feet 1 inch. On the 21st of January, 1878, the reading was 2 feet 1½ inches.

The Farmington and Black Rock pillars are 23 miles apart. The relative height of their zeros will be ascertained as soon as practicable by making coincident readings, during still weather, of the water surface at the two stations. It is already known that the Farmington zero is *approximately* 16 inches lower than the Black Rock.

A stone "bench" or monument for permanent reference has also been placed on rising ground near the observation pillar, and the two will be connected by spirit level. The Farmington bench is of gneiss, and is marked with a + in the same manner as the Black Rock. The stone was contributed by Mr. Abbott, of Farmington, and was gratuitously shaped and placed by Mr. Miller.

Mr. Miller has also voluntarily assumed charge of the record, and will make or superintend the observations. It will not be practicable to visit the pillar daily, nor even at *regular* intervals, but it is expected that the record will be as full as the one tabulated above. The following items are to be noted:

1. Time of observation, including year, month, day, and hour.
2. Reading of water surface in feet and inches.
3. Direction and force of wind.
4. Account of wind for the preceding 24 hours.
5. Name of observer.

These observations will not only determine the annual gain or loss of the lake, but will in a few years give data to construct the curve of the annual tide.

The history of past changes not having been the subject of record, it became necessary to compile it from such collateral data as were attainable. The enquiries inaugurated by Professor Henry have been prosecuted, and have resulted in a tolerably definite determination of the principal changes since 1847, together with the indication of a superior limit to earlier oscillations.

Ever since the settlement of Salt Lake City, in 1847, the islands of the lake have been used as herd grounds. Fremont and Carrington islands have been reached by boat, and Antelope and Stansbury islands partly by boat, partly by fording, and partly by land communication. A large share of the navigation has been performed by citizens of Farmington, and the shore is in that neighborhood so flat that the changes of water level have necessitated frequent changes of landing place. The pursuits of the boatmen have been so greatly affected that all of the more important fluctuations were impressed upon their memories, and most of the changes were so associated with features of the topography that some estimate of their quantitative values could be made. The data which became thus available were collated for Professor Henry by Mr. Miller, a gentleman who himself took part in the navigation, and of whom I have already had occasion to speak. His results agree very closely with those derived from an independent investigation of my own, to which I will now proceed.

Antelope Island is connected with the delta of the Jordan River by a broad, flat sand bar that has been usually submerged but occasionally exposed. It slopes very gently toward the island, and just where it joins it is interrupted by a narrow channel a few inches in depth. For a number of years this bar afforded the means of access to the island, and many persons traversed it. By combining the evidence of such persons it has been practicable to learn the condition of the ford up to the time of its final abandonment. From 1847 to 1850 the bar was dry during the low stage of each winter, and in summer covered by not more than 20 inches of water. Then began a rise which continued until 1855 or 1856. At that time a horseman could with difficulty ford in the winter, but all communication was by boat in summer. Then the water fell for a series of years until in 1860 and 1861 the bar was again dry in winter. The spring of 1862 was marked by an unusual fall of rain and snow, whereby the streams were greatly flooded and the lake surface was raised several feet. In subsequent years the rise continued, until in 1865 the ford became impassable. According to Mr. Miller the present height was attained in about 1868, and there have since occurred only minor fluctuations.

For the purpose of connecting the traditional history as derived from the ford with the systematic record that has now been inaugurated, I visited the bar in company with Mr. Miller on the 19th of October, 1877, and made careful soundings. The features of the ford had been minutely described, and there was no uncertainty as to the identification of the locality. We found 9 feet of water on the sand flat, and 9 feet 6 inches in the little channel at its edge. The examination was completed at 11 a. m.; at 5 p. m. the water stood at 0 feet 10 inches on the Black Rock pillar; and on the following day at 8 a. m. we marked its level at the place where the Farmington pillar now stands, our mark being 2 feet 2 inches above the zero of the pillar.

The Antelope Island bar thus affords a tolerably complete record from 1847 to 1865, but fails to give any later details. It happens, however, that the hiatus is filled at another locality. Stansbury Island is joined to the mainland by a similar bar, which was entirely above water at the time of Captain Stansbury's survey, and so continued for many years. In 1866, the year following that in which the Antelope bar became unfordable, the water for the first time covered the Stansbury bar, and its subsequent advance and recession have so affected the pursuits of the citizens of Grantsville, who used the island for a winter herd ground, that it will not be difficult to obtain a full record by compiling their forced observations. Since undertaking the inquiry I have had no opportunity to visit that town, but the following facts have been elicited by correspondence. Since the first flooding of the bar the depth of water has never been less than 1 foot, and it has never been so great as to prevent fording in winter. But in the summers of 1872, 1873, and 1874, during the flood stage of the annual tide, there was no access except by boat, and in those years the lake level attained its greatest height. In the spring of 1869 the depth was 4½ feet, and in the autumn of 1877, 2½ feet.

The last item shows that the Stansbury bar is 7 feet higher than the Antelope, and serves to connect the two series of observations.

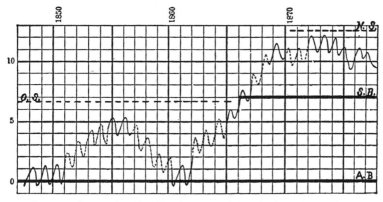

Diagram showing the rise and fall of Great Salt Lake from 1847 to 1877.

N. S. = Level of new storm line.
O. S. = Level of old storm line.
S. B. = Level of Stansbury Island bar.
A. B. = Level of Antelope Island bar.

Further inquiries will probably render the record more complete and exact, but, as it now stands, all the general features of the fluctuations are clearly indicated. In the accompanying diagram the horizontal spaces represent years, and the vertical, feet. The irregular curve shows the height of the lake in different years. Where it is drawn as a full line the data are definite; the dotted portions are interpolated.

Upon the same diagram are indicated the levels of two storm lines. The upper is the limit of wave action at the present time, and is 3 feet above the winter stage (October, 1877). It is everywhere marked by drift wood, and in many places by a ridge of sand. Above it there is a growth, on all steep shores, of sage and other bushes, but those in immediate proximity are dead, having evidently been killed by the salt spray. Below the line are still standing the stumps of similar bushes, and the same can be found 2 or 3 feet below the surface of the water.

The lower storm line was observed by Captain Stansbury in 1850, and has been described to me by a number of citizens of Utah to whom it was familiar at that time and subsequently. Like the line now visible, it was marked by drift wood, and a growth of bushes, including the sage, extended down to it; but below it there were seen no stumps. Its position is now several feet under water, and it is probable that the advancing waves destroyed most of its features, but the vestiges of the bushy growth above it remain.

The peculiarities of the two storm lines have an important bearing on the history of the lake. The fact that the belt of land between them supported sage bushes shows that previous to its present submergence the lake had not covered it for many years. Lands washed by the brine of the lake become saturated with salt to such extent that even salt-loving plants cannot live upon them, and it is a familiar fact that the sage (*Artemisia semper-virens*) never grows in Utah upon soil so saline as to be unfavorable for grain. The rains of many years, and perhaps even of centuries, would be needed to cleanse land abandoned by the lake so that it could sustain the salt-hating bushes, and we cannot avoid the conclusion that the ancient storm line had been for a long period the superior limit of the fluctuations of the lake surface.

To avoid misapprehension, it should be stated that the storm lines have been described as they appear on the eastern shore of Antelope Island, a locality where the slope of the ground amounts to three or four degrees. The circumstances are different at the margin of the mainland, and especially where the slopes are very gentle. The lake is so shallow that its equilibrium is greatly disturbed by strong winds. Its waves are small, but in storms the water is pushed high up on the land toward which the wind blows, the extreme effects being produced where the inclination is most gentle. The islands, however, are little flooded; the water does not accumulate against them, but is driven past; and the easterly gales that produced the present storm line on the east shore of Antelope Island may have driven so much water to the westward as even to have depressed the level in that locality.

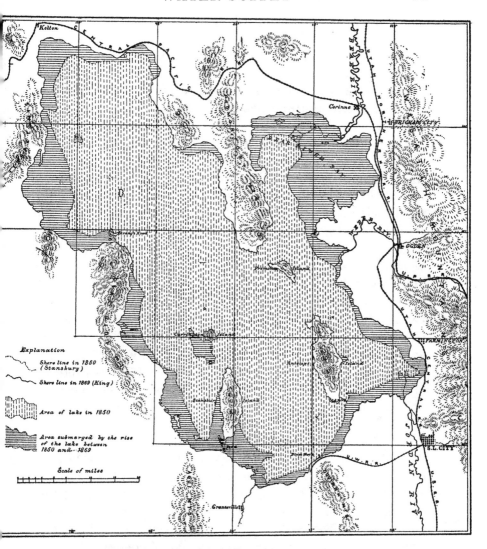

COMPARATIVE MAP OF GREAT SALT LAKE, UTAH.

Compiled to show its increase of area. The topography and later shore-line are taken from the survey of Mr. Clarence King, U.S. Geologist; the earlier shore-line from the Survey of Capt. Howard Stansbury, U.S.A.

Moreover, where the land surface is nearly level, the cleansing by rain of portions once submerged is indefinitely retarded. On all the flatter shores the lake is bordered by tracts too saline for reclamation by the farmer, and either bare of vegetation or scantily covered by salt-loving shrubs. These tracts are above the modern storm line, and they acquired their salt during some flood too remote to be considered in this connection. The largest of them is called the Great Salt Lake Desert, and has a greater area than the lake itself.

Thus it appears that in recent times the lake has overstepped a bound to which it had long been subject. Previous to the year 1865, and for a period of indefinite duration, it rose and fell with the limited oscillation and with the annual tide, but was never carried above a certain limiting line. In that year, or the one following, it passed the line, and it has not yet returned. The annual tide and the limited oscillation are continued as before, but the lowest stage of the new regime is higher than the highest stage of the old. The mean stage of the new regime is 7 or 8 feet higher than the mean stage of the old. The mean area of the water surface is a sixth part greater under the new regime than under the old.

The last statement is based on the United States surveys of Captain Stansbury [1] and Mr. King. The former gathered the material for his map in 1850, when the water was at its lowest stage, and the latter in the spring of 1869, when the water was near its highest stage. The one map shows an area of 1,750 and the other of 2,166 square miles. From these I estimate the old mean area at 1,820 miles, the new at 2,125 miles, and the increase at 305 miles, or 17 per cent.

The "abnormal change" of the lake may then be described as an infilling or rise of the water whereby its ordinary level has been raised 7 or 8 feet and its ordinary area has been increased a sixth part; and this appears to be distinct from the limited oscillation and annual tide, which may be regarded as comparatively normal. To account for it a number of theories have been proposed, and three of them seem worthy of consideration. They appeal respectively to volcanic, climatic, and human agencies.

VOLCANIC THEORY

It has been surmised that upheavals of the land, such as sometimes accompany earthquakes, might have changed the form of

[1] Howard Stansbury (1806–1863) set out in 1849 with a group that included John Williams Gunnison (1812–1853) to explore and survey the Great Salt Lake region. His report, "Exploration and Survey of the Valley of the Great Salt Lake of Utah," was printed as *Senate Doc. 3* 32nd Cong., Special Sess.

the lake bed and displaced from some region the water that has overflowed others. This hypothesis acquires a certain plausibility from the fact that the series of uplifts and downthrows by which the mountains of the region were formed have been traced down to a very recent date, but it is negatived by such an array of facts that it cannot be regarded as tenable. In the first place, the water has risen against *all* the shores and about every island of which we have account. The farmers of the eastern and southern margins have lost pastures and meadows by submergence. At the north, Bear River Bay has advanced several miles upon the land. At the west, a boat has recently sailed a number of miles across tracts that were traversed by Captain Stansbury's land parties. That officer has described and mapped Strong's Knob and Stansbury Island as peninsulas, but they have since become islands. Antelope Island is no longer accessible by ford, and Egg Island, the nesting ground of the gulls and pelicans, has become a reef. Springs that supplied Captain Stansbury with fresh water near Promontory Point are now submerged and inaccessible; and other springs have been covered on the shores of Antelope, Stansbury, and Fremont islands.

In the second place, the rise of the lake is correlated in time with the increase of the inflowing streams, which has been everywhere observed by irrigators, and it is logical to refer the two phenomena to the same cause.

And, finally, if upheaval could account for the enlargement of the lake, it would still be inadequate to account for the maintenance of its increased size, in the face of an evaporation that yearly removes a layer several feet in depth. The same compensatory principle that restricts the "limited oscillation" would quickly restore the equilibrium between inflow and evaporation, in whatever manner it was disturbed.

CLIMATIC THEORY

It is generally supposed that the change is a phenomenon of climate, and this hypothesis includes harmoniously the increase of streams with the increase of lake surface. By some it is thought that the climate of the district is undergoing, or has undergone, a permanent change; and by others that the series of oscillations about a mean condition which characterizes every climate has in this case developed a moist phase of exceptional degree and duration. The latter view was my own before I became aware of the features of the ancient storm line, but it now appears to me untenable. That a variable surface of evaporation, which had for a long period recognized a limit to its expansion, should not merely exceed that limit, but should maintain an abnormal extent for more than a decade, is in a high degree improbable.

It is far more probable that one of those gradual climatic changes, of which geology has shown the magnitude and meteorology has illustrated the slowness, here finds a manifestation. The observed change is apparently abrupt, and even saltatory; but of this we cannot be certain, since it is impossible from a record of only thirty years to eliminate the limited oscillation. It is quite conceivable that were such elimination effected, the residual change would appear as a continuous and equable increase of the lake. However that may be, a certain degree of rapidity of change is necessarily involved, for the climatic change which is able in a decade to augment by a sixth part the mean area of evaporation cannot be of exceeding slowness. If we can ascertain how great a change would be demanded, it will be well to compare it with such changes as have been observed in other parts of the country, and see whether its magnitude is such as to interfere with its assumption.

The prevailing winds of Utah are westerly, and it may be said in a general way that the atmosphere of the drainage basin of Great Salt Lake is part of an air current moving from west to east. The basin having no outlet, the precipitation of rain and snow within its limits must be counterbalanced by the evaporation. The air current must on the average absorb the same quantity of moisture that it discharges. Part of the absorption is from land surfaces and part from water, the latter being the more rapid.

If, now, the equilibrium be disturbed by an augmented humidity of the inflowing air, two results ensue. On the one hand the precipitation is increased, and on the other, the absorbent power of the air being less, the rate of evaporation is diminished. In so dry a climate the precipitation is increased in greater ratio than the humidity, and the rate of evaporation is diminished in less ratio; while of the increased precipitation an increased percentage gathers in streams and finds its way to the lake. That reservoir, having its inflow augmented and its rate of evaporation decreased, gains in volume and grows in breadth until the evaporation from the added expanse is sufficient to restore the equilibrium. Giving attention to the fact that the lake receives a greater percentage of the total downfall than before, and to the fact that its rate of evaporation is at the same time diminished, it is evident that the resultant augmentation of the lake surface is more than proportional to the augmentation of the precipitation.

We are therefore warranted in assuming that an increase of humidity sufficient to account for the observed increase of 17 per cent in the size of the lake would modify the rainfall by less than 17 per cent. The actual change of rainfall cannot be estimated with any degree of precision, but from a review of such data as are at my command I am led to the opinion that an allowance of 10 per cent would be as likely to exceed as to fall short, while an allowance of 7 per cent would be at the verge of possibility.

The rainfall of some other portions of the continent has been recorded with such a degree of thoroughness and for such a period that a term of comparison is afforded. In his discussion of the precipitation of the United States, Mr. Schott has grouped the stations by climatic districts, and deduced the annual means for the several districts. Making use of his table on page 154 (Smithsonian Contributions, No. 222), and restricting my attention to the results derived from five or more stations, I select the following extreme cases of variation between the mean annual rainfalls of consecutive decades. District I comprises the sea coast from Maine to Virginia, and the record includes five or more stations from 1827 to 1867. From the decade 1831–'40 to the decade 1841–'50 the rainfall increased 6 per cent. District II comprises the state of New York and adjacent regions, and includes five or more stations from 1830 to 1866. From the decade 1847–'56 to the decade 1857–'66 the rainfall increased 9 per cent. District IV comprises the Ohio Valley and adjacent regions, and includes five or more stations from 1837 to 1866. From decade 1847–'50 to decade 1851–'60 the rainfall diminished 8 per cent.

The case, then, stands that the best comparable districts and epochs exhibit extreme fluctuations from decade to decade of from 6 to 9 per cent, while the rise of Great Salt Lake implies a fluctuation of about 10 per cent. But before deciding that the hypothetical fluctuation in Utah is extraordinary, consideration should be given to the fact that in the dry climate of that region a given change in humidity will produce a relatively great change in rainfall, while an identical change of rainfall, measured in inches, acquires an exaggerated importance when expressed as the percentage of a small total rainfall. Giving due weight to these considerations, I am led to conclude that the assumed increase of rainfall in Utah is not of incredible magnitude, and consequently that the hypothesis which ascribes the rise of the lake to a change of climate should be regarded as tenable. It by no means follows that it is proven, and so long as it depends on an assumption the truth of which is merely possible, but not established, it can claim no more than a provisional acceptance.

It is proper to add that, so far as I entertain the idea of a change of climate, I do so without referring the change to any local cause. It is frequently asserted that the cultivated lands of Utah "draw the rain"; or that the prayers of the religious community inhabiting the territory have brought water to their growing crops; or that the telegraph wires and iron rails which gird the country have in some way caused electricity to induce precipitation; but none of these agencies seem to be competent. The weather of the globe is a complex whole, each part of which reacts on every other, and each part of which depends on every other. The weather of Utah is an interdependent part of the whole, and cannot be referred to its causes until the entire subject is mastered. The simpler and more immediate meteoric reactions have been so far analyzed that their results are daily predicted; but the remote sources of our daily changes, as well as the causes of the greater cycles of change, are still beyond our reach. Although withdrawn from the domain of the unknowable, they remain within that of the unknown.

THEORY OF HUMAN AGENCIES

The only remaining theory of value is the one advocated by Professor Powell: that the phenomena are to be ascribed to the modification of the surface of the earth by the agency of man. The rise of the lake and the increase of streams have been observed since the settlement of the country by the white man, and the sage brush on the old storm line shows that they had not been carried to the same extent at any previous period in the century. They have coincided in time with the extension of the operations of civilization; and the settlers attach this idea to the facts in detail as well as in general. They have frequently told me that wherever and whenever a settlement was established, there followed in a few years an increase of the water supply, and these statements have been supported by such enumerations of details that they seem worthy of consideration. If they are well founded, the secret of the change will surely be found among the modifications incident to the operations of the settler.

Similar testimony was gathered by Prof. Cyrus Thomas [2] in 1869 in regard to the increase of water supply at the western edge of the plains, and the following conclusion appears in his report to Dr. Hayden (page 237 of the reprint of Dr. Hayden's reports for 1867, 1868, and 1869):

All this, it seems to me, must lead to the conclusion that since the territory [Colorado] has begun to be settled, towns and cities built up, farms cultivated, mines opened, and roads made and travelled, there has been a gradual increase of moisture. Be the cause what it may, unless it is assumed that there is a cycle of years through which there is an increase, and that there will be a corresponding decrease, the fact must be admitted upon this accumulated testimony. I therefore give it as my firm conviction that this increase is of a permanent nature, and not periodical, and that it has commenced within eight years past, and that it is in some way connected with the settlement of the country, and that as the population increases the moisture will increase.

Notwithstanding the confidence of Professor Thomas's conclusions, he appears to have reached them by a leap, for he makes no attempt to analyze the influence of civilized man on nature to which he appeals. Before we accept his results, it will be necessary to inquire in what way the white man has modified the conditions by which the water supply is controlled.

To facilitate this inquiry, an attempt will be made to give a new and more convenient form to our expression of the amount of change for which it is necessary to account in the basin of Great Salt Lake.

The inflow of the lake is derived chiefly from three rivers, and

[2] Ethnologist and entomologist (1825–1910), who served 1869–1873 with The Hayden Survey and after 1882 with the Bureau of Ethnology.

is susceptible of very exact determination. Thorough measurement has not yet been made, but there has been a single determination of each river and minor stream, and a rough estimate can be based on them. The Bear and the Weber were measured in October, 1877, and I am led by the analogy of other streams and by the characters of the river channels to judge that the mean volume of the Bear for the year was twice its volume at the date of measurement, and that of the Weber four times. The mean flow of the Jordan can be estimated with more confidence, for reasons which will appear in a following chapter. The "supply from other sources" mentioned in the table includes all the creeks that flow from the Wasatch Mountains, between Draper and Hampden, together with the Malade River, Blue Creek, the creeks of Skull and Tooele Valleys, and the line of springs that encircles the lake.

Rivers, etc.	Measured volume, in feet per second	Estimated mean volume, in feet per second
Bear River, measured October 4, 1877, at Hampden Bridge	2,600	5,200
Weber River, measured October 11, near Ogden	500	2,000
Jordan River, measured July 8, near Draper	1,275	1,000
Supply from other sources	. . . .	1,800
Total	. . . .	10,000
Deduct the water used in irrigation	. . . .	600
Remainder	. . . .	9,400

The result expresses the mean inflow to the lake in 1877, and is probably not more than 25 per cent in error. The total inflow for the year would suffice to cover the lake to a depth of 60 inches. In the same year (or from October, 1876, to October, 1877) the lake fell 6½ inches, showing that the loss by evaporation was by so much greater than the gain by inflow. The total annual evaporation of inflowing water may therefore be placed provisionally at 66½ inches. If we add to this the rain and snow which fall on the lake, we deduce a total annual evaporation of about 80 inches of water; but for the present purpose it will be more convenient to consider the former figure.

The extent of the Salt Lake basin is about 28,500 square miles. The western portion, amounting to 12,500 miles, sends no water to the lake, yielding all its rainfall to evaporation within its own limits. The remaining 16,000 miles includes both plains and mountains, and its tribute is unequal. To supply 66½ inches annually to the whole area of the lake, 2,125 miles, it must yield a sheet of water with an average thickness of 8.83 inches. In former times, when the lake had an area of only 1,820 miles, the yield of the same area was 7.43 inches. The advance from 7.43 to 8.83, or the addition of 1 inch and 4 tenths to the mean outflow of the district, is the phenomenon to be accounted for.

All the water that is precipitated within the district as rain or snow returns eventually to the air, but different portions are returned in different ways. Of the snow, a portion is melted and a portion is evaporated without melting. Of the melted snow and the rain, a part is absorbed by vegetation and soil, and is afterward reabsorbed by the air; another part runs from the surface in rills, and a third part sinks into the underlying formations and afterward emerges in springs. The streams which arise from springs and rills are again divided. Part of the water is evaporated from the surfaces of the streams of fresh water lakes interrupting their courses. Another part enters the adjacent porous soils, and either meets in them the air by which it is slowly absorbed, or else so saturates them as to produce marshes from which evaporation progresses rapidly at the surface. The remainder flows to Great Salt Lake, and is in time evaporated from its surface. The lesser portion of the precipitation enters the lake; the greater is intercepted on the way and turned back to the air. Whatever man has done to clear the way for the flowing water has diminished local evaporation and helped to fill the lake. Whatever he has done to increase local evaporation has tended to empty the lake.

The white man has modified the conditions of drainage, first, by the cultivation of the soil; second, by the raising of herds; and, third, by the cutting of trees.

1. By plowing the earth the farmer has rendered it more porous and absorbent, so that a smaller percentage of the passing shower runs off. He has destroyed the native vegetation, and replaced it by another that may or may not increase the local evaporation; but this is of little moment, because his operations have been conducted on gentle slopes which in their natural condition contributed very little to the streams. It is of greater import that he has diverted water already accumulated in streams, and for the purposes of irrigation has spread it broadly upon the land,

whence it is absorbed by the air. In this way he has diminished the inflow of the lake.

Incidental to the work of irrigation has been what is known as the "opening out" of springs. Small springs are apt to produce bogs from which much water is evaporated, and it has been found that by running ditches through them the water can be gathered into streams instead. The streams of water thus rescued from local dissipation are consumed in irrigation during a few months of the year, but for the remainder go to swell the rivers, and the general tendency of the work is to increase the inflow of the lake. A similar and probably greater result has been achieved by the cutting of beaver dams. In its natural condition every stream not subject to violent floods was ponded from end to end by the beaver. Its water surface was greatly expanded, and its flood plains were converted into marshes. The irrigator has destroyed the dams and drained the marshes.

There are a few localities where drainage has been resorted to for the reclamation of wet hay lands, and that work has the same influence on the discharge to the lake.

2. The area affected by grazing is far greater than that affected by farming. Cattle, horses, and sheep have ranged through all the valleys and upon all the mountains. Over large areas they have destroyed the native grasses, and they have everywhere reduced them. Where once the water from rain was entangled in a mesh of vegetation and restrained from gathering into rills, there is now only an open growth of bushes that offer no obstruction. Where once the snows of autumn were spread on a non-conducting mat of hay, and wasted by evaporation until the sunshine came to melt them, they now fall upon naked earth and are melted at once by its warmth.

The treading of many feet at the boggy springs compacts the spongy mold and renders it impervious. The water is no longer able to percolate, and runs away in streams. The porous beds of brooklets are in the same way tramped and puddled by the feet of cattle, and much water that formerly sank by the way is now carried forward.

In all these ways the herds tend to increase the inflow of the lake, and there is perhaps no way in which they have lessened it.

3. The cutting of trees for lumber and fence material and fuel

has further increased the streams. By the removal of foliage, that share of the rain and snow which was formerly caught by it and thence evaporated, is now permitted to reach the ground, and some part of it is contributed to the streams. Snow beds that were once shaded are now exposed to the sun, and their melting is so accelerated that a comparatively small proportion of their contents is wasted by the wind. Moreover, that which is melted is melted more rapidly, and a larger share of it is formed into rills.

On the whole, it appears that the white man causes a greater percentage of the precipitation in snow to be melted and a less percentage to be evaporated directly. This follows from the destruction of trees and of grass. By reducing the amount of vegetation he gives a freer flow to the water from rain and melting snow and carries a greater percentage of it to streams, while a smaller percentage reaches the air by evaporation from the soil. By the treading of his cattle he diminishes the leakage of the smaller water channels, and conserves the streams gathered there. By the same means and by the digging of drains he dries the marshes and thereby enlarges the streams. In all these ways he increases the outflow of the land and the inflow of the lake. He diminishes the inflow in a notable degree only by irrigation.

The direct influence of irrigation upon the inflow is susceptible of quantitative statement. Four hundred square miles of land in Utah and Idaho are fertilized by water that would otherwise flow to the lake, and they dissipate annually a layer of about 20 inches. To supply these 20 inches the drainage district of 16,000 miles yields an average layer of 0.5 inch, and this yield is in addition to the 1.4 inches required to maintain the increase of lake surface. The total augmentation of the annual water supply is therefore represented by a sheet 1.9 inches in depth covering the entire district.

The indirect influence of irrigation, and the influences exerted by the grazier and the woodman, cannot be estimated from any existing data, but of their tendencies there can be no question. To some extent they diminish local evaporation, and induce a larger share of the rainfall to gather in the streams; and to one who has contrasted the district in question with similar districts in their virgin condition, there seems no extravagance in ascribing to them the whole of the observed change.

In the valley of the Mississippi and on the Atlantic coast, it has been observed that the floods of rivers are higher than formerly, and that the low stages are lower, and the change has been ascribed by Ellet [3] and others to the destruction of the native vegetation. The removal of forests and of prairie grasses is believed to facilitate the rapid discharge from the land of the water from rain and melted snow, and to diminish the amount stored in the soil to maintain springs. In an arid country like Utah, where the thirst of the air is not satisfied by the entire rainfall, any influence that will increase the rapidity of the discharge must also increase the amount of the discharge. The moisture that lingers on the surface is lost.

On the whole, it may be most wise to hold the question an open one whether the water supply of the lake has been increased by a climatic change or by human agency. So far as we now know, neither theory is inconsistent with the facts, and it is possible that the truth includes both. The former appeals to a cause that may perhaps be adequate, but is not independently known to exist. The latter appeals to causes known to exist but quantitatively undetermined.

It is gratifying to turn to the economic bearings of the question, for the theories best sustained by facts are those most flattering to the agricultural future of the Arid Region. If the filling of the streams and the rise of the lake were due to a transient extreme of climate, that extreme would be followed by a return to a mean condition, or perhaps by an oscillation in the opposite direction, and a large share of the fields now productive would be stricken by drought and returned to the desert.

If the increase of water supply is due to a progressive change of climate forming part of a long cycle, it is practically permanent, and future changes are more likely to be in the same advantageous direction than in the opposite. The lands now reclaimed are assured for years to come, and there is every encouragement for the work of utilizing the existing streams to the utmost.

And finally, if the increase of water supply is due to the changes wrought by the industries of the white man, the prospect is even

[3] Charles Ellet (1810–1862), advocate of improvement of western rivers, wrote *The Physical Geography of the Mississippi Valley* (published by the Smithsonian, 1849) and *The Mississippi and Ohio Rivers* (1853).

better. Not only is every gain of the present assured for the future, but future gain may be predicted. Not alone are the agricultural facilities of this district improving, but the facilities in the whole Rocky Mountain Region are improving and will improve. Not only does the settler incidentally and unconsciously enhance his natural privilege, but it is possible, by the aid of a careful study of the subject, to devise such systematic methods as shall render his work still more effectual.

FARMING WITHOUT IRRIGATION

The general rule that agriculture in Utah is dependent on artificial irrigation finds exception in two ways. First, there are some localities naturally irrigated; and, second, there is at least one locality of which the local climate permits dry farming.

Along the low banks of many streams there are fertile strips of land. The soil is in every such case of a porous nature, and water from the stream percolates laterally and rises to the roots of the plants. Nearly all such lands are flooded in spring time, and they are usually devoted to hay as an exclusive crop; but some of them are above ordinary floods and are suited for other uses. It rarely happens, however, that they are farmed without some irrigation, for the reason that the use of the convenient water renders the harvest more secure and abundant.

The same fertility is sometimes induced by subterranean waters which have no connection with surface streams. In such cases there is usually, and perhaps always, an impervious subsoil which retains percolating water near the surface. A remarkable instance of this sort is known at the western base of the Wasatch Mountains. A strip of land from 20 to 40 rods broad, and marking the junction of the mountain slope with the plain, has been found productive from Hampton's Bridge to Brigham City, a distance of 18 miles. In some parts it has been irrigated, with the result of doubling or trebling the yield, but where water has not been obtained, the farmer has nevertheless succeeded in extracting a living. A similar but narrower belt of land lies at the eastern base of the Promontory range, and a few others have been found. In each locality the proximity of subterranean water to the surface is shown by the success of shallow wells, and there is evidently a natural irrigation.

There is one region, however, where natural irrigation is out of the question, but where crops have nevertheless been secured. Bear River "City" was founded by a company of Danes, who brought the water of the Malade River to irrigate their fields. After repeated experiment they became satisfied that the water was so brackish as to be injurious instead of beneficial, and ceased to use it; and for a number of years they have obtained a meagre subsistence by dry farming. A district lying south of Ogden and east of Great Salt Lake, and known as "the Sand Ridge," has recently been brought in use, and in 1876 and 1877 winter wheat was harvested with a yield variously reported as from 10 to 15 bushels per acre. This success is regarded by some of the older settlers as temporary and delusive, for it is said to have depended on exceptional spring rains; but the majority of the community have faith in its permanence, and the experiment is being pushed in many valleys. In Bear River City and on the Sand Ridge water is not found by shallow wells, and the land is naturally dry. In these localities, and, so far as I am aware, in all others where dry land has been successfully farmed, the soil is sandy, and this appears to be an essential condition. Success has moreover been restricted to the line of valleys which lie at the western base of the Wasatch Mountains and near Great Salt Lake.

This last feature depends, as I conceive, on a local peculiarity of climate. The general movement of the atmosphere is from west to east, and the air which crosses the lake is immediately lifted from its level to the crest of the Wasatch. Having acquired from the lake an addition to its quota of moisture, it has less power of absorption and a greater tendency to precipitation than the atmosphere in general, and it confers on the eastern shore of the lake a climate of exceptional humidity.

The character of this climate is clearly indicated by the assemblage of the observed facts in regard to precipitation. Through the kindness of Prof. Joseph Henry I have been permitted to examine the rain records accumulated by the Smithsonian Institution, including not only those which have been embodied in the published "Tables," but the more recent data to be included in the forthcoming second edition. The following table shows the mean annual precipitation for all stations in Utah, Nevada, Wyoming, and Colorado, which have a record two years or more in extent, together with certain other facts for comparison. The temperature means are taken from the Smithsonian Temperature Tables and the United States Signal Service Reports.

Station	Annual precipita-tion	Mean temperature		Height above sea	Latitude	Length of record	
		Spring	Summer				
	Inches	Deg. F.	Deg. F.	Feet	o ′	Yrs.	Mos.
Salt Lake City, Utah	24.81	50	74	4,354	40 46	9	2
Camp Douglas, Utah	18.82	49	73	5,024	40 46	10	3
Colorado Springs, Colo.	17.59	44	68	5,970	38 49	3	0
Camp Winfield Scott, Nev.	17.33	47	74	. . .	41 34	2	8
Fort Massachusetts, Colo.	17.23	. .	. .	8,365	37 32	5	1
Golden City, Colo.	17.01	. .	72	5,240	39 44	2	3
Fort Sedgwick, Colo.	15.44	47	74	3,600	40 58	2	1
Fort Fred., Steele, Wyo.	15.38	41	66	6,845	41 47	5	5
Fort Fetterman, Wyo.	15.10	41	67	5,012	42 50	5	7
Fort Garland, Colo.	14.86	43	64	7,864	37 25	13	1
Fort Laramie, Wyo.	14.45	47	73	4,472	42 12	17	8
Fort D. A. Russell, Wyo.	14.09	36	64	6,000	41 12	5	1
Denver, Colo.	13.77	46	69	5,250	39 45	5	1
Harrisburg, Utah	13.74	. .	. .	3,275	37 10	2	2
Fort Reynolds, Colo.	13.26	52	75	4,300	38 12	2	8
Fort Lyon, Colo.	12.56	51	77	4,000	38 08	7	9
Fort Sanders, Wyo.	11.46	38	62	7,161	41 17	6	10
Saint George, Utah	11.39	. .	. .	2,800	37 13	2	11
Camp Halleck, Nev.	10.98	45	68	5,790	40 49	5	8
Cheyenne, Wyo.	10.14	40	66	6,075	41 08	3	9
Camp McDermitt, Nev.	8.53	46	70	4,700	41 58	6	4
Fort Bridger, Wyo.	8.43	39	63	6,656	ₒ 41 20	12	10
Fort Churchill, Nev.	7.43	52	75	4,284	39 17	3	9
Camp Floyd, Utah	7.33	49	74	4,867	40 16	2	6
Means	13.80	45	70	5,300	40 05	. .	. .

Two of the stations, Salt Lake City and Camp Douglas, lie within the zone of climate modified by Great Salt Lake, and a brief inspection of the table will show how greatly their climate is influenced. As a general rule, the localities of greatest precipitation in the Rocky Mountain Region have so great altitude that their summer temperature does not permit agriculture, but Salt Lake City, with an altitude 1,000 feet below the average of the 24 stations, and a temperature 4° above the average, has a rainfall 11 inches greater than the average; and Camp Douglas, 3° warmer than the average and 250 feet lower, has a rainfall 5 inches greater. If the two stations are compared with those which lie nearest them, the contrast is still more striking. Camp Halleck, 130 miles west of the lake, and 600 feet higher than Camp Douglas, has a rainfall of 11 inches only. Fort Bridger, 90 miles east of the lake and 1,600 feet higher than Camp Douglas, has a rainfall of 8 inches. Camp Floyd, 30 miles south of the lake and sheltered from its influence by mountains, receives only 7⅓ inches. But Salt Lake City and Camp Douglas, lying between the lake and the Wasatch Range, record respectively 24.8 and 18.8 inches.

In fine, it appears that the climate of the eastern shore of Great Salt Lake is decidedly exceptional and approximates in humidity to that of Central Kansas. The fact that it admits of dry farming gives no warrant for the belief that large areas in the Arid Region can be cultivated without irrigation, but serves rather to confirm the conclusion that the limit to remunerative dry farming is practically drawn by the isohyetal line of 22 inches. Even in this most favored district the yield is so small that it can be doubled by irrigation, and eventually water ditches will be carried to nearly all the land that has yet been plowed.

CHAPTER V

CERTAIN IMPORTANT QUESTIONS
RELATING TO IRRIGABLE LANDS

THE UNIT OF WATER USED IN IRRIGATION

THE unit of water employed in mining as well as manufacturing enterprises in the west is usually the inch, meaning thereby the amount of water which will flow through an orifice one inch square. But in practice this quantity is very indefinite, due to the "head" or amount of pressure from above. In some districts this latter is taken at six inches. Another source of uncertainty exists in the fact that increase in the size of the orifice and increase in the amount of flow do not progress in the same ratio. An orifice of one square inch will not admit of a discharge one-tenth as great as an orifice of ten square inches. An inch of water, therefore, is variable with the size of the stream as well as with the head or pressure. For these reasons it seemed better to take a more definite quantity of water, and for this purpose the *second-foot* has been adopted. By its use the volume of a stream will be given by stating the number of cubic feet which the stream will deliver per second.

THE QUANTITATIVE VALUE OF WATER IN IRRIGATION

In general, throughout the Arid Region the extent of the irrigable land is limited by the water supply; the arable lands are much greater than the irrigable. Hence it becomes necessary, in determining the amount of irrigable lands with reasonably approximate accuracy, to determine the value of water in irrigation; that is, the amount of land which a given amount of water will serve.

All questions of concrete or applied science are more or less complex by reason of the multifarious conditions found in nature, and this is eminently true of the problem we are now to solve, namely, how much water must an acre of land receive by irrigation to render agriculture thereon most successful; or, how much land will a given amount of water adequately supply. This will be affected by the following general conditions, namely, the amount of water that will be furnished by rainfall, for if there is rainfall in the season of growing crops, irrigation is necessary only to supply the deficiency; second, the character of the soil and subsoil. If the conditions of soil are unfavorable, the water supply may be speedily evaporated on the one hand, or quickly lost by subterranean drainage on the other; but if there be a soil permitting the proper permeation of water downward and upward, and an impervious subsoil, the amount furnished by artificial irrigation will be held in such a manner as to serve the soil bearing crops to the greatest extent; and, lastly, there is a great difference in the amount of water needed for different crops, some requiring less, others more.

Under these heads come the general complicating conditions. In the mountainous country the areal distribution of rainfall is preëminently variable, as the currents of air which carry the water are deflected in various ways by diverse topographic inequalities. The rainfall is also exceedingly irregular, varying from year to year, and again from season to season.

But in all these varying conditions of time and space there is one fact which must control our conclusions in considering most of the lands of the Arid Region, namely: any district of country which we may be studying is liable for many seasons in a long series to be without rainfall, when the whole supply must be received from irrigation. Safety in agricultural operations will be secured by neglecting the rainfall and considering only the supply of water to be furnished by artificial methods; the less favorable seasons must be considered; in the more favorable there will be a surplus. In general, this statement applies throughout the Arid Region, but there are some limited localities where a small amount of rainfall in the season of growing crops seems to be constant from year to year. In such districts irrigation will only be used to supply deficiencies.

The complicating conditions arising from soil and subsoil are many. Experience has already shown that there are occasional conditions of soil and subsoil so favorable that the water may be supplied before the growing season, and the subsoil will hold it for weeks, or even months, and gradually yield the moisture to the overlying soil by slow upward percolation or capillary attraction during the season when growing crops require its fertilizing effect. When such conditions of soil and subsoil obtain, the construction of reservoirs is unnecessary, and the whole annual supply of the streams may be utilized. On the other hand, there are extremely pervious soils underlaid by sands and gravels, which speedily carry away the water by a natural under drainage. Here a maximum supply by irrigation is necessary, as the soils must be kept moist by frequent flowing. Under such conditions the amount of water to be supplied is many fold greater than under the conditions previously mentioned, and between these extremes almost infinite variety prevails.

Practical agriculture by irrigation has also demonstrated the fact that the wants of different crops are exceedingly variable, some requiring many fold the amount of others. This is due in part to the length of time necessary to the maturing of the crops, in part to the amount of constant moisture necessary to their successful growth. But by excluding the variability due to rainfall, and considering only that due to differences of soils and crops, and by taking advantage of a wide experience, a general average may be obtained of sufficient accuracy for the purposes here in view.

In examining the literature of this subject it was found that the experience in other countries could not be used as a guide in considering our problems. In general, irrigation in Europe and Asia is practiced only to supply deficiencies, and the crops there raised are only in part the same as with us, and the variation on account of the crops is very great. Certain statements of Marsh [1] in his *Man and Nature* have been copied into the journals and reports published in the United States, and made to do duty on many occasions; but these statements are rather misleading, as the experience of farmers in the Arid Region has abundantly demonstrated. The writers who have used them have in general overestimated the quantitative value of water in irrigation. The facts in Italy, in Spain, in Grenada, and India are valuable severally for discussion in the countries named, but must be used

[1] George Perkins Marsh (1801–1882), whose *Man and Nature; or Physical Geography as Modified by Human Action* (1864) is considered influential in the conservation movement.

in a discussion of the arid lands of the United States with much care. It seemed better, under these circumstances, to determine the quantitative value of water in irrigation in Utah from the experience of the farmers of Utah. Irrigation has there been practiced for about thirty years, and gradually during that time the area of land thus redeemed has been increased, until at present about 325,000 acres of land are under cultivation. A great variety of crops have been cultivated — corn, wheat, oats, rye, garden vegetables, orchard trees, fruits, vines, etc., etc.; and even the fig tree and sugar cane are there raised.

During the past six or seven years I have from time to time, as occasion was afforded, directed my attention to this problem, but being exceedingly complex, a very wide range of facts must be considered in order to obtain a reasonably approximate average. During the past year the task of more thoroughly investigating this subject was delegated to Mr. Gilbert. The results of his studies appear in a foregoing chapter, written by him; but it may be stated here that he has reached the conclusion that a continuous flow of one cubic foot of water per second, i. e., a *second-foot* of water, will, in most of the lands of Utah, serve about 100 acres for the general average of crops cultivated in that country; but to secure that amount of service from the water very careful and economic methods of irrigation must be practiced. At present, there are few instances where such economic methods are used. In general, there is a great wastage, due to badly constructed canals, from which the water either percolates away or breaks away from time to time; due, also, to too rapid flow, and also to an excessive use of the water, as there is a tendency among the farmers to irrigate too frequently and too copiously, errors corrected only by long experience.

The studies of Mr. Gilbert, under the circumstances, were quite thorough, and his conclusions accord with my own, derived from a more desultory but longer study of the subject.

AREA OF IRRIGABLE LAND SOMETIMES NOT LIMITED BY WATER SUPPLY

While, as a general fact, the area of arable land is greater than the area of irrigable land, by reason of the insufficient supply of water, yet in considering limited tracts it may often be found that the supply of water is so great that only a part of it can be used thereon. In such cases the area of irrigable land is limited by the extent to which the water can be used by proper engineering skill. This is true in considering some portions of Utah, where the waters of the Green and Colorado cannot all be used within that territory. Eventually these surplus waters will be used in southern California.

METHOD OF DETERMINING THE SUPPLY OF WATER

To determine the amount of irrigable land in Utah, it was necessary to consider the supply; that is, to determine the amount of water flowing in the several streams. Again, this quantity is variable in each stream from season to season and from year to year. The irrigable season is but a small portion of the year. To utilize the entire annual discharge of the water, it would be necessary to hold the surplus flowing in the non-growing season in reservoirs, and even by this method the whole amount could not be utilized, as a great quantity would be lost by evaporation. As the utilization of the water by reservoirs will be to a great extent postponed for many years, the question of immediate practical importance is resolved into a consideration of the amount of water that the streams will afford during the irrigating season. But in the earlier part of the season the flow in most of the streams in this western region is great, and it steadily diminishes to the end of the summer. Earlier in the season there is more water, while for the average of crops the greater amount is needed later.

The practical capacity of a stream will then be determined by its flow at the time when that is least in comparison with the demands of the growing crops. This will be called the critical period, and the volume of water of the critical period will determine the capacity of the stream. The critical period will vary in different parts of the region from the latter part of June until the first part of August. For the purposes of this discussion it was only necessary to determine the flow of the water during the critical period. This has been done by very simple methods. Usually in each case a section of the stream has been selected having the least possible variation of outline and flow. A cross-section of the stream has been measured, and the velocity of flow determined. With these factors the capacity of the streams has been obtained. In some cases single measurements have been made; in others several at different seasons, rarely in different years. The determination of the available volume of the several streams by such methods is necessarily uncertain, especially from the fact that it has not always been possible to gauge the streams exactly at the critical period; and, again, the flow in one season may differ materially from that in another. But as the capacity of a stream should never be rated by its volume in seasons of abundant flow, we have endeavored as far as possible to determine the capacity of the streams in low water years. Altogether the amount of water in the several streams has been determined crudely, and at best the data given must be considered tolerable approximations. In considering the several streams experience may hereafter discover many errors, but as the number of determinations is great, the average may be considered good.

METHODS OF DETERMINING THE EXTENT OF IRRIGABLE LAND UNLIMITED BY WATER SUPPLY

In the few cases where the water supply is more than sufficient to serve the arable lands, the character of the problem is entirely changed, and it becomes necessary then to determine the area to which the waters can be carried. These problems are hypsometric; relative altitudes are the governing conditions. The hypsometric methods were barometric and angular; that is, from the barometric stations vertical angles were taken and recorded to all the principal points in the topography of the country; mercurial and aneroid barometers were used, chiefly the former; the latter to a limited extent, for subsidiary work. Angular measurements were made with gradientors to a slight extent, but chiefly with the orograph, an instrument by which a great multiplicity of angles are observed and recorded by mechanical methods. This instrument was devised by Professor Thompson for the use of the survey, and has been fully described in the reports on the geographical operations. To run hypsometric lines with spirit levels would have involved a great amount of labor and been exceedingly expensive, and such a method was entirely impracticable with the means at command, but the methods used give fairly approximate results, and perhaps all that is necessary for the purposes to be subserved.

THE SELECTION OF IRRIGABLE LANDS

From the fact that the area of arable lands greatly exceeds the irrigable, or the amount which the waters of the streams will serve, a wide choice in the selection of the latter is permitted. The considerations affecting the choice are diverse, but fall readily into two classes, viz: physical conditions and artificial conditions. The mountains and high plateaus are the great aqueous condensers; the mountains and high plateaus are also the reservoirs that hold the water fed to the streams in the irrigating season, for the fountains from which the rivers flow are the snow fields of the highlands. After the streams leave the highlands they steadily diminish in volume, the loss being due in part to direct evaporation, and in part to percolation in the sands from which the waters are eventually evaporated. In like manner irrigating canals starting near the mountains and running far out into the valleys and plains rapidly diminish in the volume of flowing water. Looking to the conservation of water, it is best to select lands as high along the streams as possible. But this consideration is directly opposed by considerations relating to temperature; the higher the land the colder the climate. Where the great majority of streams have their sources, agriculture is impossible on account of prevailing summer frosts; the lower the altitude the more genial the temperature; the lower the land the greater the variety of crops which can be cultivated; and to the extent that the variety of crops is multiplied the irrigating season is lengthened, until the maximum is reached in low altitudes and low latitudes where two crops can be raised annually on the same land. In the selection of lands, as governed by these conditions, the higher lands will be avoided on the one hand because of the rigor of the climate; if these conditions alone governed, no settlement should be made in Utah above 6,500 feet above the level of the sea, and in general still lower lands should be used; on the other hand the irrigable lands should not be selected at such a distance from the source of the stream as to be the occasion of a great loss of water by direct and indirect evaporation. For general climatic reasons, the lands should be selected as low as possible; for economy of water as high as possible; and these conditions in the main will cause the selections to be made along the middle courses of the streams. But this general rule will be modified by minor physical conditions relating to soil and slope — soils that will best conserve the water will be selected, and land with the gentlest slopes will be taken.

In general, the descent of the streams in the arid land is very great; for this reason the flood plains are small, that is, the extent of the lands adjacent to the streams which are subject to overflow at high water is limited. In general, these flood-plains should not be chosen for irrigation, from the fact that the irrigating canals are liable to be destroyed during flood seasons. Where the plan of irrigation includes the storage of the water of the nongrowing season, by which all the waters of the year are held under control, the flood-plain lands can be used to advantage, from the fact that they lie in such a way as to be easily irrigated and their soils possess elements and conditions of great fertility.

Other locally controlling conditions are found in selecting the most advantageous sites for the necessary water works.

These are the chief physical factors which enter into the problem, and in general it will be solved by considering these factors only; but occasionally artificial conditions will control.

The mining industries of the Arid Region are proportionately greater than in the more humid country. Where valuable mines are discovered towns spring up in their immediate vicinity, and they must be served with water for domestic purposes and for garden culture. When possible, agriculture will be practiced in the immediate vicinity for the purpose of taking advantage of the local market. In like manner towns spring up along the railroads, and agriculture will be carried on in their vicinity. For this and like reasons the streams of the Arid Region will often be used on lands where they cannot be made the most available under physical conditions, and yet under such circumstances artificial conditions must prevail.

In the indication of specific areas as irrigable on the accompanying map of Utah, it must be considered that the selections made are but tentative; the areas chosen are supposed to be, under all the circumstances, the most available; but each community will settle this problem for itself, and the circumstances which will control any particular selection cannot be foretold. It is believed that the selections made will be advantageous to the settler, by giving him the opinions of men who have made the subject a study, and will save many mistakes.

The history of this subject in Utah is very instructive. The greater number of people in the territory who engage in agriculture are organized into ecclesiastical bodies, trying the experiment of communal institutions. In this way the communal towns are mobile. This mobility is increased by the fact that the towns are usually laid out on Government lands, and for a long time titles to the land in severalty are not obtained by the people. It has been the custom of the church to send a number of people, organized as a community, to a town site on some stream to be used in the cultivation of the lands, and rarely has the first selection made been final. Luxuriant vegetation has often tempted the settlers to select lands at too great an altitude, and many towns have been moved down stream. Sometimes selections have been made too far away from the sources of the streams, and to increase the supply of water, towns have been moved up stream. Sometimes lands of too great slope have been chosen, and here the waters have rapidly cut deep channels and destroyed the fields. Sometimes alkaline lands are selected and abandoned, and sometimes excessively sandy lands have caused a change to be made; but the question of the best sites for the construction of works for controlling and distributing the water has usually determined the selection of lands within restricted limits.

To a very slight extent indeed have artificial conditions controlled in Utah; the several problems have generally been solved by the consideration of physical facts.

INCREASE IN THE WATER SUPPLY

Irrigation has been practiced in different portions of the Arid Region for the last twenty-five or thirty years, and the area cultivated by this means has been steadily increasing during that time. In California and New Mexico irrigation has been practiced to a limited extent for a much longer time at the several Catholic missions under the old Spanish regime. In the history of the settlement of the several districts an important fact has been uniformly observed — in the first years of settlement the streams have steadily increased in volume. This fact has been observed alike in California, Utah, Colorado, and wherever irrigation has been practiced. As the chief development of this industry has been within the last fifteen years, it has been a fact especially observed during that time. An increase in the water supply, so universal of late years, has led to many conjectures and hypotheses as to its origin. It has generally been supposed to result from increased rainfall, and this increased rainfall now from this, now from that, condition of affairs. Many have attributed the change to the laying of railroad tracks and construction of telegraph lines; others to the cultivation of the soil, and not a few to the interposition of Divine Providence in behalf of the Latter Day Saints.

If each physical cause was indeed a *vera causa*, their inability to produce the results is quite manifest. A single railroad line has been built across the Arid Region from east to west, and a short north and south line has been constructed in Colorado, another in Utah, and several in California. But an exceedingly small portion of the country where increase of water supply has been noticed has been reached by the railroads, and but a small fraction of one per cent of the lands of the Arid Region have been redeemed by irrigation. This fully demonstrates their inadequacy. In what manner rainfall could be affected through the cultivation of the land, building of railroads, telegraph lines, etc., has not been shown.[2] Of course such hypotheses obtain credence because of a lack of information relating to the laws which govern aqueous precipitation. The motions of the earth on its axis and about the sun; the unequal heating of the atmosphere, which decreases steadily from equator to poles; the great ocean currents and air currents; the distribution of land and water over the earth; the mountain systems — these are all grand conditions affecting the

[2] Henry Nash Smith, in "Man and Climate on the Great Plains, 1867–1880," and also in "Rain Follows the Plow: The Notion of Increased Rainfall for the Great Plains, 1844–1880," *Huntington Library Quarterly*, X, 169–193 (February 1947), has discussed at length the origins and development of the fantasies about a changing Plains climate. He traces their beginnings to Ferdinand Vandiveer Hayden in 1867. That Powell's careful, point-by-point disproving of most of these fantasies was not wholly successful is indicated by the fact that when I was a boy on the Saskatchewan plains from 1914 to 1920 there were still men who believed a plowed-up prairie drew down the rain. As recently as August 13, 1961, an article in the *New York Times*, under the head of "Farmer Runs Risk on Great Plains," mentions the old fallacies but concludes with, "Soil conservation and crop diversification have reduced the impact of the recent droughts, but Great Plains farmers still have to be optimists."

distribution of rainfall. Many minor conditions also prevail in topographic reliefs, and surfaces favorable to the absorption or reflection of the sun's heat, etc., etc., affecting in a slight degree the general results. But the operations of man on the surface of the earth are so trivial that the conditions which they produce are of minute effect, and in presence of the grand effects of nature escape discernment. Thus the alleged causes for the increase of rainfall fail. The rain gauge records of the country have been made but for a brief period, and the stations have been widely scattered, so that no very definite conclusions can be drawn from them, but so far as they are of value they fail to show any increase. But if it be true that increase of the water supply is due to increase in precipitation, as many have supposed, the fact is not cheering to the agriculturist of the Arid Region. The permanent changes of nature are secular; any great sudden change is ephemeral, and usually such changes go in cycles, and the opposite or compensating conditions may reasonably be anticipated.

For the reasons so briefly stated, the question of the origin and permanence of the increase of the water supply is one of prime importance to the people of the country. If it is due to a temporary increase of rainfall, or any briefly cyclic cause, we shall have to expect a speedy return to extreme aridity, in which case a large portion of the agricultural industries of the country now growing up would be destroyed.

The increase is abundantly proved; it is a matter of universal experience. The observations of the writer thereon have been widely extended. Having examined as far as possible all the facts seeming to bear on the subject, the theory of the increase of rainfall was rejected, and another explanation more flattering to the future of agriculture accepted.

The amount of water flowing in the streams is but a very small part of that which falls from the heavens. The greater part of the rainfall evaporates from the surfaces which immediately receive it. The exceedingly dry atmosphere quickly reabsorbs the moisture occasionally thrown down by a conjunction of favoring conditions. Any changes in the surfaces which receive the precipitation favorable to the rapid gathering of the rain into rills and brooks and creeks, while taking to the streams but a small amount of that precipitated, will greatly increase the volume of the streams themselves, because the water in the streams bears so small a proportion to the amount discharged from the clouds. The artificial changes wrought by man on the surface of the earth appear to be adequate to the production of the observed effects. The destruction of forests, which has been immense in this country for the past fifteen years; the cropping of the grasses, and the treading of the soil by cattle; the destruction of the beaver dams, causing a drainage of the ponds; the clearing of drift wood from stream channels; the drainage of upland meadows, and many other slight modifications, all conspire to increase the accumulation of water in the streams, and all this is added to the supply of water to be used in irrigation.

Students of geology and physical geography have long been aware of these facts. It is well known that, under the modifying influences of man, the streams of any region redeemed from the wilderness are changed in many important characteristics. In flood times their volumes are excessively increased and their powers of destruction multiplied.[3] In seasons of drought, some streams that were perennial before man modified the surface of the country become entirely dry; the smaller navigable streams have their periods of navigation shortened, and the great rivers run so low at times that navigation becomes more and more difficult during dry seasons; in multiplied ways these effects are demonstrated. While in the main the artificial changes wrought by man on the surface are productive of bad results in humid regions, the changes are chiefly advantageous to man in arid regions where agriculture is dependent upon irrigation, for here the result is to increase the supply of water. Mr. Gilbert, while engaged during the past season in studying the lands of Utah, paid especial attention to this subject, and in his chapter has more thoroughly discussed the diverse special methods by which increase in the flow of the streams is caused by the changes wrought by man upon the surface of the earth. His statement of facts is clear, and his conclusions are deemed valid.

[3] See Powell's article, "Our Recent Floods," *North American Review*, CLV, 149–159 (August 1892).

CHAPTER VI

THE LANDS OF UTAH[1]

A zone of mountains and high plateaus extends from the northern nearly to the southern boundary of Utah Territory. The Wasatch Mountains constitute the northern portion of this zone, the High Plateaus the southern. This central zone has a general altitude above the sea of from nine to eleven thousand feet. Many peaks are higher, a few reaching an altitude of about twelve thousand feet. On the other hand many cañons and valleys have been excavated by the running waters far below the general level thus indicated.

The Uinta Mountains stretch eastward from the midst of the Wasatch. This region is a lofty table land carrying many elevated peaks whose summits are from twelve to nearly fourteen thousand feet above the level of the sea. This is the highest portion of Utah, and among its peaks are the culminating points.

South from the Uinta Region, and from the southern extremity of the Wasatch Mountains, another elevated district extends east-southeast beyond the borders of Utah. This table land is cut in

---

[1] Since the Powell Survey worked from 1870 to 1879 in the plateau country of which Utah was the heart, and since Powell's explorations of 1868 and 1869 had also led him into that in part unmapped and unexplored region, the data utilized by Powell for this report are the earliest scientific information on the area. The fact that the Mormons had from the beginning made use of the streams for irrigation and had developed co-operative methods of building and maintaining irrigation works gave a strong impetus to Powell's interest in that subject. On the country of his particular interest all the publications of his survey are relevant, especially C. E. Dutton, *Geology of the High Plateaus of Utah* (Washington, 1880) and *Tertiary History of the Grand Canyon District*, United States Geological Survey Monograph 2 (Washington, 1882); G. K. Gilbert, *Report on the Geology of the Henry Mountains* (Washington, 1878), and *Lake Bonneville*, United States Geological Survey Monograph 1 (Washington, 1890); and Powell's own *Report on the Geology of the Eastern Portion of the Uinta Mountains and a Region of Country Adjacent Thereto*, United States Geographical and Geological Survey of the Territories (Washington, 1876), and *Exploration of the Colorado River of the West and Its Tributaries* (Washington, 1875).

twain by two great gorges of the Green River — the Cañon of Desolation and Gray Cañon. The eastern portion is called East Tavaputs Plateau, the western West Tavaputs Plateau.

Between the Uinta Mountains and the Tavaputs table land is the Uinta-White Basin, a low synclinal valley, drained by the Uinta and its ramifications on the west, and the lower portion of the White River on the east.

The district of country lying south of the Tavaputs table land, and east and south of the High Plateaus, is traversed by many deep cañons. This is the Cañon Land of Utah. In its midst the Green and Grand unite to form the Colorado. The Price and San Rafael are tributary to the Green. The Fremont, Escalante, Paria, Kanab, and Virgin are directly tributary to the Colorado from the north and west. From the east the San Juan flows to the Colorado, but its drainage area is not included in our present discussion.

West of the lofty zone lie low, arid valleys, interrupted by short and abrupt ranges of mountains whose naked cliffs and desolate peaks overlook the still more desolate valleys. These short longitudinal ranges are but a part of the Basin Ranges, a mountain system extending through Nevada and northward into Idaho and Oregon. That portion of the Basin Range System which lies in Utah, and which we now have under consideration, is naturally divided into two parts, the northern embracing the drainage area of Great Salt Lake, the southern embracing the drainage area of Sevier Lake, giving the Great Salt Lake District and the Sevier Lake District.

To recapitulate, the grand districts into which Utah is naturally divided are as follows: The Wasatch Mountains and the High Plateaus, constituting the lofty zone above mentioned; the Uinta Mountains, the Tavaputs table lands, the Uinta-White Basin, the Cañon Lands, the Sevier Lake Basin, and the Great Salt Lake Basin, the two latter being fragments of the great Basin Range Province.

The eastern portion of the Territory of Utah is drained by the Colorado River by the aid of a number of important tributaries. The western portion is drained by streams that, heading in the mountains and high plateaus of the central portion, find their way by many meanderings into the salt lakes and desert sands to the westward.

Considered with reference to its drainage, Utah may thus be divided into two parts — the Colorado drainage area and the Desert drainage area; the former is about two-fifths, the latter three-fifths of the area of the territory.

All of the Wasatch Mountains lie west of the drainage crest; a part of the High Plateaus are drained to the Colorado, a part to the deserts. This great water divide, commencing north of the Pine Valley Mountains in the southwest corner of the territory, runs north of the Colob Plateau and enters the district of the High Plateaus. It first runs eastward along the crest or brink of the Pink Cliffs that bound the Markagunt and Paunsagunt Plateaus, and then north and east in many meandering ways, now throwing a plateau into the western drainage, and now another into the eastern, until it reaches the western extremity of the Tavaputs table lands. Thence it runs around the western end of the Uinta Valley, throwing the Tavaputs table lands, the Uinta Valley, and Uinta Mountains into the Colorado drainage, and the Wasatch Mountains into the Desert drainage.

These two regions are highly differentiated in orographic structure and other geological characteristics. The sedimentary formations of the eastern region are in large part of Cenozoic and Mesozoic age, though Paleozoic rocks appear in some localities. The Cenozoic and Mesozoic formations are largely composed of incoherent sands and shales with intercalated beds of indurated sandstone and limestone. The great geological displacements are chiefly by faults and monoclinal flexures, by which the whole country has been broken up into many broad blocks, so that the strata are horizontal or but slightly inclined, except along the zones of displacement by which the several blocks are bounded. Here the strata, when not faulted, are abruptly flexed, and the rocks dip at high angles.

The Uinta Mountains are storm carved from an immense uplifted block. The mountains of the Cañon Lands are isolated and volcanic. In the High Plateaus sedimentary beds are covered by vast sheets of lava. The sedimentary beds exposed in the mountains of the Desert region are of Paleozoic age, and many crystalline schists appear, while the sedimentary beds exposed in the valleys are Post-Tertiary. The crystalline schists and ancient sedimentaries of the mountains are often [overlain by?] extensive masses of extravasated rocks. The prevailing type of orographic structure is that of monoclinal ridges of displacement. Blocks of strata have been turned up so as to incline at various angles, and from their upturned edges the mountains have been carved. But these monoclinal ridges are much complicated by mountain masses having an eruptive origin.

In the eastern districts the materials denuded from the mountains and plateaus have been carried to the sea, but in the western districts the materials carried from the mountains are deposited in the adjacent valleys, so that while the mountains are composed of rocks of great age, the rocks of the valleys are of recent origin. In that geological era known as the Glacial epoch the waters of a great lake spread over these valleys, and the mountains stood as islands in the midst of a fresh-water sea. For the history of this lake we are indebted to the researches of Mr. Gilbert. It had its outlet to the north by way of the Shoshoni River and the Columbia to the North Pacific. These later beds of the valleys are in part the sediments of Lake Bonneville, the great lake above mentioned, and in part they are subaërial gravels and sands.

The Wasatch system of mountains is composed of abrupt ranges crowned with sharp peaks. The several minor ranges and groups of peaks into which it is broken are separated only in part by structural differences, since ridges with homogeneous structure are severed by transverse valleys. The drainage of the whole area occupied by the Wasatch Mountains is westward to the Great Salt Lake. The streams that head in the western end of the Uinta Mountains and West Tavaputs Plateau cut through the Wasatch Mountains.

Great Salt Lake and its upper tributary, Utah Lake, exist by virtue of the presence of the Wasatch Mountains, for the mountains wring from the clouds the waters with which the lakes are supplied.

Walled by high ridges and peaks, many elevated valleys are found. In the midsummer months these valleys are favored with a pleasant, invigorating climate. Occasionally showers of rain fall. Vegetation is vigorous. The distant mountain slopes bear forests of spruce, pine, and fir: the broken foot hills are often covered by low, ragged piñon pines and cedars; and the flood plains of the streams are natural meadows. About the springs and streamlets groves of aspen stand, and the streams are bordered with willows, box elders, and cottonwoods. Now and then a midsummer storm comes, bringing hail, and even snow. When the short summer ends, the aspen and box elder foliage turns to gold flecked with scarlet; the willows to crimson and russet; the meadows are quickly sered, and soon the autumn verdure presents only the somber tints of the evergreens; early snows fall, and the whole land is soon covered with a white mantle, except that here and there bleak hills and rugged peaks are swept bare by the winds. The brief, beautiful summer is followed by a long, dreary winter, and during this winter of snowfall are accumulated the waters that are to be used in fertilizing the valleys away below in the border region between the mountains and the desert basins.

From the Wasatch on the north to the Colob on the south are elevated tables, in general bounded by bold, precipitous escarpments. The lands above are highly and sharply differentiated from the lands below in climate, vegetation, soil, and other physical characters. These high plateaus are covered with sheets and beds of lava, and over the lava sheets are scattered many volcanic cinder cones. The higher plateaus bear heavy forests of evergreens, and scattered through the forests are many little valleys or meadow glades. The gnarled, somber forests are often beset with fallen timber and a vigorous second growth, forming together a dead and living tangle difficult to penetrate. But often the forest aisles are open from glade to glade, or from border cliff to border cliff. In the midst of the glades are many beautiful lakelets, and from the cliffs that bound the plateaus on every hand the waters break out in innumerable springs.

Here, also, a brief summer is followed by a long winter, and through its dreary days the snow is gathered which fills the lakelets above and feeds the springs along the bordering cliffs. The springs of the cliffs are the fountains of the rivers that are to fertilize the valleys lying to the east, south, and west.

The Uinta Mountains constitute an east and west range. From a single great uplift, nearly 200 miles long and from 40 to 50 miles wide, valleys and cañons have been carved by rains and rivers, and table lands and peaks have been left embossed on the surface. Along its middle belt from east to west the peaks are scattered in great confusion, but in general the highest peaks are near the center of the range. The general elevation descends abruptly both on the north and south margins of the uplift, and at the crest of each abrupt descent there are many limestone ridges and crags. Between these ridges and crags that stand along the bordering crests, and the peaks that stand along the meandering watershed, there are broad tables, sometimes covered with forests, sometimes only with grass.

This is a third region of short summers and long winters, where the waters are collected to fertilize the valleys to the north and south.

Away to the southward are the twin plateaus, East and West Tavaputs, severed by the Green River. These plateaus culminate at the Brown Cliffs, where bold escarpments are presented southward.

Outlying the Brown Cliffs are the Book Cliffs. These, also, are escarpments of naked rock, with many salient and reëntrant angles and outlying buttes. The beds of which they are composed are shales and sandstones of many shades of blue, gray, and buff. In the distance, and softly blended by atmospheric haze, the towering walls have an azure hue. Everywhere they are elaborately water carved, and bold battlements above are buttressed with sculptured hills. In 1869, when the writer first saw this great escarpment, he gave it the name of the Azure Cliffs, but an earlier traveler, passing by another route across the country, had seen them in the distance, and, seizing another characteristic feature, had called them the Book Mountains. Gunnison saw, however, not a range of mountains, but the escarped edge of a plateau, and this escarpment we now call the Book Cliffs. From the Brown Cliffs northward these plateaus dip gently north to the Uinta-White Basin. From the very crest of the Brown Cliffs the drainage is northward.

This is a fourth region of short summers and long winters, where the moisture is collected to fertilize adjacent lands; but the altitude is not great enough nor the area large enough to accumulate a large supply of water, and the amount furnished by the Tavaputs Plateaus is comparatively small.

Such are the lofty regions of Utah that furnish water to irrigate the lowlands.

TIMBER

In these elevated districts is found all the timber of commercial value. This is well shown on the map. The map also exhibits the fact that many portions of the elevated districts are devoid of timber, it having been destroyed by fire, as explained in a former chapter. Doubtless, if fires could be prevented, the treeless areas would in due time be again covered with forests, but in such a climate forest growth is slow. At present, the treeless areas will afford valuable summer pasturage for cattle, and doubtless such pasturage would be advantageous to the growth of new forests, by keeping down the grasses in which in part the fires spread. It has already been shown that, to a great extent, the fires which destroy the forests are set by Indians while on their hunting excursions. The removal of the Indians from the country will further protect the forests. Eventually, the better class of timber lands will fall into the hands of individual owners, who will be interested in protecting their property from devastation by this fierce element. By all of these means the standing timber will be preserved for economic uses; but it will be a long time before complete immunity from fires will be secured.

The demand for lumber will never be very great. A variety of causes conspire to this end. The adjacent country will sustain but a small agricultural population, because the irrigable lands are of limited extent. The people of the lowlands will eventually supply themselves with fuel by cultivating timber along the water courses and by using the coal so abundant in some portions of Utah. The lumber will never be carried to a foreign market because of the expense of transportation: first, it will be expensive to get it down from the highlands to the lowlands, and, second, there are no navigable streams by which lumber may be cheaply transported from the country. In general, the lumber is of inferior quality, and cannot successfully compete for a permanent place in the markets of the world. But there will be a demand for lumber for building and fencing purposes in the valleys, and for mining purposes in the mountains.

If the timber region can be protected from fire, the supply of timber will equal the demand.

From the brief description given above, it will be seen that the timber region will never support agriculture. Much of it is mountainous and inhospitable, and the climate is cold. The timber region is ever to be such; mining industries will slightly encroach on it on the one hand, and pasturage industries on the other, but lumbermen will control the country.

The forests of these upper regions are monotonous, as the variety of tree life is very small. All of the timber trees proper are coniferous, and belong to the pine, fir, and juniper families. The pine of chief value is *Pinus ponderosa*, locally distinguished as the "Long leaved pine"; the wood is very heavy and coarse grained, but is suitable for the ruder building and mining purposes. It is usually found on the slopes between eight and nine thousand feet above the level of the sea. It attains a large size, and is a stately tree, contrasting grandly with the darker and smaller firs that usually keep it company.

Pinus aristata is of no commercial value, as it is much branched and spreading with limbs near the base; it grows on the crags at an altitude of from nine to eleven thousand feet.

Pinus flexilis grows at the same altitude as the last mentioned, and often shows a similar habit of growth. On the southern plateaus it is less branched and has a tolerably straight trunk, but it is too small and scarce to be important as timber. It is highly resinous, and is called "Pitch pine."

Pinus monticola, or Sugar pine, is found on the southern plateaus, but is not abundant, and rarely attains milling size.

Pinus edulis is the well known "Piñon pine." It covers the foot hills and less elevated slopes adjacent to the river valleys. The tree is low, diffusely branched and scrubby, and is of no use for lumber; but the wood is well supplied with resin and makes excellent fuel, for which purpose it is extensively used in consequence of its accessibility.

There are three valuable species of Abies, namely: A. *Douglasii*, A. *concolor*, and A. *Engelmanni*. *Abies Douglasii*, or Douglas' spruce, bears some resemblance to the eastern spruce, A. *Canadensis*, but it is a finer tree, and the wood is much superior. Though rather light, it is tough and exceedingly durable. The heart wood is red, from which circumstance lumbermen distinguish it as the "Red pine." In building it is used for all the heavier parts, as frames, joists, rafters, etc., and it makes excellent flooring. Its value is still further enhanced from the fact that it occupies a belt of from seven to nine thousand feet altitude, and thus is easily obtained. It may readily be distinguished by its cones, the bracts of which are trifurcate, sharp, pointed, and conspicuously exserted, and they are unlike those of any other species.

Abies concolor, known in Utah as the "Black balsam," grows at about the same altitude as the last mentioned species, and though rather crossgrained makes good lumber, being quite durable and strong. From its silvery foliage, the leaves being glaucous on both sides, this tree is known to tourists as the "White silver fir." Lumbermen sometimes call it the "Black gum," the wood being very dark colored.

Abies Engelmanni, or Engelmann's spruce, occupies the highest elevations, and constitutes the only timber above 11,000 feet in altitude. Above 11,500 feet it is reduced to a dwarf. On the terraces of the high plateaus, at about 10,000 feet altitude, it appears to flourish best, and here it becomes a large, beautiful tree. The leaves are needle shaped, and thus differ from both the preceding species. The trunks are straight and free from limbs or knots, making fine saw logs. The wood is white and soft, but fine grained and durable, and being easily worked is held in high esteem for all the lighter uses, such as sash, doors, etc. Its place in the lumber industries of Utah is about the same as that of the "White pine" (*Pinus Strobus*) in the east. Lumbermen usually call it "White pine." Because of the altitude of its habitat it is difficult to obtain, yet it is systematically sought, and large amounts are yearly manufactured into lumber; it also makes good shingles.

Abies Menziesii, or Menzies's spruce, usually called "Spruce" by lumbermen of the country, is botanically very similar to the species last described, but the cones are larger and the leaves sharper pointed. It bears a large quantity of cones, which are generally aggregated near the top, obscuring the foliage, and giving the trees a peculiar tawny appearance. The wood is light, white, and fine grained, and would rival that of the last named species but for the fact that the trunk has a number of slight curves, so that it is impossible to obtain good saw logs of sufficient length from it. Its habitat is along the cañons from seven to nine thousand feet altitude, and seems to end about where *A. Engelmanni* begins. It is, however, a smaller tree, and less abundant.

Abies subalpina is of little value as a timber tree; the wood is soft and spongy, from which circumstance it is locally known as "Pumpkin pine," but the more appropriate name of "White balsam" is also applied to distinguish it from *A. concolor*, which is called "Black balsam." This species grows high up on the mountains and plateaus, generally from nine to eleven thousand feet. It is very tall, often attaining a height of 80 or 90 feet. Its trunk is straight and limbless for a great distance. This species has been but little known to botanists heretofore, from the fact that it has been confounded with *A. grandis*, but Mr. Engelmann [2] decides, from specimens collected by Mr. L. F. Ward,[3] that it must be considered as a new species.

Abies amabilis and *Abies grandis*, spruces resembling the "White balsam" in their general appearance, occur in the Wasatch Mountains, but are not abundant.

Juniperus Californicus, var. *Utahensis*, or White cedar, is very abundant over the foot hills and lower mountain slopes, and, like the piñon pine, is much used for fire wood. It has also the characteristic durability of the junipers, and makes excellent fence posts. It grows low, is diffusely branched, and is valueless for milling purposes.

Juniperus Virginiana, or Red cedar, is also found in this region. Its habitat is near the streams and at moderate altitudes. It is said to lack the durable qualities for which it is noted at the east, and which seem to be transferred to the other species.

Populus angustifolia, or Cottonwood, is the chief representative of the poplar family in this region. The people of the country distinguish two varieties or species, the Black cottonwood and Yellow cottonwood. The former is said to be useless for lumber, while the latter has some slight value. It forms no part of the forest proper, but fringes the lower reaches of the streams, rarely occurring higher in altitude than 6,000 feet. Its rapid growth and

[2] George Engelmann (1809–1884), pioneer botanist.
[3] Lester Frank Ward (1841–1913), geologist in the U. S. Geological Survey 1882, but known best as a leader in American sociology.

its proximity to the irrigable lands make it valuable for fuel, although it is not of superior quality.

Populus monilifera, the Cottonwood of the Mississippi Valley, grows with the above in the southern part of the Territory, and has about the same value.

Populus tremuloides, or Aspen, is found about the moist places on the mountain sides, and often borders the glades of the plateaus. The long poles which it furnishes are sometimes used for fencing purposes; it makes a fair fuel; the quantity found is small.

Acer grandidentata, a species of Maple, abounds at the north as a bush, and rare individuals attain the rank of small trees. Its wood is highly prized for the repair of machinery, but is too scarce to be of great service.

Negundo aceroides, or Box elder, is found along the water courses in many places. Sometimes along the larger streams it attains a height of 25 or 30 feet. It makes a good fuel, but is found in such small quantities as to be scarcely worthy of mention.

Quercus undulata, or White oak, is very abundant as a bush, and sometimes attains a diameter of six or eight inches. It is too rare as a tree to deserve more than mere mention.

Betula occidentalis, a species of Birch, grows about the upland springs and creeks. Its habit is bushlike, but it often has a height of 20 feet, and it makes a tolerable fuel.

The Hackberry (*Celtis occidentalis*) and two species of Ash (*Fraxinus coriacea* and *F. anomala*) grow as small trees, but are exceedingly rare.

The above is a nearly complete list of the forest trees of Utah. The number of species is very small; aridity on the one hand, and cold on the other, successfully repel the deciduous trees. The oak, hickory, ash, etc., necessary to such a variety of industries, especially the manufacture of agricultural machinery, must all be imported from more humid regions. The coniferous trees, growing high among the rocks of the upper regions and beaten by the cold storms of a long winter, are ragged and gnarled, and the lumber they afford is not of the finest quality; and the finishing lumber for architectural purposes and furniture must also be imported from more humid regions.

Uinta-White Basin

The Uinta-White Valley is a deep basin inclosed by the Uinta Mountains on the north and the Tavaputs highlands on the south. Eastward the basin extends beyond the limits of Utah; westward the Uinta Mountains and West Tavaputs Plateau nearly inclose the head of the Uinta Valley, but the space between is filled with a section of the Wasatch Mountains. From the north, west, and south the Uinta Valley inclines gently toward the Duchesne River. Many streams come down from the north and from the south. In the midst of the valley there are some small stretches of bad lands.

Along the lower part of the Uinta and the Duchesne, and the lower courses of nearly all the minor streams, large tracts of arable land are found, and from these good selections can be made, sufficient to occupy in their service all the water of the Uinta and its numerous branches. The agricultural portion of the valley is sufficiently low to have a genial climate, and all the crops of the northern States can be cultivated successfully.

Stretching back on every hand from the irrigable districts, the little hills, valleys, and slopes are covered with grasses, which are found more and more luxuriant in ascending the plateaus and mountains, until the peaks are reached, and these are naked.

On the north of the Uinta, and still west of the Green, the basin is drained by some small streams, the chief of which is Ashley Fork. Except near the lower course of Ashley Fork, this section of country is exceedingly broken; the bad lands and hogbacks are severed by deep, precipitous cañons.

From the east the White River enters the Green. Some miles up the White, a cañon is reached, and the country on either hand, stretching back for a long distance, is composed of rugged barren lands. But between the highlands and the Green, selections of good land can be made, and the waters of the White can be used to serve them. From the White, south to the East Tavaputs Plateau, the grass lands steadily increase in value to the summit of the Brown Cliffs. Many good springs are found in this region, and eventually this will be a favorite district for pasturage farms.

Fine pasturage farms may be made on the southern slope of the Yampa Plateau, with summer pasturage above and winter pasturage below. Altogether, the Uinta-White Basin is one of the favored districts of the west, with great numbers of cool springs issuing from the mountains and hills; many beautiful streams of clear, cold water; a large amount of arable land from which irrigable tracts may be selected; an abundance of fuel in the piñon pines and cedars of the foot hills; and building timber farther back on the mountains and plateaus.

The whole amount of irrigable land is estimated at 280,320 acres.

The Cañon Lands

South of the Tavaputs highlands, and east and south of the High Plateaus, the Cañon Lands of Utah are found. The lower course of the Grand, the lower course of the Green, and a large section of the Colorado cuts through them, and the streams that head in the High Plateaus run across them. All the rivers, all the creeks, all the brooks, run in deep gorges — narrow, winding cañons, with their floors far below the general surface of the country. Many long lines of cliffs are found separating higher from lower districts. The hills are bad lands and alcove lands.

The Sierra la Sal and Henry Mountains are great masses of lava, wrapped in sedimentary beds, which are cut with many dikes. South of the High Plateaus great numbers of cinder cones are found.

On the Grand River there are some patches of land which can be served by the waters of that river. On the Green, in what is known as Gunnison Valley, patches of good land can be selected and redeemed by the waters of that river.

Castle Valley is abruptly walled on the west, north, and northeast by towering cliffs. East of its southern portion a region of towers, buttes, crags, and rocklands is found, known as the San Rafael Swell. In this valley there is a large amount of good land, and the numerous streams which run across it can all be used in irrigation. Farther south, on the Fremont, Escalante, and Paria, some small tracts of irrigable land are found, and on the Kanab and Virgin there are limited areas which can be used for agricultural purposes. But all that portion of the cañon country south of

Castle Valley and westward to the Beaver Dam Mountains is exceedingly desolate; naked rocks are found, refusing footing even to dwarfed cedars and piñon pines; the springs are infrequent and yield no bountiful supply of water; its patches of grass land are widely scattered, and it has but little value for agricultural purposes.

A broad belt of coal land extends along the base of the cliffs from the Tavaputs Plateau on the northeast to the Colob Plateau on the southwest. At the foot of the cliffs which separate the lowlands from the highlands, many pasturage farms may be made; the grass of the lowlands can be used in the winter, and that of the highlands in summer, and everywhere good springs of water may be found.

The extent of the irrigable lands in this district is estimated at 213,440 acres.

The Sevier Lake District

This district embraces all the country drained by the waters which flow into the Sevier Lake, and the areas drained by many small streams which are quickly lost in the desert. The greater part of the irrigable land lies in the long, narrow valleys walled by the plateaus, especially along the Sevier, Otter Creek, and the San Pete. The arable lands greatly exceed the irrigable, and good selections may be made. Most of the irrigable lands are already occupied by farmers, and the waters are used in their service. In the valleys among the high plateaus, and along their western border, the grasses are good, and many pasturage farms may be selected, and the springs and little streams that come from the plateau cliffs will afford an abundant supply of water. The summits of the plateaus will afford an abundant summer pasturage.

Westward among the Basin Ranges feeble and infrequent springs are found; there is little timber of value, but the lower mountains and foot hills have cedars and piñon pines that would be valuable for fuel if nearer to habitations. The cedar and piñon hills bear scant grasses. The valleys are sometimes covered with sage, sometimes with grease wood, sometimes quite naked.

The amount of irrigable land in this district is estimated at 101,700 acres.

The Great Salt Lake District

This district has already become famous in the history of western agriculture, for here the Latter Day Saints first made "a home in the valleys among the mountains."

The rivers and creeks bring the waters down from the Wasatch Mountains on the east. The high valleys among the mountains have to some extent been cultivated, and will hereafter be used more than at present for meadow purposes. In general the people have selected their lands low down, in order to obtain a more genial climate. Yet the irrigable lands are not very far from the mountains, as a glance at the map will reveal. Utah Lake constitutes a fine natural reservoir and discharges its waters into Salt Lake by the Jordan, and from its channel the waters may be conducted over a large area of country. The waters of the Weber and Bear Rivers, now flowing idly into the lake, will soon be spread over extensive valleys, and the area of agricultural lands be greatly increased. Westward the influence of the mountains in the precipitation of moisture is soon lost, and beyond the lake an irreclaimable desert is found.

Near to the mountains the grass lands are fair but they have been overpastured and greatly injured. Out among the Basin Ranges little grass land of value is found.

The amount of irrigable land in this district is estimated at 837,660 acres.

The lofty zone of mountains and table lands with arms stretching eastward, with its culminating points among summer frosts and winter storms, is the central region about which the human interests of the country gather. The timber, the water, the agricultural lands, the pasturage lands, to a large extent the coal and iron mines, and to some extent the silver mines, are all found in these higher regions or clinging closely to them.

GRASSES

While the forests present but a few species of trees, the pasturage lands present a great variety of grasses. Between fifty and sixty species have been collected by parties connected with the survey under the direction of the writer, and these are distributed among twenty-six or twenty-seven genera. Most of them belong to the mountains or highlands, and are rich and sweet. Nearly all of them are bunch grasses. The spaces by which the bunches are separated are bare or occupied with weeds and shrubs. This is often the case on the mountains and high plateaus. A continuous turf is never seen. Where a sward is seen in moist places, about springs and in glades, the verdure consists in chief part of other plants, sedges and reeds.

Of the bunch grasses the *Poas* are by far the most abundant. Of this genus nine species were obtained, but this gives an inadequate idea of the variety. Of one species alone Dr. Vasey [4] has enumerated nine varieties, and advances the opinion that several will be eventually considered as species. They are found at all altitudes, mostly on the slopes. Perhaps the most important single species in that region is the *Bouteloua oligostachya*, the so called "Circle grass." It has a peculiar habit of forming partial or complete circles on the ground, with areas of bare ground in the center. These turfy rings are comparatively narrow, often not more than three or four inches in width, while the circles are from two to four feet in diameter. The form is not always circular, but often assumes irregular shapes. The grass is sweet and nutritious, but its chief value consists in its power to resist inclement seasons, as it cures standing, like the "Buffalo grass" of the Great Plains.

Another very valuable grass is the *Eriocoma cuspidata*, which is known by the name of "Sand grass." It grows at much lower altitudes, and is properly a valley grass. It has a solitary, scattering habit, or at least the bunches are small and turfless. Horses and cattle select it with care from among other species, and it seems especially nutritious. It has a large black grain, which is often collected by the Indians for food.

A remarkable lowland grass is the Vilfa (*Sporobolis airoides*). It has something of the appearance of "Hair grass," with a widely spreading purple panicle and large perennial roots. The old culms persist at the base, and with the new ones form thick and almost woody tufts. These tufts are scattered about in the strongly akaline soils of the river bottoms, and are extensively pastured by

---

[4] George Vasey (1822–1893), botanist associated with Powell on his Colorado exploration, and botanist of the U. S. Department of Agriculture. He made a catalog of the trees and grasses of the United States.

large herds of cattle. A marked characteristic of this grass, common, however, to several others, is its power to take up saline matter, which gives to the whole plant a salty taste. The effect of this upon the stock feeding upon it is doubtful, judging from the conflicting reports of the inhabitants; but it seems that when cattle are first pastured upon it they are injured by the excess of salt, but that after a time they cease to be injured by it. All of the so called "Salt grasses" are cropped to a greater or less extent by stock.

The chief grasses of the elevated timber tracts belong to the genus *Bromus*. When young they are good, but they become stale and valueless with age. The only grass that can compare with those of the eastern meadows, and which forms a continuous sod and covers the ground with a uniform growth, is a variety of *Aira cœspitosa*, a red topped grass, which was found surrounding the small lakes of the mountains and plateaus, at elevations of 11,000 feet and over. This is an exceedingly beautiful grass as it waves in the gentle breezes that fan the lakelets of the upper regions.

Phragmites communis, the so-called "Cane," is common in the glades and sloughs; and, though large and rather dry, it furnishes the only verdure obtainable for months in severe seasons.

Much of the hay and pasturage of the country, which is there called grass, consists of plants of different families. Notable among these are several species of *Carex* (sedges), particularly *Carex Jamesii*, which springs up wherever artificial meadows are made by the system of flooding commonly practiced. The plants have large, strong, subterranean rootstocks, forming a tangled mass which, when once established, cannot easily be eradicated. The leaves are broad and grasslike, and, though coarse and comparatively insipid, form a good sward which can be mowed — a rare condition in that country; and hence such meadows are highly prized.

Juncus Balticus, var. *montanus*, which has a blue color, terete culms, and tough fiber, and which the settlers call "Wire grass," is very abundant. It is cut for hay, and is said to serve a good purpose as such.

There are some shrubs that furnish excellent browsing, among which, perhaps, the grease wood takes the first rank. The sage brush, *Artemisia*, on the contrary, is seldom resorted to. There is one shrub to which great virtues are ascribed which may be mentioned in this connection. This is the *Cercocarpus parvifolius*, which occupies the mountain sides for a wide zone of altitude. The foliage, though not strictly evergreen, remains most of the winter, and is said to afford the only food for horses and cattle that can be obtained during some seasons of deep snows. This shrub is a congener of the well known mountain mahogany, *C. ledifolius*, which grows at higher altitudes, and has truly evergreen foliage.

The small perennial plant *Eurotia lanata*, or "White sage," found growing in the valleys and plains, is held in high esteem as winter food for stock.

The growth of grass, even on the plateaus, is often scant; on the foot hills it becomes less, and farther away from the highlands it still diminishes in quantity until absolute deserts are found. Most of the grasses seem to protect themselves from the great aridity by growing in bunches. They appear to produce proportionately a greater amount of seeds than the grasses of the Humid Region, and their nutritive qualities, especially in winter, seem to be due thereto. In general, the grasses seem to have large, strong stems, and are not so easily broken down as those of the Humid Region, and the rains and snows by which they would be so broken down are infrequent. Again, for these reasons, the grasses, standing long after they are cut by frosts, cure themselves, forming thereby a winter pasturage.

The irrigable lands of Utah will be discussed more thoroughly and in detail in subsequent chapters by Mr. G. K. Gilbert, who has made the Great Salt Lake District his study; by Capt. C. E. Dutton, who has prepared the chapter on the irrigable lands of the Sevier Lake Drainage, and by Prof. A. H. Thompson, who has written the chapter on the irrigable lands of the Colorado Drainage.

The following is a table of the irrigable lands, arranged by districts, as discussed in the present chapter. The table is compiled from those presented in subsequent chapters.

Table of irrigable lands in Utah Territory

	Square miles	Acres	Cultivated in 1877 Square miles	Acres
Salt Lake drainage system				
Base of Uinta Mountains	2.5	1,600	1.6	1,024
Yellow Creek and Duck Creek	2.0	1,280	..	...
Randolph Valley and Saleratus Creek	69.0	44,160	9.6	6.344
Shores of Bear Lake	9.0	5,760	5.0	3,200
Cache Valley	250.0	160,000	50.0	32,000
Bear River Delta, Malade Valley, and Connor's Spring Valley	218.0	139,520	22.0	14,080
Box Elder Valley (Mantua)	1.5	960	1.1	704
Weber Valley from Peoa to Hennefer, inclusive	9.0	5,760	8.5	5,440
Parley's Park	3.2	2,048	3.2	2,048
Uptown	2.0	1,280	.5	320
Echo Creek	0.9	576	.3	192
Croydon	0.5	320	.4	256
Round Valley	0.5	320	.5	320
Morgan Valley	6.9	4,416	6.0	3,840
Ogden Valley	8.0	5,120	4.1	2,624
Weber Delta Plain	219.0	140,160	91.0	58,240
Kamas Prairie	13.0	8,320	4.7	3,003
Hailstone Ranche and vicinity	2.0	1,280	2.0	1,280
Provo Valley	16.0	10,240	6.0	3,840
Waldsburg	2.0	1,280	2.0	1,280
Utah Valley	190.0	121,600	59.0	37,760
Salt Creek	16.0	10,240	14.0	8,960
Salt Lake Valley (including Bountiful and Centerville)	192.0	122,880	89.9	57,412
Tooele Valley	45.0	28,800	5.4	3,456
Cedar Fort	1.5	1,000	1.2	800
Fairfield	1.5	900	1.2	800
Vernon Creek	2.0	1,200	1.5	900
Saint Johns	1.1	700	1.1	700
East Cañon Creek (Rush Valley)	1.5	900	.8	500
Stockton	.3	500	.3	200
Skull Valley	4.0	2,500	1.6	1,000
Government Creek	.5	300	.5	300
Willow Spring, T. 10 S., R. 17 W.	.4	250	.4	250
Redding Spring	.1	50	..	20
Dodoquibe Spring	.1	50	..	...
Deep Creek, T. 9 S., R. 19 W.	1.6	1,000	.8	500
Pilot Peak	.3	200	..	...
Grouse Valley	2.4	1,500	.8	500
Owl Spring	.1	10	..	...
Rosebud Creek	.6	400	.2	150
Muddy Creek, T. 10 N., R. 15 W.	.5	300	.5	300
Park Valley	3.5	2,300	1.1	700
Widow Spring	.1	20	..	...
Indian Creek, T. 13 N., R. 12 W.	.2	100	..	...
East base Clear Creek Mountains	.2	150	..	5
Cazure Creek	.3	200	..	...
Clear Creek, T. 15 N., R. 12 W.	.3	200	.1	80
Junction Creek	.7	500	..	...
Goose Creek	.3	200	..	...
Pilot Spring	.1	15	..	...
Deseret Creek (or Deep Creek)	4.5	3,000	.5	300
Crystal Springs, T. 14 N., R. 7 W.	.2	100	.1	60
Antelope Springs, T. 9 N., R. 6 W.	.1	30	..	30

Table of irrigable lands in Utah Territory — Continued

	Square miles	Acres	Cultivated in 1877 Square miles	Acres
Salt Lake drainage system — Continued				
Hanzel Spring	.1	15	..	15
Promontory, east base	.9	600	.5	300
Blue Creek	2.3	1,500	..	...
Brackish Springs, near Blue Creek	1.5	1,000	.3	200
Antelope Island	.1	50	..	...
The valley of the Sevier River				
San Pete Valley	31.2	20,000	17.0	10,880
Gunnison	6.2	4,000	44.4	2,800
Sevier Valley, above Gunnison	54.7	35,000	16.5	10,500
Circle Valley	6.3	4,000	1.1	750
Panguitch and above	10.9	7,000	2.8	1,800
Irrigable lands of the desert drainage of southwestern Utah				
Cherry Creek	.2	100	..	...
Judd Creek	.2	100	..	...
Levan	3.4	2,000	..	...
Scipio	2.6	1,700	..	...
Holden	1.6	1,000	..	...
Filmore and Oak Creek	5.5	3,500	..	...
Meadow Creek	1.9	1,200	..	...
Kanosh	3.1	2,000	..	...
Beaver Creek and tributaries	21.9	14,000	..	...
Paragoonah	1.6	1,000	..	...
Parowan	1.6	1,000	..	...
Summit	.6	400	..	...
Cedar City, Iron City, and Fort Hamilton	3.6	2,300	..	...
Mountain Meadows	.3	200	..	...
Pinto	.3	200	..	...
Hebron	1.6	1,000	..	...
Irrigable lands of the Colorado drainage				
Virgin River	30	19,200	11.0	7,040
Kanab Creek	2.5	1,600	1.1	700
Paria River	6	3,840	..	...
Escalante River	6	3,840	..	...
Fremont River	38	24,320	..	...
San Rafael River	175	112,000	..	...
Price River	11	7,040	..	...
Minnie Maud Creek	3	1,920	..	...
Uinta River	285	182,400	.5	300
Ashley Fork	25	16,000	.1	50
Henrys Fork	10	6,400	..	...
White River	75	48,000	..	...
Browns Park } Green River	10	6,400	..	...
Below Split Mountain Cañon } Green River	50	32,000	..	...
Gunnison Valley } Green River	25	16,000	..	...
Grand River	40	25,600	..	...
Total	2,262.4	1,447,920	..	...

CHAPTER VII

IRRIGABLE LANDS OF THE SALT LAKE DRAINAGE SYSTEM

By G. K. GILBERT

THE field of my work in 1877 included so large a portion of the drainage basin of Great Salt Lake and so little else that it has proved most convenient to report on all of that basin, or rather on that part of it which lies within the Territory of Utah. In so doing, I have depended, for nearly all the lands draining to Utah Lake, upon the data gathered by Mr. Renshawe, of this survey, in connection with his topographic work. The remainder of the district, with very slight exception, I have myself visited.

The officials and citizens of the Territory have all freely contributed such information as I have sought, and have aided me in many ways; but I have been especially indebted to Mr. Martineau and Mr. Barton, the surveyors of Cache and Davis Counties; to Mr. Fox, the territorial surveyor; and to the Hon. A. P. Rockwood, the statistician of the Deseret Agricultural Society. Mr. Rockwood prepared a statistical report on the Territory in 1875, which has been of great service to me, and he has kindly placed at my disposal the manuscript details of his work as well as the published summary.

METHOD AND SCOPE OF INVESTIGATION

Where agriculture is dependent upon irrigation, the extent of land that can be put to agricultural use is determined by the relation of the quantity of available water to the quantity of available land. There is a certain amount of water needed by a unit of land, and wherever the land susceptible of cultivation requires more water than is obtainable, only a portion of the land can be utilized. But there is also a limit to the amount of water that can be profitably employed on a unit of land, and where the supply of water is in excess of the quantity required by such lands as are properly disposed to receive and use it, only a portion of the water can be utilized. In order to ascertain, therefore, the extent of agricultural land in a given district, it is necessary to make a measurement of land, or a measurement of water, or perhaps both, and it is necessary to know the amount of water demanded by a unit area of the land under consideration.

The proper quota of water for irrigation depends on climate and soil and subsoil, as well as on the nature of the crop, and varies indefinitely under diverse conditions. As a rule, the best soils require least water; those which demand most are light sands on one hand and adhesive clays on the other. Where the subsoil is open and dry, more water is needed than where it is moist or impervious. Wherever there is an impervious substratum, the subsoil accumulates moisture and the demand for water diminishes from year to year. These and other considerations so complicate the subject that it is difficult to generalize, and I have found it more practicable to use in my investigations certain limiting quantities than to attempt in every case a diagnosis of the local conditions. By comparing the volumes of certain streams in Utah, that are now used in irrigation to their full capacity, with the quantities of land that they serve, I have found that one hundred acres of dry bench land (*i. e.*, land with a deep, dry, open subsoil) will not yield a full crop of grain with less than one cubic foot of water per second, and this under the most favorable climate of the Territory. Where the climate is drier, a greater quantity is required. Where there is a moist subsoil, a less may suffice.

In the drier districts, where the streams are small, they are usually employed upon the dry benches, because these are most convenient to their sources; and it is very rarely the case that their utility is increased by the presence of a moist subsoil. But it is also in the drier districts that the extent of agricultural land is ascertained by the measurement of streams; and hence there is little danger of error if we use in all cases the criterion that applies to dry bench land. In the discussion of the lands of northern Utah, I have therefore assigned to each cubic foot per second of perennial flow the reclamation of one hundred acres of land, with the belief that the consequent estimates would never underrate, though they might sometimes exaggerate, the agricultural resources of the districts examined.

In the measurement of streams the following method was employed: A place was sought where the channel was straight for a distance equal to several times the width of the stream, and where for some distance there was little change in the dimensions of the cross section. Measurement was then made of the width (in feet), of the mean depth (in feet), and of the maximum surface current (in feet per second). The mean current was assumed to be four-fifths of the maximum current; and fourth-fifths of the product of the three measured elements was taken to give the flow in cubic feet per second. This method of measurement is confessedly crude, and is liable to considerable error, but with the time at my disposal no better was practicable, and its shortcomings are less to be regretted on account of the variability of the streams themselves.

All the streams of Utah that flow from mountain slopes are subject to great fluctuations. They derive a large share of their water from the melting of snow, and not only does the melting vary as to its rapidity and season, but the quantity of snow to be melted varies greatly from year to year. A single measurement standing alone is quite inadequate to determine the capacity of a stream for irrigation, and as it was rarely practicable to visit a stream more than once, an endeavor was made to supplement the single determination by collating the judgments of residents as to the relative flow of the several creeks and rivers at other seasons and in other years. In districts where the water is nearly all used and its division and distribution are supervised by "watermasters," those functionaries are able to afford information of a tolerably definite character, but in other districts it was necessary to make great allowance for errors of judgment. Certainly, that element of my estimates which is based on inquiries cannot claim so small a probability of error as the element based on measurements.

Streams that are formed in high mountains reach their highest stage in June, and their lowest in September or October. Streams from low mountains attain their maxima in April or May, and reach their low stages by August or September. In the low valleys the irrigation of wheat and other small grains begins about the first of June, and continues until the latter part of July. The irrigation of corn and potatoes begins in the early part of July, and continues until the middle of August. In the middle of July all of the land calls for water, and if the supply is sufficient at that time, it is sure to meet all demands at other times. It will be convenient to call that time *the critical season*. In the higher agricultural valleys corn and potatoes are not grown, but the irrigation of small grains and hay is carried on from the middle of June to the middle or latter part of August. Through all this time the volume of the streams is diminishing, and if they fail at all it is at the end of the season. The critical season for the higher valleys is about the middle of August.

In order to estimate properly the agricultural capability of a stream, it is necessary to ascertain its volume at its critical season. In the investigations of the past summer, this was accomplished by direct measurement in but a limited district. For the remainder of my field of operations I was compelled to depend on the estimates of others as to the relation between the volumes of streams at the time of measurement and at the critical season.

As will appear in the sequel, the uncertainty attaching to these determinations of volumes affects the grand total in but small degree. The utility of the large streams it not limited by their volumes so much as by the available land suitable for overflow, a quantity susceptible of more accurate determination, and the extent of land irrigable by the large streams is many times greater than that irrigable by the small.

No streams are used throughout the year, and few can be fully utilized during the spring flood. Wherever it is practicable to store up the surplus water until the time of need, the irrigable area is correspondingly increased. Enough has been accomplished in a few localities to demonstrate the feasibility of reclaiming thousands of acres by the aid of reservoirs, and eventually this will be done; but except in a small way it is not a work of the immediate future. For many years to come capital will find greater remuneration in taking possession of the large rivers.

In estimating the agricultural resources, it was, of course, necessary to take account of all future increase, and wherever storage by reservoirs seemed practicable a rough estimate was made of the extent of land that could be thus reclaimed.

There are a few restricted areas in Utah that yield remunerative crops to the farmer without the artificial application of water. Their productiveness is doubled or trebled by the use of water, and so far as they are susceptible of irrigation they need not be distinguished from the irrigable lands. When the greater rivers shall have been diverted to the work of irrigation, nearly all such areas will be supplied with water, but a few will not. The endeavor has been to include the latter as well as the former in the estimate of the agricultural land.

The term "agricultural land" is construed to include that which is used or may be used for the production of hay as well as that cultivated by the plow. Most irrigable lands may be utilized in either way, but there are some tracts which, on account of the severity of the climate or the impurity of the water, are adapted to the growth of grass only.

I have sought in the foregoing remarks to set forth as briefly as possible the methods and scope of my investigations, and to indicate the degree of accuracy to be anticipated in the resulting estimates. To these estimates we will now proceed.

IRRIGATION BY THE LARGE STREAMS

Three rivers enter Great Salt Lake — the Bear, the Weber, and the Jordan, and upon their water will ultimately depend the major part of the agriculture of Utah. By a curious coincidence, the principal heads of the three rivers lie close together in the western end of the Uinta range of mountains.

The *Bear River* runs northward at first, and a little beyond the foot of the mountains enters the Territory of Wyoming. Swerving to the left, it passes again into Utah, and swerving again to the right returns to Wyoming. From Wyoming it runs northward into Idaho, and after making a great detour to the north returns on a more westerly line to Utah. It reënters in Cache Valley, and passes thence by a short cañon to its delta plain on the northwestern border of Great Salt Lake. Its principal tributaries are received in Idaho and in Cache Valley. Bordering upon the upper reaches of the river, there is little land available for cultivation, and the climate forbids any crop but hay. I am informed that the meadow land there somewhat exceeds two square miles in area. Where the river next enters Utah it runs for 30 miles through an open valley, the valley that contains the towns of Woodruff and Randolph.

At the head it passes through a short defile, and can readily be thrown into two canals at such a level as to command the greater part of the valley, bringing about 90 square miles of land "under ditch." For the irrigation of this amount the river is sufficient, but if the necessary water were thus appropriated, too little would remain for the use of the lands which border the contiguous portions of the river in Wyoming. These have equal claim to the use of the river, and a proper distribution of the water would assign it to the reclamation of the best selection of land in the two Territories. I estimate that such an adjustment would permit the Utah valley to irrigate 45 square miles with the water of the river. The minor streams of the valley will serve, in addition, 24 square miles. The climate is unfavorable to grain and the chief crop must be of hay.

Where the river next enters Utah it has acquired so great a volume that it is impracticable to make use of its entire amount. The portion of Cache Valley which lies in Utah can nearly all be irrigated. What is on the left bank of Bear River can be served by Logan River and other tributaries without calling on the main stream. The right bank will have to be served in connection with an adjacent tract in Idaho, and by a canal lying entirely in that Territory. The expense will be great, but not greater than the benefit will warrant. I estimate that the Utah division of Cache Valley will ultimately contain 250 square miles of irrigated land. The climate admits of the growth of wheat, oats, and corn, and such fruits as the apple, pear, and the apricot.

In leaving Cache Valley the river tumbles through a short, narrow cañon, and then enters the plain that borders the lake. The limestone walls of the cañon offer a secure foundation for the head works to a system of canals to supply the plain. Here, again, a large outlay is necessary, but the benefits will be more than commensurate. Not only will the entire alluvial plain of the Bear be served, but the valley of the Malade, as far as Oregon Springs, and the valley which extends from Little Mountain to Connor's Spring. After deducting from these areas the land along the margin of the lake that is too saline to afford hope of reclamation, there remains a tract of 214 square miles. One-tenth of this is now in use, being in part watered by Box Elder Creek and other small creeks, and in part cultivated without irrigation.

In the following table are summed the agricultural resources of that portion of the Bear River drainage basin which lies in Utah:

Tracts	Square miles —	
	Cultivated in 1877	Cultivable
Base of Uinta Mountains	1.6	2.5
Yellow Creek and Duck Creek	0.0	2.0
Randolph Valley and Saleratus Creek	9.6	69.0
Shores of Bear Lake	5.0	9.0
Cache Valley	50.0	250.0
Delta Plain, Malade Valley, and Connor's Spring Valley	22.0	218.0
Box Elder Valley (Mantua)	1.1	1.5
Total	89.3	552.0

The entire area of the Bear River District is about 3,620 square miles, 2½ per cent being now under cultivation, and over 15 per cent susceptible of cultivation.

The *Weber River* runs with a general northwesterly course from the Uinta Mountains to Great Salt Lake, entering the latter at the middle of its eastern shore. The Ogden is its only important tributary. At the foot of the mountains it enters Kamas Prairie, in which it can be made to irrigate a few square miles. Thence to Hennefer, a distance of 30 miles, it is continuously bordered by a strip of farming land about one-third of a mile broad. Then it passes a series of three close cañons — in the intervals of which are Round Valley, with a few acres of land, and Morgan Valley, with 7 square miles — and emerges upon its delta plain. Within this plain are no less than 219 square miles of farming land, of which about two-fifths are now in use. A part is unwatered, a part is watered by the Ogden River and by a number of creeks, and the remainder is watered by the Weber. To serve the higher portions of the plain a great outlay would be required, and I am of opinion that the highest levels cannot profitably be supplied. Still, a great extension of the irrigated area is inevitable, and I anticipate that when the water of the Weber has been carried as far as is economically practicable, not more than 15 miles of the plain will remain unsupplied. Deducting this amount, as well as the area served by the minor streams and springs of the plain, there remain 185 square miles dependent on the Weber and Ogden Rivers. The Ogden River has also to water 8 square miles in its upper course, and the Weber 34, making a total of 227 square miles dependent on the two streams. Whether they are competent to serve so great an area may well be questioned. On the 8th of October I found in the Ogden River, at the mouth of its cañon, a flow of 115 feet per second, and three days later the Weber showed 386 feet. There was almost no irrigation in progress at that time, and the total of 501 feet included practically all the water of the streams. To irrigate 227 square miles, the rivers need to furnish at the critical season (in this case about the 10th of July) 1,450 feet, or nearly three times their October volume. Of the ratio between their July and October volumes I have no direct means of judging, and the problem is too nice a one to be trusted to the estimates of residents unaided by measurements; but indirectly a partial judgment may be reached by comparing the rivers with certain tributaries of the Jordan which were twice observed. City Creek was measured on the 5th of July, and again on 1st of September, and Emigration and Parley creeks were measured July 5th, and again September 3rd. These streams rise in mountains that are about as high as those which furnish the Weber and its branches, and their conditions are generally parallel. Their measured volumes were as follows:

Streams	I. — July volume, in feet per second	II. — September volume, in feet per second	III. — Ratio of I to II
City Creek	119	32	3.7
Emigration Creek	24	8	3.0
Parley's Creek	72	29	2.5

The comparison is not decisive, but it seems to show that the problem demands for its solution a careful examination at the "critical season." If the Ogden and Weber had been measured in September, as were the other streams, their volumes would probably have been found less than in October; and this consideration appears to throw the balance of evidence against the competence of the rivers to water the contiguous lands.

But if their incompetence shall be proved, it does not follow that the lands must go dry. The Bear at the north and the Jordan at the south have each a great volume of surplus water, and either supply can be led without serious engineering difficulty to the lower levels of the delta of the Weber.

In the following table are summed the agricultural resources of the Weber drainage basin:

Tracts	Square miles —	
	Cultivated in 1877	Cultivable
Kamas Prairie (northern edge)	.7	3.0
Peoa to Hennefer, inclusive	8.5	9.0
Parley's Park	3.2	3.2
Uptown	.5	2.0
Echo Creek	.3	.9
Croydon	.4	.5
Round Valley	.5	.5
Morgan Valley	6.0	6.9
Ogden Valley	4.1	8.0
Delta Plain	91.0	219.0
Total	115.2	253.0

The estimate of 219 miles of cultivable land on the Delta Plain includes 15 miles that will probably never be irrigated, but may nevertheless be farmed.

The total area of the Weber basin (including the whole plain from Bonneville to Centerville, and excluding the main body of Kamas Prairie) is 2,450 square miles; 4¾ per cent of the area is now under cultivation, and 10⅓ per cent is susceptible of cultivation.

The *Jordan River* is the outlet of Utah Lake, and runs northward, entering Great Salt Lake at its southeastern angle. On the right it receives a number of large tributaries from the Wasatch Range. The largest tributary of Utah Lake is the Provo River, which rises in the Uinta Mountains close to the head of the Weber and Bear.

From the mouth of its mountain cañon the Provo enters Kamas Prairie, and it hugs the south margin of the plain just as the Weber hugs the north margin, passing out by a narrow defile at the southwest corner. At one time in the history of the prairie the Provo flowed northward through it and joined itself to the Weber. The surface of the prairie was then lower than now, and the sand and gravel which the river brought from the mountains accumulated upon it. Eventually the Provo built its alluvium so high that its water found a new passage over the wall of the valley. The new channel, affording a more rapid descent than the old, quickened the current through the valley, and caused it to reverse its action and begin the excavation of the material it had deposited. So long as the river built up its bed, its channel was inconstant, shifting from place to place over the whole plain; but so soon as it began to cut away the bed, its position became fixed and the plain was abandoned. The river now flows in a narrow valley of its own making, 150 feet below the surface of the plain. As a result of this mode of origin, Kamas Prairie slopes uniformly from the Provo to the Weber, and it would be an immense undertaking to irrigate it with the water of the Weber. But the Provo River can be returned to its ancient duty with comparative ease. A few miles of canal will suffice to carry its water to the upper edge of the plain, and thence it can be led to every part. Already a small canal has been constructed, and its enlargement may convert the whole prairie into a meadow. Thus the prairie, although part of the drainage basin of the Weber, belongs to the irrigation district of the Provo.

The Provo next follows a narrow rock bound valley for 7 miles, being skirted by bottom lands that admit of some farming. It then enters Provo Valley, an opening about as large as the last, and favored by a warm climate that permits the growth of breadstuffs. Thence to Utah Valley it follows a deep, close cañon.

The volume of the Provo is sufficient to water about 100 square miles. If it be permitted to serve 28 miles in Kamas Prairie and 40 miles in Provo Valley and its adjuncts, there will remain for Utah Valley the quota for 32 miles. The minor streams of the valley, American Fork, Spanish Fork, Hobble Creek, Payson Creek, etc., will irrigate 120 miles, making a total of 152 square miles supplied with water. The total land of the valley which might be irrigated if the water were sufficient amounts to no less than 225 miles.

Thus it appears that if all available lands on the upper Provo are reclaimed, one-third of Utah Valley must go unwatered, while if none of them are irrigated, nearly the whole of the valley will be supplied. A middle course would appear most wise, and will undoubtedly be followed. A gradual extension of the canals, as the demands and means of the communities dictate and permit, will bring lands successively into use in the order of their value and convenience, and when the limit is reached and title has been acquired to all the water, the most available lands in each of the three valleys traversed by the Provo will have been reclaimed.

The residents of Kamas Prairie will probably have increased their meadows so as to furnish winter hay for herds sufficient to stock the summer pastures of the vicinity; Provo Valley, having a less favorable climate than Utah Valley, will have irrigated only its choicest soils; and the major part of the river will belong to Utah Valley. The apportionment may be roughly estimated as — Kamas Prairie, 10 miles; Provo Valley and Waldsburg, 20 miles, and Utah Valley, 70 miles.

Below Utah Lake there is little inequality of volume dependent on season. The lake is a natural reservoir 127 square miles in extent, and so far equalizes the outflow through the Jordan that the volume of that stream is less affected by the mean level of the lake than by the influence of northerly and southerly winds. With suitable head works its volume can be completely controlled, and, if desirable, the entire discharge of the lake can be concentrated in the season of irrigation.

The highest stage of the lake is in July, and the lowest in March or April; and the natural volume of its outlet has of course a corresponding change. In July I found that volume to be 1,275 feet per second, and I am informed by residents that the stream carried more than one-half as much water in its low stage; 1,000 feet is perhaps not far from the mean volume. When all possible use is made of Provo River and other tributaries the annual inflow of the lake will be diminished by about one-eighth, and the outflow by a greater fraction, which we will assume to be one-quarter. (This postulates that the evaporation is at the rate of 90 inches per year for the whole lake surface.) The remaining perennial outflow of 750 feet per second, if concentrated into four months, would irrigate for that period 350 square miles. It will be practicable to include under canals from the Jordan only about 160 square miles of farming land, and I think it safe to assume that the supply of water will be greatly in excess of the demand.

At the present time the Jordan is little used, the chief irrigation of Salt Lake Valley being performed by the large creeks that flow from the mountains at the east. It will not be long, however, before large canals are constructed to carry the Jordan water to all parts of the valley that lie below the level of Utah Lake. They will include 120 square miles of farming land.

The mountain streams, being no longer needed in the lower

parts of the valley, will be carried to higher land and made to serve the benches at the base of the mountains. By these means the total agricultural area of the valley will be increased to 192 square miles. Eventually, the western canal will be carried about the north end of the Oquirrh range and made to irrigate the northern third of Tooele Valley. It will pass above the farming lands of E. T. City and Grantsville, and enable the streams which irrigate the latter town to be used upon the higher slopes. The service of the Jordan will amount to no less than 40 miles and the agricultural area of the valley will be increased to about 45 square miles.

Including Tooele Valley and Kamas Prairie with the drainage basin of the Jordan, its agricultural resources sum up as follows:

Tracts	Square miles —	
	Cultivated in 1877	Cultivable
Kamas Prairie	4.0	10.0
Hailstone Ranch and vicinity	2.0	2.0
Provo Valley	6.0	16.0
Waldsburg	2.0	2.0
Utah Valley	59.0	190.0
Goshen ⎫		
Mona ⎬ Salt Creek	14.0	16.0
Nephi ⎭		
Salt Lake Valley (including Bountiful and Centerville)	89.8	192.0
Tooele Valley	5.4	45.0
Total	182.2	473.0

The drainage district has an area of 4,010 miles; 4½ per cent are cultivated, and 11¾ per cent may be cultivated.

It will be observed that in these estimates the available water above Utah Lake is regarded as insufficient for the available land, while below the lake there is a superabundance of water, and yet the lower stream is only a continuation of the upper streams. The difference arises from the function of the lake as a reservoir. Below the reservoir the whole of the annual supply can be controlled, but above it I have assumed that irrigation will merely make use for the irrigating season of the quantity which flows at the critical period. If artificial reservoirs can be constructed so as to store water for use in Utah Valley, a greater area can be cultivated. With adequate storage facilities the streams tributary to the lake can irrigate in Kamas Prairie 28 miles; in Provo Valley and vicinity

40 miles; in Thistle Valley 6 miles; on Salt Creek 16 miles, and in Utah Valley 225 miles, making a total of 315 miles; and there will still escape to the Jordan enough water to serve all the land assigned to that stream. If such storage is practicable, the estimate tabulated above should show 552 instead of 473 miles of cultivable land. The region most likely to afford storage facilities lies in the mountains where the waters rise. I did not visit it, and until it has been examined I shall not venture to increase the estimate.

The following table gives a summary for the Great Salt Lake river system:

Districts	Areas, in square miles			
	Whole district	Under cultiva-tion in 1877	To be reclaimed in the future	Total cultivable
Bear River	3,620	89.3	462.7	552.0
Weber River	2,450	115.2	137.8	253.0
Jordan River	4,010	192.2	280.8	473.0
Total	10,080	396.7	881.3	1,278.0
Ratios	1,000	.039	.088	.127

This region includes an eighth part of the land area of the Territory, and more than one-half the agricultural land. It is the richest section of Utah. Nearly one-third of its available land is already in use. The cost of the canals by which its cultivated lands have been furnished with water has been about $2,000,000. To complete its system of irrigation will probably cost $5,000,000 more.

IRRIGATION BY SMALL STREAMS

Through the remainder of the drainage basin of Great Salt Lake there are no large bodies of farming land. At wide intervals are small tracts, dependent on springs and small creeks, and the available land is in nearly every case greatly in excess of the available water. A few exceptional spots are cultivated without irrigation, but so far as they have been discovered they are so situated as to be moistened from beneath. No crops have been raised on dry bench lands.

The principal facts are gathered in the following table:

Localities	No. of distinct tracts	Acres in cultivation in 1877	Acres cultivable	Cultivable acres not included in existing surveys	Remarks
Cedar Fort	1	800	1,000	...	With aid of reservoirs.
Fairfield	1	800	900	...	
Vernon Creek	1	900	1,200	...	With aid of reservoirs.
Saint Johns	1	700	700	...	
East Cañon Creek, Rush Valley	1	500	900	...	
Stockton	1	200	500	...	
Skull Valley	11	1,000	2,500	(?)	With aid of reservoirs; visited in part only.
Government Creek	1	300	300	...	Not visited.
Willow Spring, township 10 south, range 17 west	1	250	250	...	Do.
Redding Spring	1	20	50	...	
Dodoquibe Spring	1	...	50	...	Not visited.
Deep Creek, township 9 south, range 19 west	1	500	1,000	...	With aid of reservoirs.
Pilot Peak	1	...	200	200	Not visited.
Grouse Valley	6	500	1,500	...	With aid of reservoirs.
Owl Spring	1	...	10	10	
Rosebud Creek	1	150	400	...	With aid of reservoirs.
Muddy Creek, township 10 north, range 15 west	1	300	300	300	
Park Valley	6	700	2,300	...	With aid of reservoirs.
Widow Spring	1	...	20	20	Not visited.
Indian Creek, township 13 north, range 12 west	1	...	100	100	With aid of reservoirs.
East base Clear Creek Mountains	6	5	150	100	Do.
Cazure Creek	1	...	200	200	Not visited.
Clear Creek, township 15 north, range 12 west	1	80	200	200	
Junction Creek	1	...	500	500	Not visited.
Goose Creek	2	...	200	200	Do.
Pilot Spring	1	...	15	...	
Deseret Creek (or Deep Creek)	1	300	3,000	...	With aid of reservoirs.
Crystal Springs, township 14 north, range 7 west	1	60	100	100	Do.
Antelope Spring, township 9 north, range 6 west	1	30	30	30	Not visited.
Hanzel Spring	1	15	15	15	
Promontory, east base	1	300	600	600	The greater part is not irrigated.
Blue Creek	1	...	1,500	...	
Brackish Springs near Blue Creek	1	200	1,000	...	
Antelope Island	1	...	50	50	Not visited.
Total	60	8,610	21,740	1,625	
Total in square miles	..	13.5	33.9	2.5	

Nineteen tracts have not yet been surveyed by the land office. The total area of the district is 13,370 square miles, of which one-tenth of one per cent is cultivated, and one-fourth of one per cent may be cultivated.

The contrast between the districts east and west of Great Salt Lake illustrates the combination of physical conditions essential to agriculture in our arid territories. An atmosphere endowed with but a small share of moisture precipitates freely only when it is reduced to a low temperature. Agriculture is dependent on the precipitation of moisture, but cannot endure the associated cold climate. It can flourish only where mountain masses turn over the aqueous product of their cold climates to low valleys endowed with genial climates. The Wasatch and Uinta crests stand from 6,000 to 9,000 feet higher than the valleys bordering Great Salt Lake. Their climate has a temperature from 20° to 30° lower. The snows that accumulate upon them in winter are not melted by the first warmth of spring, but yield slowly to the advancing sun, and all through the season of growing crops feed the streams that water the valleys. The Bear, the Weber, and the Jordan carry the moisture of the mountains to the warmth of the valleys, and fertility is the result.

To the north and west of the lake there are many mountains, but they are too low and small to store up snow banks until the time of need. Their streams are spent before the summer comes; and only a few springs are perennial. The result is a general desert, dotted by a few oases.

CHAPTER VIII

IRRIGABLE LANDS OF THE VALLEY
OF THE SEVIER RIVER

By Captain C. E. Dutton

As an agricultural region, the valley of the Sevier River and of its tributaries is one of the most important in Utah. The amount of arable land which may be reached by the waters of the stream is very much larger than the stream can water advantageously, and the time is probably not far distant when all the water that can be obtained will be utilized in producing cereals, and there is probably no other region in Utah where the various problems relating to the most economic use of water will be solved so speedily. It is, therefore, a region of unusual interest, regarded in the light of the new industrial problems which the irrigation of these western lands is now bringing forward. Fortunately, there is a smaller prospect of difficulty and obstruction in the settlement of the legal controversies which must inevitably arise elsewhere out of disputes about water rights than will be encountered in other regions, for the Mormon Church is an institution which quietly, yet resistlessly, assumes the power to settle such disputes, and the Mormon people in these outlying settlements yield to its assumptions an unhesitating obedience. Whatever the church deems best for the general welfare of its dependencies it dictates, and what it dictates is invariably done with promptitude, and none have yet been found to resist. This communal arrangement has been attended with great success so far as the development of the water resources are concerned, and the system of management has ordinarily been so conducted that the general welfare has been immensely benefited; and if individuals have suffered, it has not been made manifest by any apparent symptoms of general discontent or of individual resistance. The system is by no means perfect as yet, but its imperfections may be found in details which produce no present serious inconvenience, and they will no doubt be remedied as rapidly as they attain the magnitude of great evils.

The Sevier River has its course along the southeastern border of the Great Basin of the west, and its upper streams head in the lofty divide which separates the drainage system of the Colorado River on the south and east from the drainage system of the Great Basin on the north and west. The general course of the upper portion of the stream is from south to north, though its tributaries flow in many directions. The lower portion of the stream, within 60 miles of its end, suddenly breaks through one of the Basin Ranges on the west — the Pavant — and then turns south-westward and empties into Sevier Lake, one of the salinas of the Great Basin.

The main valley of the Sevier River has a N. S. trend, and begins on the divide referred to, about 270 miles almost due south of Great Salt Lake, and continues northward a distance of about 170 miles. There are three principal forks of this stream. The lowest fork is at Gunnison, 140 miles south of Salt Lake City, and called the San Pete, which waters a fine valley about 45 miles in length, and which is at present the most important agricultural district in Utah. About 80 miles farther up the stream, at Circle Valley, the river divides into very nearly equal branches; one coming from the south, the other breaking through a great plateau on the east. These are called, respectively, the South and East Fork of the Sevier. The South Fork has its principal fountains far up on the surface of a great plateau — the Panguitch Plateau — whose broad expanse it drains by three considerable streams, which finally unite in the valley at the foot of its eastern slope.

The East Fork of the Sevier receives the waters of a beautiful valley lying to the eastward of and parallel to the main valley of the Sevier, and separated from it by a lofty plateau 90 miles in length from north to south, and from 10 to 20 miles in breadth, called the Sevier Plateau. Through this great barrier the stream has cut a wide gorge 4,000 feet in depth and 10 miles long, called East Fork Cañon, and right at its lower end it joins the South Fork of the Sevier.

The physical geography of the region drained by the waters of the river is highly interesting, and has an important relation to the subject. The area in question consists of a series of tabular blocks, of vast proportions, cut out of the general platform of the country by great faults, and lifted above it from 2,000 to nearly 6,000 feet, so that the absolute altitudes (above sea level) of the tables range from 9,000 to 11,500 feet. Where the valleys are lowest the tables are highest, and *vice versa*. The valleys or lowlands stand from 5,000 to 7,500 feet above the sea. The plateaus have areas ranging from 400 to 1,800 square miles, and collectively with the included lowlands within the drainage system of the Sevier have an area of about 5,400 square miles. The tables front the valleys with barriers which are more continuous and which more closely resemble long lines of cliffs than the mountain chains and sierras of other portions of the Rocky Mountain Region, and there are stretches of unbroken walls, crowned with vast precipices, 10, 20, and even 40 miles in length, which look down from snowy altitudes upon the broad and almost torrid expanses below. If the palisades of the Hudson had ten times their present altitude and five or six times their present length, and if they had been battered, notched, and crumbled by an unequal erosion, they would offer much the same appearance as that presented by the wall of the Sevier Plateau which fronts the main valley of the Sevier. If they were from six to eight times multiplied, and extended from Hoboken to West Point, and were similarly shattered, they would present the appearance of the eastern wall of Grass Valley. If they were eight to ten times multiplied, and imagined to extend around three-fourths of the periphery of an area 40 miles by 20, and but little damaged by erosion, they would represent the solemn battlements of the Aquarius Plateau. These great plateaus are masses of volcanic rock overlying sedimentaries, the latter so deeply buried that they are seldom seen even in the deepest chasms, while superposed floods of volcanic outflows are shown in sections, reaching sometimes a thickness of 5,000 feet. The dark colors of these rocks give a somber aspect to the scenery, and the gloomy fronts of the towering precipices are rendered peculiarly grand and imposing.

The prevailing winds of this region are from the west, northwest, and southwest, and are a portion of the more general movement of the atmospheric ocean which moves bodily from the Pacific to the heart of the continent. In crossing the Sierra Nevada a large portion of its moisture is wrung from the air, which blows hot and arid across the Great Basin. Notwithstanding the aridity of the basin area, the air gains about as much moisture as it loses in crossing it, until it strikes the great barriers on the east side of the basin — the Wasatch and the chain of high plateaus which are mapped as its southerly continuation. Here the winds are projected by the bold fronts several thousands of feet upward. The consequent cooling and rarefaction condense from them an amount of moisture which, relatively to that arid country, may be called large, though far less than that of more favored regions. In the valleys the rainfall is exceedingly small; almost the whole of the precipitation is in the high altitudes. It is no uncommon thing to see the heavy masses of the cumulus clouds enveloping the summits of all the plateaus while the valleys lie under a sky but little obscured. The plateaus, then, are the reservoirs where the waters accumulate, and from which they descend in many rivulets and rills, while around their bases are copious springs fed by the waters which fall above. The rainfall in the valleys is very small, as compared with that upon the plateaus, and it is also highly variable. No record has been kept of the precipitation within the drainage system of the Sevier, and the nearest point where such a record has been kept is at Fort Cameron, near Beaver, at the western base of the Tushar Mountains. These observations cover but a brief period, and no doubt represent a much larger precipitation than that which occurs in the valleys and plains generally, because the situation of the point of observation is just at the base of the loftiest range in southern Utah, where the air currents from the west first strike it. Moreover, these observations are not yet published, and are not at present available. In the narrow valleys between closely approximated and lofty mountain walls, like the valley of the Sevier at Marysvale, the rainfall is greater than where the valley is wider, with lower walls, as at Panguitch, Richfield, and Gunnison. An estimate of the amount would be very hazardous; but, judging from what is known of similar localities, the amount in the wider valleys may be as low as 7 or 8 inches, or as high as 10 or 11. In the narrower and deeper valleys it may be between 10 and 12 inches. Upon the plateaus it may be as large as 30 to 35 inches. The principal fall is in the winter and spring months, from the middle of November to the first of

June; and in this period at least seven-eighths of the precipitation must be accomplished in the valleys and three-fourths upon the plateaus. There is, however, a large amount of variation in the distribution of the monthly falls from year to year. No two consecutive years correspond in this respect. In 1876 a heavy storm, with great rainfall and snow, occurred in the month of October, but in 1875 and 1877 no such storm occurred. In 1875 many drenching showers occurred in the months of July and August, but none occurred at the same months of 1877. In general, however, no summer rainfall has ever been known of such extent as to dispense with the necessity of irrigation, or even to materially reduce the necessary amount. Great variability in the distribution of the fall over different months of the year is one of the characteristics of the climate. But whatever the distribution, it is never such as to affect this one conspicuous feature — that the season in which crops must have their chief growth and reach their maturity is the dry season.

Connected with the irrigation of the Sevier Valley is a limiting condition, which rarely has to be considered in connection with the lands watered by the Bear and Weber Rivers, and which does not enter at all into the lands lying about Great Salt Lake. It is the dependence of climate upon altitude. There are lands along the upper portions of the forks of the Sevier which can be irrigated easily enough, but which are not cultivable for grain on account of the shortness of the summer and of the danger of frosts during the growth and ripening of the grain. This in turn is directly connected with the altitude. At the point where the Sevier leaves its main valley and enters the Pavant range, its altitude is 5,050 feet above sea-level. At Gunnison it is 5,150 feet.

The altitudes of the San Pete Valley are approximately as follows:

	Feet
Manti	5,350
Ephraim	5,450
Moroni	5,500
Springtown	5,550
Mount Pleasant	5,600
Fairview	5,725
Fountain Green	5,650

Beginning at Gunnison and ascending the Sevier along its main course, the altitudes are as follows:

	Feet
Gunnison	5,100
Salina	5,175
Richfield	5,300
Monroe	5,350
Joseph City	5,375
Marysvale	5,600
Circle Valley	6,000

Taking the East Fork in Grass Valley:

	Feet
Head of East Fork Cañon	6,300
Cousharem	6,700
Daniels' Ranch	7,000

Taking the South Fork:

	Feet
Head of Panguitch Cañon	6,250
Panguitch	6,400
Hillsdale	6,550
Junction of Mammoth Creek	6,900

In the San Pete Valley, which has been cultivated as far up as Mount Pleasant for twenty years, I cannot learn that any crop has ever been injured by frosts, and we may therefore conclude that this valley is safe from such an attack, unless a most abnormal one. The same may be said of the main Sevier Valley from Joseph City downward. From Joseph City to Circle Valley there is a relatively small portion of irrigable land, but such as there is may, I think, be regarded as safe from frost. Circle Valley, where the two forks unite, has been cultivated for cereals for four years, and has not yet suffered from frost, and it is fair to assume that such a calamity will be very infrequent there, though it may not be possible to say there is no danger. In Panguitch Valley, a severe frost in August, 1874, inflicted great injury upon the crops, and only a small quantity of very inferior grain was harvested. But in 1875, 1876, and 1877, excellent crops were secured. Above Panguitch the amount of arable land is not great, and the danger to crops is increased. In Grass Valley there is a magnificent expanse of fertile arable land, but there can be no question that a large portion of it is so liable to killing frosts in August, or even in July, that the cereals cannot flourish there. The lower portion of the valley, near the head of East Fork Cañon, is more hopeful, and it is probable that a large majority of crops planted there will mature, though occasional damage may be reasonably looked for. The general result may be summarized as follows: Below 6,000 feet crops may be considered as safe from serious damage by frosts. From 6,000 to 7,000 feet crops are liable to damage in a degree proportional to the excess of altitude above 6,000 feet. Above 7,000 feet the danger is probably such as to render agriculture of little value to those who may pursue it.

The climate has shown in past times a longer period of variation than the annual one. Panguitch was settled once in 1860, but was abandoned on account of the destruction of crops by the frosts. The settlement was renewed in 1867, and again abandoned, in consequence of the attacks of Indians. It was settled a third time in 1870, and, though crops have occasionally been injured, the agriculture has on the whole proved remunerative.

Let us now look at the irrigable lands of the Sevier and its tributaries. Above the town of Panguitch, on the South Fork, there is a considerable area of arable land, which could be easily reached by canals from the main stream and below 7,000 feet altitude, but for want of a detailed survey it is impossible to do more than guess at the area. I think, however, that 8,000 acres would be the maximum limit. This portion of the valley is liable to killing frosts, though during the last three years it has not suffered from this cause. In the long run, I believe agriculture will not prove remunerative here. From Panguitch northward to the head of the Panguitch Cañon, a distance of 18 miles, is a broad valley, averaging 5 miles in width, a very large portion of which is irrigable, provided the water supply is adequate. At least 24,000 acres may be cultivated without resort to anything more than the usual methods of distributing the water; but not the whole of this area is fertile. The greater part of the area of Panguitch Valley is composed of alluvial slopes, or, as they have been termed by geologists, alluvial cones. Although these surface features are presented in a somewhat more typical and striking manner in Grass Valley, yet they are well enough exhibited here; and as they have an important relation to the subject, I will briefly discuss them.

In a mountainous country like this, where the melting of the snows in spring or heavy rainfalls at other seasons create sudden and great torrents, large quantities of detritus are carried down from the mountains into the valleys. These mountain streams, which in summer, autumn, and early winter are ordinarily either very small or wholly dried up, may upon certain occasions become devastating floods. The bottoms of the ravines are steep water courses, down which the angry torrents rush with a power which is seldom comprehended by those who dwell in less rugged regions. Huge boulders weighing several tons, great trees, with smaller débris of rocks, gravel, sand, and clay, are swept along with resistless force, until the decreasing slope diminishes the energy sufficiently to permit the greater boulders to come to rest, while the smaller ones are still swept onward. The decrease of slope is continuous, so that smaller and smaller fragments reach a stable position, and only cobblestones, gravel, or sand reach the junctions of the streams with the main rivers. Around the openings of the greater gorges and ravines the deposits of coarser detritus build up in the lapse of time the alluvial cones. As it accumulates, each torrent builds up its bed and constantly changes the position of its channel, and with the mouth of the ravine for a center it sweeps around from right to left and left to right like a radius, adding continually, year after year, to the accumulations of detritus. Thus a portion of a flat cone is formed, having its apex at the mouth of the ravine. At the foot of mountain ranges these alluvial cones are formed at the mouth of every ravine, and are sometimes so near together that they intersect each other, or become confluent. They are composed of rudely stratified materials, ranging in size or grain from fine silt and sand to rounded stones of several hundredweight, and occasionally a block of a ton or more may be seen near the apex of the cone. In regions where the rocks are soft and readily disintegrated the stones are more worn, less in number, and smaller in size, and this is the case generally with unaltered sedimentary rocks. But in valleys running among volcanic ranges, the much greater hardness and durability of the materials preserve them from disintegration, and the stones are more numerous, larger, and less worn by attrition, composing indeed a very large proportion of the bulk of the alluvial cones. A large portion of the valley of the

Sevier lies in the midst of a volcanic region, and its sides are everywhere flanked with these alluvial cones, which are very stony and gravelly. The lower portion of the Sevier is in a country made of sedimentary beds, and though the alluvial cones are equally common, they consist of finer material, and are less burdened with stones.

The Panguitch Valley is between volcanic plateaus, and most of its area consists of alluvial cone land, which is no doubt fertile wherever the stones and rubble are not sufficient to prevent plowing and planting, but this difficulty must render it at least very undesirable. There is, however, a large area of land of another description in Panguitch Valley, composed of the finest silt brought down by the gentler current of the river itself, and deposited within its own basin. This is good bottom land, and the amount of it I estimate at not less than 7,000 acres. It has already been remarked that Panguitch Valley stands at an altitude above 6,000 feet, and is not free from danger of summer frosts. These have been known to destroy or seriously injure the grain, though in a majority of years crops will no doubt be safely harvested. Whether the danger is such as to make agriculture unremunerative in the long run experience can alone demonstrate.

Following the South Fork of the Sevier downward through the Panguitch cañons, the next important agricultural area is Circle Valley. This is a broad, nearly circular area, situated in the midst of scenery of the most magnificent description. Upon the east and west sides rise those gigantic cliffs which are the peculiar feature of the scenery of this elevated region, looking down upon the valley from altitudes of 4,000 to 5,000 feet. This valley also has upon its sides long sloping areas of stony alluvial cones, full of blocks of trachyte and basalt washed down from the cliffs above. It has also a large area of arable land. There is in addition, a certain area of sandy land of an inferior degree of excellence. The area of best bottom land will probably reach as high as 6,000 acres. In this area there is probably very little danger from early frosts, as the 6,000 feet contour passes through the middle of the valley, and, as already stated, the areas which lie within this limit are reasonably safe from this occurrence. At the north end of Circle Valley we find the junction of the two main forks of the Sevier River. From the junction the main stream runs northward for nearly 20 miles, and throughout this entire stretch there is but little arable land. Upon both sides of the river there are long alluvial slopes, made up of stony materials and coarse gravels, through which a plow could scarcely be driven. A portion of the way the river runs between rocks and low cliffs and in abrupt cañons, cutting through old trachyte and basaltic outflows. Reaching Marysvale, we find a sufficient area for three or four good sized farms, consisting of bottom land of the finest quality, which can be watered either from the Sevier River itself or from two considerable affluents which come roaring down out of the Beaver Mountains. North of Marysvale is a barrier thrown across the valley, consisting of rugged hills of rhyolitic rocks, through which the river has cut a deep cañon; but agriculture in any portion of this barrier is out of the question. The river emerges from it at the head of what may be called its main or lower valley, near the Mormon settlement called Joseph City. From this point northward we find what must undoubtedly become the great agricultural area of southern Utah. It is a magnificent valley, nowhere less than 5 miles in width, and at least 60 miles in length, with abrupt mountain walls on either side, and almost the whole of its soil consisting of alluvial cones, and susceptible of a high degree of cultivation. The limit of the amount of land in this valley which can be irrigated is measured by the quantity of water which can be found to turn upon it. The western side of the valley is flanked by abrupt walls of sedimentary rocks. As I have before stated, the alluvial cones which find their origin in the degradation of these sedimentary walls are invariably composed of finer materials than those which come from the breaking up of volcanic rocks. The soil, therefore, is much more readily plowed and planted than the corresponding cones farther up the river. The surface of these cones, moreover, is coated with a thick layer of fine loam, and it is not until penetrated to a considerable depth that we come upon a coarser material. This portion of the valley of the Sevier has been under cultivation for more than eight years. The art of irrigation has also reached a certain stage of advancement, at which it can be studied with some interest. A canal of sufficient magnitude to carry the entire body of the water of the Sevier during the dry season has been run for a distance of 8 miles, and is used for irrigating the large grain fields which lie around Richfield; and, as irrigation is now conducted, the entire flow of the stream is turned through this canal after having been employed for irrigating the various fields, which extend for the distance of nearly 7 miles. The total amount of irrigable land which may be found between Joseph City on the south and the point where the Sevier leaves its proper valley, 65 miles to the northward, cannot be much less than 90,000 acres. The limit of irrigation throughout this entire valley is the limit of the water supply.

There is one other valley to which we must advert, namely, the valley of the San Pete. This is fully equal in fertility and in the convenience of every element connected with irrigation to the best part of the main valley of the Sevier. The San Pete is a stream of considerable magnitude, and experience has shown that it is probably capable, under a more improved system of irrigation than that now in use, of watering the greater portion of its valley. The cultivable acreage of the San Pete Valley is about 55,000 acres, provided the whole could be watered.

The quantity of water carried by the Sevier will now be considered. This, of course, is highly variable from month to month. The time for measurement, if the true irrigating capacity of the stream is to be considered, should be that time at which the ratio of water in the stream to the amount required is smallest. At different stages of growth of the crops the amount of water required differs considerably. The largest amount is needed about the time the seeds of the grain begin to fill out. Ordinarily this is in the latter part of July and early August throughout the lower and most extensive portion of the valley, and a week later in the upper portions. At this season the water is not at its minimum. There is a gradual diminution of the flow during July, but the great shrinkage of the stream occurs during the middle of August, just after, or sometimes even during, those irrigations in which the greatest amount is required. The critical period of the crops occurs, therefore, just before, and sometimes dangerously near, the period of rapid decline in the water supply. It will therefore be evident that it is not a very easy matter to determine the exact stage of water which can serve as a criterion of the irrigating capacity. My own measurements, however, were hardly a matter of choice, but were made at the most advantageous period which could be selected without interfering with the primary objects of the expedition.

The Sevier was measured at the junction of the two main forks, at the north end of Circle Valley, on the 6th and 7th of July. The method adopted was first to find a section of the water at a given point by soundings and by actual measurement of the width of the water surfaces, and measuring the surface velocity by means of floats. The most probable mean result of several measurements was found to be 410 cubic feet per second for the East Fork, and 450 feet per second for the South Fork, or a total of 860 feet.

While this measurement was made the South Fork was being drawn upon above for the watering of about 1,100 acres near Panguitch, 35 miles farther up the stream, and also for watering about 600 acres in Circle Valley, about 3 to 4 miles above. The amount of water used in Circle Valley was probably greater than that at Panguitch, since the method employed was much more wasteful, and no provision made for returning the tail water to the stream. On the other hand, a large proportion of the tail water from both places finds its way back to the channel in spite of waste, but how much it is impossible to conjecture. I think, however, that 75 cubic feet per second would cover the loss from these sources.

Below the point of measurement the Sevier receives the following affluents: At Van Buren's ranch is a cluster of very large springs, furnishing about 55 cubic feet per second. Between Van Buren's and Marysvale are three streams, yielding together about 30 feet, and Bullion Creek at Marysvalle carries about 40 feet. There is still another affluent at Marysvale with about 30 feet. Finally, Clear Creek, north of Marysvale Cañon, gives about 45 feet, making the total contributions between the junction of the forks and Joseph City about 200 feet.

At Monroe a stream issues from the Sevier table, and is used for the irrigation of the field cultivated by that settlement. Its flow is estimated at 40 feet in the middle of July. At Richfield, on the other side of the valley, is a stream coming from the Pavant, with a flow of about 20 feet, and at Glencove a stream of 25 feet. At Salina is a large tributary issuing from a great cañon through the north end of the Sevier Plateau, and its measurement indicated a flow of 165 feet. The total between Monroe and Salina, inclusive, would thus reach 250 feet, to which might be added some smaller tributaries, not specifically mentioned, amounting perhaps to 10 feet, giving a total of 260 feet. Adding this to the tributaries between the upper forks and Joseph City, and to the main river itself, we have, as the total above Gunnison, 1,320 feet. This estimate being for the early part of July, and obviously largely in excess of the amount which is available at the critical period, in the last week of that month and the first week in August, what allowance should be made for the diminution of supply during the month of July it is difficult to determine. The smaller tributaries, as a rule, shrink much more than the larger. Those which enter the stream lower down decline more during July than those which join it farther up. Taken altogether, I am satisfied that it would be unsafe to estimate the irrigating capacity in the first week of August at more than 60 per cent of that found in the first week of July, and I regard 50 per cent as a much more probable estimate. For want of a better one, I adopt it, and this gives the estimated irrigating capacity of the Sevier and its tributaries above the junction of the San Pete at 660 cubic feet per second during the critical period.

The water supply in the San Pete Valley was measured by Mr. Renshawe during the latter part of July, and found by him to be as follows:

Volume of flowing water, in cubic feet per second,
of streams in San Pete Valley

	Feet
Pleasant Creek	28
Ephraim Creek	28
Manti Creek	28
Springtown Creek	14
Fairview Creek	10
Wales Creek	6
Fountain Green	10
Moroni	10
Creek between Ephraim and Manti	5
Creek between Manti and Gunnison	5
Creek above Fairview	2½
Twelve-mile Creek	28
San Pete at Gunnison	60
Total	234½

This estimate is also liable to reduction, being undoubtedly a little in excess of the amount available at the critical period. This reduction may be as great as 15 per cent, which would leave very closely 200 cubic feet as the water supply of the San Pete Valley, which, added to the total of the Sevier above Gunnison, gives for the whole drainage system of the Sevier River a water supply of 860 feet per second at the time when the greatest amount is required.

The next factor to be inquired into is the amount of land which a cubic foot per second of water can irrigate. This is, of course, highly variable, depending upon the nature of the soil, and the economy with which the water is applied, and the frequency of the irrigations. New lands freshly broken require much more water than the older ones which have been planted and watered for several years; and in fact the quantity diminishes with each season for a long term of years. In the San Pete Valley, which has been longest cultivated, the decrease in the amount of water applied to the oldest lands has not yet ceased, though some fields have been cultivated with regularity since 1857. The fresh soils are highly porous and absorptive, requiring a large quantity of water for their irrigation, and not retaining this moisture well under the great evaporative power of a dry and hot atmosphere. With successive irrigations, the pores of the soil are gradually closed and the earth is slowly compacted by the infiltration of impalpable silt brought by the irrigating waters. It absorbs water much more slowly, and retains it a much longer time. There is, however, a check to this increased irrigating power, arising from a wasteful mode of agriculture. It has not been the practice to employ fertilizers, nor any other conservative means of keeping up the fertility of the soil, and the yield of the crops growing smaller, the old lands are frequently abandoned, and fresh adjoining lands are broken, planted, and watered. It has been the practice to cut the straw, which is never returned as mulch; and, as there is but little rotation in crops, the result can be easily comprehended. So long as new land costs nothing but the labor to clear of the *Artemisia* or sage brush, there is always the tendency to invade it as rapidly as the old lands show signs of fatigue. Thus the waters are constantly irrigating every year a large proportion of new land, and the consumption of water is correspondingly great.

A serious loss of water and fertility is produced by any method of irrigation which employs more water than is just sufficient to saturate the soil. Whatever water runs off from a field carries with it great quantities of mud and fine silt, together with the most precious elements of fertility. These elements are the soluble alkaline salts and organic matter which are readily taken up by the water, and once removed are not speedily restored. A field which is so irrigated that a large surplus of water is continually running from the tail ditches during the flow will rapidly deteriorate in fertility. But a field which receives water which is allowed to stand until it has soaked into the earth, without any surplus passing into the tail ditches, will increase in fertility. These irrigating waters bring with them a sufficiency of plant food to compensate, and more too, for the drain upon the soil caused by the harvest; but they will carry off more than they bring if they are permitted to run over the field and escape from it, instead of being caught and held until they are absorbed. It is not always practicable to attain this exact distribution of water, and many cases occur where great expense and labor might be required to arrange the ditches and fields in this manner. Ordinarily, it is cheaper to throw away old land and take up new than to improve the system of irrigation, and there are many fields in the valley of the Sevier which have been abandoned because the fertility of the soil has been washed out by a reckless method of irrigation. Connected with this is another source of waste, arising from very unequal requirements of contiguous areas, in consequence of which many lands, especially old ones, are liable to be excessively watered. When a community farms a large number of small fields, using water from the same canals, it is usually impossible so to regulate the distribution of the privilege that each field will receive the exact amount it needs. Some fields can remain unwatered much longer than others, and the tendency always is to get as much water as possible — each farmer fearing a deficiency of water and wasting its surplus. Experience on the part of the watermasters and a more and more settled habit in the lands themselves gradually diminish this source of loss and create economy. Far better results, therefore, may ordinarily be anticipated in old lands than in new. Better results, also, are found where circumstances render difficult or impracticable the abandonment of old fields for new, and this is ordinarily in those portions where the water is nearly or quite sufficient for all the irrigable land, and where all the irrigable land is taken up.

Recurring, then, to the inquiry as to the amount of land which a cubic foot per second of running water will irrigate, this area is in many of the new lands as low as 40 acres, and it seldom exceeds 80 acres with the old lands. Probably there are very few regions in the world where the demand of the soil for water is so great as here where the supply is so small. In California a cubic foot of water is said to be capable of irrigating more than a hundred acres, in India 200, and in Spain and Italy a much larger area. The reason is obvious. It is the direct consequence of the extreme aridity of the climate of Utah. The irrigating capacity of the unit of water is even less in the southern counties of Utah than in those around Great Salt Lake. Mr. Gilbert's estimate of 100 acres for this last locality being accepted as the best that can be hoped for, it will not be rating the factor too low to say that 80 acres is the best that can be hoped for in the valley of the Sevier. The present factor will not, I am convinced, have a higher average value than 50 acres.

The total acreage, therefore, which can be irrigated in the drainage system of the Sevier by the present system of watering and of agriculture may be estimated at about 43,000 acres, and the greatest improvements and economies in the system of farming and watering cannot, with the present water supply, be expected to raise the irrigable area above 70,000 acres.

Districts	Square miles cultivated during 1877	Acres cultivated during 1877	Square miles of irrigable land	Acres irrigable land
San Pete Valley	17	11,000	31.2	20,000
Gunnison	4.4	2,800	6.2	4,000
Sevier Valley above Gunnison	16.5	10,500	54.7	35,000
Circle Valley	1.2	750	6.3	4,000
Panguitch and above	2.8	1,800	11	7,000
Total	41.9	26,850	109.4	70,000

Nevertheless, I am persuaded that it will be practicable to extend the possibility of irrigation by an increase of water supply to a degree sufficient to irrigate every acre of the main valley of the Sevier which can be reached by canals, and which is also fit for cultivation. It is by the method of artificial reservoirs. There is probably no region in the world more admirably suited to the easy, cheap, and efficient application of this method than this very region drained by the Sevier River. The sources of this river are found at high altitudes, but these high places are not mountains in the ordinary sense, but great plateaus with broad summits. These table tops have vast numbers of large basins broad enough for great ponds, which are now drained by narrow gorges cut through volcanic sheets and leading down to lower levels. These gorges are in most cases narrow cañons, which, being once barred across, will dam the waters above them. I could not select a better example than the following: About 15 miles southwest of the town of Panguitch is a broad basin, the central part of which is occupied by a shallow lake, about $1\frac{1}{4}$ miles long and nearly a mile wide, called Panguitch Lake. Its altitude is about 8,200 feet. It is completely surrounded with barriers, nowhere less than 100 feet in height, and finds its drainage through a narrow cleft on the northeast side. It receives the influx of two fine streams, which in May and June must carry heavy floods of water from the lofty rim and broad watershed of the Panguitch Plateau lying to the westward. Even in August their united flow must reach 50 feet per second. By throwing a dam 30 feet high and 50 or 60 feet long across the outlet between its walls of solid trachyte, a lake would be formed with an area of 6 or 7 square miles. There are many such basins upon the Panguitch Plateau, and it would be a low estimate to say that it would be possible, at comparatively small expense, to create 30 or 40 square miles of lake surface, with an average depth of 20 feet, upon that plateau alone. The precipitation upon its surface would be more than sufficient to fill these lakes every year. A dam across the upper part of East Fork Cañon would create a lake behind it which might have an area of 12 to 15 square miles. Numerous reservoirs could be created at small expense in Grass Valley, upon the Fish Lake Plateau, and upon the Sevier Plateau, and in those valleys which are drained by Salina Creek and its tributaries. The Sevier River itself can be cheaply dammed at several gorges and made to overflow swampy flats above — notably at the head of Marysvale Cañon, and again just north of Van Buren's ranch. Other things equal, it would be better, as well as cheaper, to build dams at higher levels, since the evaporation is much less there than in the valleys, and the natural facilities for creating lakes are also greater.

In this way, I believe it to be practicable to reserve a store of water sufficient to irrigate every acre of ground in the Sevier Valley, which is by the nature of its soil and its situation suitable for irrigation. It may be noted, too, that the "tank system" thus suggested would not interfere with or take the place of the present system, but would be supplementary to it. The streams would in June and early July run through the lakes and over the dams, yielding about as much water as they now yield in these months, and the reservoirs would not have to be drawn upon before the middle of July.

A very interesting subject connected with the peculiar conditions of agriculture in the west is the origin and distribution of alkaline salts in the soil. In moist regions such occurrences are rare. They are peculiar to arid regions, and, in truth, very few arid regions fail to exhibit them. The cause in a general way is well known. The small amount of rain which falls during the wet season penetrates deeply into the earth, where it gradually takes up such soluble salts as it encounters there. During the dry season which follows, there is always going on an evaporation from the surface, however dry it may appear to the senses. It is a mistake to suppose that because the saline soil is as dry as ashes no evaporation is in progress. In many cases this may be true; but often in the most arid regions there are many localities where the water collects far below the immediate surface. By capillary action, this water always tends to diffuse itself throughout the loose materials which make up the overlying soils. As fast as it is evaporated at the surface, more water from below rises by capillary action to take its place. When the air is exceedingly dry, as it invariably is in summer throughout the whole Rocky Mountain Region at moderate altitudes, the evaporative power becomes so great and extends to such a depth below the immediate surface, that we are unable to recognize the slightest traces of moisture indicating that evaporation is going on. The water which may have accumulated beneath has gradually risen by percolation through the interstices of the unconsolidated materials of the soil, bringing with it whatever soluble salts it may have taken into solution during its sojourn beneath the surface. These soluble salts are left at the surface by the final evaporation of the water, and, as the process is continuous until the reservoir beneath is exhausted, the salts accumulate. Contrast this now with the action going on in a moist country. Here the copious waters wash the soils as rapidly as the salts come up from below, and carry them in solution into the drainage channels. During the greater part of the year the movement of the waters is partly from the surface downward into the subterranean water courses, from which they emerge in springs; partly by surface drainages into rills, and thence into living streams. By both movements, any tendency to accumulate soluble salts at the surface during the relatively brief periods of dryness is prevented. In a dry country the periods of dryness are very much longer, and the rainfall is seldom sufficient to wash the accumulated salts from the soil. There is, however, usually a limit to this accumulation, since at long intervals rains occur sufficient to remove a large portion of the salts. The difference between a dry and wet country in this respect is therefore one of degree rather than of kind. In a dry country the periods of accumulation of salts at the surface are long and continuous, while the washings of the soil are rare and imperfect. In a wet country the periods of accumulation are short and rare, while the washings are frequent, copious, and thorough.

The saline materials vary widely in character and constitution. They are, however, chiefly salts of soda, lime, potash, and magnesia. Sometimes they exist in the condition of chlorides, sometimes of carbonates, and sometimes of sulphates. The reactions from which they are derived are many, and it will be proper here to give only a few illustrations. A portion of the salts of magnesia and soda are derived from the decomposition, by atmospheric influences, of volcanic, granitic, and other crystalline rocks. Where these materials exist in the form of feldspar, hornblende, and pyroxene, the great decomposing agent is water charged with the carbonic acid of the atmosphere, by the action of which soda, magnesia, and lime are, with inconceivable slowness, dissolved out of the constituents of these rocks. There is no stream, however pure it may apparently be, which does not carry more or less of chlorides and carbonates in solution. The sulphates are derived mainly from subterranean sources. In the Rocky Mountain

Region, one of the most common forms of sulphate is found very abundantly in the rocks of the Carboniferous, Triassic, Cretaceous, and Tertiary Ages, in the forms of gypsum and selenite, which are sulphates of lime. Whenever waters containing carbonate of soda are filtered through strata containing these sulphates, a double decomposition takes place, by which carbonate of lime and sulphate of soda are formed. The carbonate of lime is very slightly soluble in water, while the sulphate of soda is highly so, and it is well known that waters emanating from the sedimentary rocks just spoken of are very frequently highly charged with it. Such, doubtless, is the origin of this mineral in the so called alkaline waters of the west, and of all the soluble minerals which pass under the name of alkali it is one of the most common. Carbonate of soda is also abundant in the soils. It is frequently found in the summer time, coating the surface of bottom lands which earlier in the season have been submerged by the augmented streams. Common salt (chloride of sodium) is even more abundant than the sulphate. It is well known, however, that many of the sedimentary rocks, particularly those of the Triassic and Jurassic Age, contain an abundance of it, and there are many localities in the west where a very fair article of common salt is obtained by the lixiviation of the detritus of the red Triassic rocks. Incrustations of these soluble saline materials occur most abundantly in the vicinity of the rivers and in the bottom lands. This may at first seem somewhat strange, but it is susceptible of a ready explanation. In order that these salts may accumulate at the surface, there must be going on continually a slow transmission of moisture from under ground upward, and since a continuous supply of water is more frequently found in the bottom lands than elsewhere, it follows that the conditions of these accumulations are here more frequently fulfilled. They may, however, and do occur at localities which probably contain subterranean reservoirs of water, which are annually filled during the wet season. Sometimes these salts are so abundant that the land requires a thorough washing before it is fit for agriculture, and the Mormons have on several occasions, when founding settlements, been obliged to allow the waters from their ditches to leach the land for many months, and in one or two cases for two, and even three, years, before a good crop could be raised. There is no difficulty, however, in removing any quantity of these readily soluble salts from the soil, provided this leaching process be continued long enough; and it is usually found that lands which were originally highly akaline become, when reclaimed from their alkalinity, among the most fertile.

There yet remains for mention a number of small areas served by some minor streams in southwestern Utah. These little creeks head in the mountains, but are soon lost in the deserts of that arid and torrid region, none of their waters finding their way to the ocean. The greater number of them belong to the drainage basin of Sevier Lake. In each case the water supply is small, and inadequate to supply the available land. In nearly every case the competence of the supply has been determined in the most practical way — by the operations of settlers; but some allowance has been made for an increase of the irrigable land by the more economic use of the water. This can be accomplished by the construction of better waterways, and by more carefully flowing the water over the lands.

The following table exhibits the extent of these areas:

Districts	Square miles	Acres
Cherry Creek	.2	100
Judd Creek	.2	100
Levan	3.1	2,000
Scipio	2.6	1,700
Holden	1.6	1,000
Fillmore and Oak Creek	5.5	3,500
Meadow Creek	1.9	1,200
Kanosh	3.1	2,000
Beaver Creek and tributaries	21.9	14,000
Paragoonah	1.5	1,000
Parowan	1.5	1,000
Summit	.6	400
Cedar City, Iron City, and Fort Hamilton	3.6	2,300
Mountain Meadows	.3	200
Pinto	.3	200
Hebron	1.6	1,000
Total	49.5	31,700

CHAPTER IX

IRRIGABLE LANDS OF THAT PORTION OF UTAH DRAINED BY THE COLORADO RIVER AND ITS TRIBUTARIES

By A. H. Thompson

That portion of Utah drained by the Colorado River and its tributaries belongs to a great basin limited on the north by the Uinta Mountains and on the west by the high plateaus that separate the drainage of the Colorado from that of the salt lakes of the interior, and extending beyond the limits of the Territory on the east and south. The floor of this basin is extremely rough, being broken by isolated groups of rugged mountains, by plateaus encircled with cliffs of almost vertical rock, by mesas and amphitheaters, and huge monumental and castellated buttes. Everywhere the surface is cut and carved with a network of cañons, hundreds and often thousands of feet in depth.

The main channel through which its drainage passes to the sea is the Colorado, and its proper upper continuation, the Green River.

The principal tributaries to these streams from the east are the White, the Grand, and the San Juan Rivers — all rising in the high mountains east of the Territory and flowing in a general westerly course — the White entering the Green River, the Grand uniting with the Green to form the Colorado, and the San Juan entering the latter about 125 miles below the junction of the Grand and the Green. The Virgin, the Kanab, the Paria, the Escalante, the Fremont, the San Rafael, the Prince, the Minnie Maud, the Uinta, and Ashley Fork are the principal tributaries from the west.

This portion of Utah is but sparsely settled by white people, the only permanent locations being in the southwestern part, and in the Uinta Valley at the north. Information concerning its agricultural resources is limited, being confined, except in relation to the localities before mentioned, to data collected by the geographical and geological parties of this survey. Many of the streams have been visited but a single time, and different streams at widely different dates, during a field season. Often the exigencies of the survey prevented as close an examination into the flow of water, and the location and character of the soil of the arable tracts, as was desirable; yet, on the whole, it is thought that the data collected can be relied upon as a very close approximation.

The climate of the basin is one of extreme aridity. The prevailing wind is westerly. The high plateaus and mountains forming the western rim of the basin force these winds up to an altitude above the sea of over 10,000 feet, and thus act as great condensers to deprive them of their moisture. Flowing down from the higher lands into the warmer regions below, their capacity for absorption is increased, and during the greater portion of the year the winds abstract from rather than add to the humidity of the lower altitudes. But little is known concerning the actual amount of precipitation of moisture within the basin. Below an altitude of 7,000 feet it is very small, probably not over an average of 5 inches yearly. At higher altitudes it is much greater, probably reaching 24 inches, but this is mostly during the winter months and in the form of snow.

The elevation of the region under consideration is from 2,500 feet to 11,500 feet above the sea, thus giving great range in temperature. In the valleys of the extreme southwestern portion an almost subtropical warmth is experienced, and [leaving?] the different valleys containing arable lands we pass from these by insensible gradations to those where frosts occur during every month in the year. Generally, the limit of successful cultivation of the soil is below 7,000 feet.

In this portion of Utah irrigation is essential to agriculture. If all the single acres it is possible to cultivate without artificial irrigation were aggregated, I do not believe the sum would reach one-fourth of one square mile, and every foot of this meager amount is irrigated naturally. Springs are of infrequent occurrence. The great source of water supply is the streams fed by the rains and snows of the high table lands and mountains. All these streams have a rapid fall in their upper courses, and are here often of considerable size; but upon reaching the lower and more level country their waters are rapidly absorbed by the porous soil and evaporated by the higher temperature. So great is the loss from these causes that some streams fail to reach the main drainage channel during the warmer months, and all are greatly shrunken in volume. All the arable lands — or lands where altitude, slope of surface, and quality of soil permit successful cultivation, if a supply of water can be obtained, and from which lands to irrigate, or irrigable lands, may be selected — are in the valleys adjacent to the streams. Usually this area in many valleys is in excess of that which the water in the streams can irrigate, and choice in the location of lands to cultivate is often practicable. In this report I have considered irrigable lands to be such only as possess all the necessary qualifications of altitude, slope of surface, and fertility of soil, and have, in addition, an available supply of one cubic foot of water per second for each hundred acres. The great dissimilarity between the valleys makes it desirable to consider the drainage basin of each separately, in respect to arable lands, irrigable lands, volume of water, and practicability of increasing this supply during the irrigating season.

THE VIRGIN RIVER

This stream is in the extreme southwest corner of the area under consideration. Its branches rise in the Colob Plateau, at altitudes varying from 8,000 to 10,000 feet above the sea. It flows in a southwesterly course, and joins the Colorado beyond the boundaries of Utah. The smaller creeks draining the eastern portion of the plateau unite, after descending to an altitude of 5,500 feet above the sea, and form what is called the Pa-ru-nu-weap Fork of the Virgin. At and below the junction of these creeks, the cañon valley in which they flow widens into what is known as Long Valley. There a considerable area of available land is found. The soil is excellent, and wherever cultivated yields abundant crops. Below Long Valley the stream enters Pa-ru-nu-weap Cañon, and is simply a series of cascades for 15 miles, descending in this distance from 5,000 to 3,500 feet above the sea level. Emerging, it enters the valley of the Virgin. This valley is 44 miles in length. Its upper portion is only an enlargement of the cañon, in which small areas of available land are found. Its lower portion is a broader valley, much broken by low, basalt covered mesas, and sharp ridges of tilted sedimentary rocks. In the upper portion of the valley the river receives several accessions, the principal ones being Little Zion, North Fork, La Verkin, and Ash Creeks. With the exception of the Ash, but very little cultivable land is found along these creeks. Midway in the valley two streams enter, coming from the Pine Valley Mountains and having small areas of irrigable land along their courses, and near the foot the Santa Clara River adds its water. The united streams leave the valley by a deep cañon cut through the Beaver Dam Mountains. The valley of the Virgin has a lower altitude than any other portion of Utah, and a warmer climate. The soil of the arable lands is usually good, and wherever it is possible to irrigate produces abundant crops. Some little difficulty is occasionally experienced in the first years of cultivation from an excess of alkaline constituents in the soil, but plentiful applications of water soon remove this difficulty, and these lands often become the most productive. No reliable data concerning the amount of arable land in the drainage basin, or the volume of water carried by the Virgin River and its tributaries, have been collected. From the best information attainable, the amount of land actually irrigated in 1875, is placed at eleven square miles. This conclusion is based in the main upon returns made in 1875 to the Deseret Agricultural and Manufacturing Society, the amount under cultivation in Long Valley having been ascertained by Mr. J. H. Renshawe, of this survey. To irrigate this, all the water in most of the tributary streams is used, but a large surplus remains in the main river. The amount of arable land is far in excess of the water supply, but some considerable expense for dams and canals would be necessary to utilize the whole amount.

It is probable that a portion of the Virgin River can be used to advantage below the Beaver Dam Mountains in Nevada, and that a sufficient amount to irrigate 25 square miles can be used to good advantage in Utah.

The time when the volume of available water furnished by any stream bears the least ratio to the demands of the growing crops is the most critical period in the cultivation of the soil where artificial irrigation is a necessity. This time, depending as it does upon the crops cultivated, the character of the soil, and the source of the water supply, whether from springs or from melting snows, differs in different localities. In the valley of the Virgin it occurs in June.

At this time the river, though not at flood height, which occurs in April, carries a large volume of water, and, by reason of the source of this supply being in the rapidly melting snows of the Colob Plateau, is decreasing but slowly, and thus the amount available at this critical period bears a greater ratio to the flood of the stream than is usual in Utah. But little information has been obtained concerning the amount of water necessary to irrigate an acre. It is thought, however, to be much greater than in any other portion of Utah.

KANAB CREEK

Kanab Creek rises in springs bursting from underneath the cliffs forming the southern boundary of the Pauns-a-gunt Plateau, and flows southward until it joins the Colorado River in Arizona. Small areas of arable land are found along its course after it has descended to an altitude of 7,500 feet, and thence until it passes beyond the boundaries of Utah. The largest area in one body is in Kanab Valley, at the foot of the Vermilion Cliffs. It is greatly in excess of the water supply, is at an altitude of about 5,000 feet, has a fertile soil, and requires but comparatively a small amount of irrigation. The amount actually under cultivation in 1877 is placed by the best information attainable at 700 acres. The critical period in the cultivation of this area occurs in June. At that time the stream is falling rapidly, and crops have sometimes been seriously damaged. Estimates of the volume of water in the stream, made at different seasons and in different years, give 15 cubic feet per second as the flow in June. Some desultory attempts have been made to increase the supply by ponding, the cañon through the Vermilion Cliffs above the arable lands affording many opportunities. When this improvement is made on some well considered and well executed plan, and the waterways flumed through some bad sandy ground that now absorbs much water, the amount available at the critical period can be at least doubled.

Some years ago a settlement was established at the foot of the Pink Cliffs, on the headwaters of the Kanab, but the town site was eventually abandoned because of the deep snows of winter and the frosts of summer.

THE PARIA RIVER

The Paria River rises under the eastern escarpment of the Pauns-a-gunt Plateau, at about the same altitude as Kanab Creek, and flows in a southwesterly course for 100 miles, joining the Colorado in Arizona. Through the greater part of its course the river flows in a deep cañon, but near its head, and at an altitude of 6,000 feet, the cañon expands into a valley. Lower in its course, and at an altitude of 4,500 feet, the cañon again widens into a smaller valley. These are the only areas of arable lands within its drainage basin in Utah. The larger contains 15 and the smaller 10 square miles. In August, 1874, this stream flowed 30 cubic feet per second in the upper valley. The flow in the lower would be one-third greater. High water occurs in April or early in May. At this time the volume is three times greater than in August. Settlements have been made in both valleys, and quite a large area is under cultivation. The soil is excellent.

The critical period in irrigation is the latter part of June or early in July. At this time the stream probably carries 40 feet per second. The land in the lower valley is much subject to flooding from heavy showers that, falling on the table lands and mesas in the upper portion of the drainage basin, pour a torrent often beyond the capacity of the channel to convey through the lower valley. So great was the damage done by these floods in sweeping away dams, breaking through ditches, and inundating the growing crops at the site first selected for settlement, that it was abandoned after three years' occupation, and other parts, where these sudden rushes could be controlled, selected. Considerable difficulty has been experienced in the lower valley from the vast amount of argillaceous sediment deposited on it. So great during the floods is this deposit from the water used in irrigation that the ground becomes completely coated with an impervious layer, and growing crops, especially of small grains, suffer from the inability of the soil to absorb the water conducted on it. The irrigating capacity of this stream during the critical period could be greatly increased by the construction of reservoirs in which to store the great surplus of water that flows earlier in the season. The cañons above the valleys offer very favorable opportunities for building the necessary dams and embankments.

THE ESCALANTE RIVER

This stream enters the Colorado next north of the Paria. It rises under the wall forming the eastern face of the Aquarius Plateau; flows first northeast, then east, and finally southeast, before reaching the Colorado. Its length is 90 miles, the lower three-fourths being in a narrow cañon having vertical walls ranging from 900 to 1,200 feet in height. Through this gorge the river sweeps, sometimes filling the whole space from wall to wall; sometimes winding from side to side in a flood plain of sand, and always shifting its bed more or less with every freshet. Not an acre of accessible arable land is known in the whole length of the cañon, and its depth precludes the possibility of using the waters of the river on the lands above. Near the head of the southern branch of the Escalante, in what is known as Potato Valley, and at an elevation of about 5,000 feet, is an area of about 6 square miles of available land. The flow of water in this branch was 90 cubic feet per second in July, 1875. A portion of this area is now under cultivation, and is said to produce good crops. A portion of the east flank of the Aquarius Plateau is drained by a number of creeks that join the Escalante in the deep gorge below Potato Valley; but they all enter close cañons, in which no areas of arable land are known at an altitude low enough for successful cultivation. Part of the waters of these creeks might be used to irrigate grass lands at an altitude of about 8,000 feet; but the conditions of pasturage are such in this region that the amount practically available is small.

THE FREMONT RIVER

The largest branch of this stream rises in the Un-ca-pa-ga Mountains, and after flowing in an easterly direction for 125 miles enters the Colorado about 40 miles below the junction of the Grand and Green. It is joined by one considerable tributary, Curtis Creek, from the north, and another smaller, Tantalus Creek, from the south. The lower half of its course is through two deep cañons, separated by an intervening valley called Graves Valley, in which is an area of 10 square miles of arable land, with an altitude of 4,500 feet above sea level. On the upper waters of the main river, in what is known as Rabbit Valley, and at an altitude of nearly 7,000 feet, are 25 square miles of arable land of good quality. This area, from its altitude, should be subject to late and early frosts, but the warm sandy soil and southeastern slope of the whole valley will probably prevent much damage from this cause. The valley is now used as a herd ground for cattle belonging to the settlements in Sevier Valley, and the few experiments made by the herdsmen in cultivating the soil also indicate that the danger to be apprehended is slight. The volume of water flowing through Rabbit Valley in July, 1875, was 175 cubic feet per second.

Tantalus Creek drains the northern portion of the eastern slope of the Aquarius Plateau. It enters a close cañon at 8,000 feet altitude, and continues in cañons until it has passed through Water Pocket Fold. It then flows along a desolate valley at the foot of the fold until it joins the Fremont River. During the warmer months the water in this creek is usually absorbed and evaporated before reaching its mouth. In the valley at the foot of Water Pocket Fold are about 10 square miles of arable land; but the almost inaccessible situation of the valley and the desolation and ruggedness of the surrounding country may present insurmountable obstacles to its settlement.

Curtis Creek, the northern tributary of Fremont River, is formed by the union of several smaller streams that rise in the Wasatch Plateau. Debouching from the plateau, these branches flow across what is known as Castle Valley, and here, at an altitude of 6,000 feet, are 25 square miles of good arable land. They were measured in September, 1876, and gave an aggregated flow of 47 cubic feet per second. As they derive a greater part of their waters from the melting snows on the plateau, double this amount, or 94 cubic feet, would not be an overestimate of the volume during the irrigating season. After the union of these branches, the united

stream flows in a deep cañon until near its junction with the Fremont River in Graves Valley. Both Curtis Creek and the Fremont
receive some accessions to their volume from springs in the
cañons through which they flow above this valley. If all the
water in their upper courses should be used to irrigate lands in
Castle and Rabbit Valleys, a sufficient amount would be returned
to their channels by percolation to irrigate, with the addition of
the accessions in the cañons, all the arable land in Graves Valley.

THE SAN RAFAEL RIVER

This stream flows in an easterly course, and enters the Green
32 miles above the junction of that stream with the Grand. It has
three principal branches — Ferron, Cottonwood, and Huntington
Creeks — all rising in the Wasatch Plateau at an altitude of about
10,000 feet. These streams have a rapid fall in their upper courses,
and leave the plateau through almost impassable cañons cut in
its eastern wall overlooking Castle Valley. They flow across that
at intervals of a few miles apart, and, then uniting, cut a deep,
narrow cañon through the San Rafael Swell. Emerging from the
swell, the river flows across a low, broken country until its junction with the Green. The largest body of arable land within the
drainage basin of the San Rafael is in Castle Valley, a long,
narrow depression lying between the eastern escarpment of the
Wasatch Plateau and the San Rafael Swell. It is nearly 60 miles
in length from north to south, and has an average elevation of
6,000 feet above the sea. Its southern end, as has been before
mentioned, is drained by the tributaries of Curtis Creek, the
central portion by the three streams forming the San Rafael, and
the northern by Price River. No permanent settlements have
been made in the valley, but it is much used as a winter herding
ground for stock owned by the settlers in other portions of Utah.
Lying near the branches of the San Rafael that cross it, and in
such position that the water can be easily conducted over it, are
200 square miles of arable land, generally of good quality. East
of the San Rafael Swell, and lying on both sides of the river, at an
altitude of 4,000 feet, are 20 square miles of arable land, which
could be easily irrigated. The river was carefully measured in July,
1876, and the volume of flow found to be 1,676 cubic feet per

second. The three branches in Castle Valley were also measured, with results closely approximating the measurement of the united streams. These measurements were made at high water, though not when the streams were at their flood. As most of this volume is derived from the melting snow, which rarely disappears from the high plateau before the middle of July, the flow would be maintained with considerable steadiness during a large part of what would be the critical period in the irrigation of this valley. After the middle of July the decrease would be very rapid until September, and the lowest stage of water reached about the first of October, when the river would not flow probably more than 400 cubic feet.

THE PRICE RIVER

This river rises in the angle formed by the intersection of the Wasatch and Western Tavaputs Plateaus, receiving tributaries from both these table lands, and has a general easterly course for 100 miles. It crosses the northern end of Castle Valley, and then flows through a broken country near the foot of the escarpment called the Book Cliffs, forming the southern boundary of the Tavaputs Plateau, till within 20 miles of the Green River, when it cuts through this escarpment into the plateau and joins the Green a few miles above the foot of Gray Cañon. The arable lands along its course are mostly found in Castle Valley, where there are at least 50 square miles — a quantity considerably in excess of the irrigating capacity of the stream. The volume of water was measured in July, 1877, a few miles below where it debouches into Castle Valley, and found to be 189 cubic feet per second. It must suffer great loss from absorption, as the volume when leaving the cliffs is much greater, and the aggregated flow of the branches on the plateaus is at least twice as great.

MINNIE MAUD CREEK

This stream rises in the broken country, where the Western Tavaputs and Wasatch Plateaus break into the Uinta Mountains. It has a general easterly course, and joins the Green midway in the Cañon of Desolation. For the greater part of its course it flows in a cañon that widens enough occasionally to give a small area of arable land. One such area, containing 6 square miles, occurs at an altitude of 5,500 feet. Here the volume of water was measured in July, 1877, and found to be 16 cubic feet per second.

THE UINTA RIVER

This is the largest tributary emptying into the main drainage channel from the west. It rises in the Uinta Mountains, and has a southerly course for 65 miles. The Duchesne River, its western branch, rises in the same mountains, and the two streams unite only a few miles before the Uinta joins the Green. The drainage basin of the Uinta has an area of 1,300 square miles, lying between the altitudes of 4,500 and 7,000 feet above the sea. It has, generally speaking, a regular slope from the foot of the Uinta Mountains to the mouth of the streams, or in a direction toward the southeast. The surface of the basin is greatly diversified, consisting of broad reaches of bottom lands along the rivers; elevated, level, or gently sloping benches, sometimes partially arable, but oftener gravelly barrens; broken, rock-faced terraces; and low cliffs and ridges. It is difficult to estimate the amount of arable land. All the bottom lands are such, and can be easily irrigated. The streams have a rapid fall, but flow near the surface, and no deep cañons are found anywhere in the basin. This renders it possible to conduct the water over considerable areas of bench land, and wherever the soil of these is sufficiently fertile, selections of good farming land can be made. Above the limit in altitude for successful cultivation, large tracts of meadow lands can be irrigated. Those best acquainted with the extent of these classes of land place the arable, including irrigable natural meadow lands, at 40 per cent of the whole basin. This would give an area of 520 square miles, and I do not think it is an overestimate. The volume of water flowing in the Duchesne River above its junction with Lake Fork was measured in August, 1877, and found to be 1,011 cubic feet per second. The Uinta was measured above its junction with the Duchesne in October, 1877, and then flowed 214 cubic feet per second. These streams all rise in high mountains, from whose summits the snow is never completely melted. The line of highest water is usually in June, but the flow is well sustained through July. After that the volume rapidly decreases, and lowest water occurs in October. The critical period in the irrigation of this basin would occur in August. I think it may safely be assumed that the measurements of the Duchesne and the Uinta represent the flow at the critical period, but that Lake Fork should be doubled. This would give 1,825 cubic feet per second, or enough to irrigate, at the assumed standard, 285 square miles, or 22 per cent. of the whole area of the basin, and indicates the Uinta drainage as one of the best, if not the best, agricultural valley in Utah.

ASHLEY FORK

This stream is the most northern tributary of the Green River south of the Uinta Mountains. It rises in that range, but at a lower altitude than the branches of the Uinta, and has a south-easterly course 48 miles in length. On its lower course, at an altitude of 5,500 feet, are 75 square miles of arable land of excellent quality, a few acres of which are now cultivated. There is sufficient water in the stream during the critical season to irrigate 25 square miles.

HENRYS FORK

But a small portion of the valley of Henrys Fork lies within the Territory of Utah, but this portion includes its best lands. A beautiful natural meadow is here found, affording a large quantity of hay to the ranchmen of that country. The altitude is great, the valley being 6,000 feet above the level of the sea, and hence liable to late and early frosts.

About 10 square miles can be redeemed by irrigation. The volume of the stream is sufficient to irrigate a much larger tract, but a part is needed for other lands which lie farther up the river, within the Territory of Wyoming.

THE WHITE RIVER

The White River enters the Green from the east, about two miles below the mouth of the Uinta. This stream rises in Colorado, and has only a small portion of its course in Utah, but lying within the boundaries of the Territory are 75 square miles of arable land which may be irrigated with its water. The river was measured in October, 1877, near its mouth, and flowed 734 cubic feet per second. High water usually occurs in June, and the critical period in the irrigation of the land is probably in August, when the stream should flow at least double the volume of October, or, 1,468 cubic feet per second. This would be greatly in excess of the amount needed to irrigate the available land in Utah, and, from the best information attainable, it seems doubtful if it could be used higher up on the course of the stream.

THE GREEN RIVER

Brown's Park. — Brown's Park is a valley through which the Green River meanders. Three or four small streams head in the mountains to the north and a like number in the mountains to the south and find their way into the river in the midst of the park. But a small portion of the park lies within Utah and the small streams will be used for irrigation in the portion which falls in Colorado. The flood plain lands of the Green are extensive, and here many natural meadow lands are found, interspersed with fine groves of cottonwood. Some of the bench lands are well adapted to irrigation, but a portion of them and the foot hills back of them are naked, valueless bad-lands.

When the general industries of the country shall warrant the great expenditure necessary, the Green will be taken out to irrigate the bench lands on either side. About 10 square miles of these bench lands will fall within Utah.

Below Split Mountain Cañon — Lying along the Green, and between the foot of Split Mountain Cañon and the mouth of the Uinta, are 50 square miles of arable land. Some portions of this may be subject to inundations at times of extraordinary floods, but the greater part is above high water mark. Green River here carries sufficient water to irrigate many times this amount of land, and while the cost for the construction of suitable dams and canals would be greater than on smaller streams, neither this nor the engineering skill required would be beyond the resources of any ordinary settlement.

Gunnison Valley — In Gunnison Valley, below the foot of Gray Cañon, are 25 square miles of arable land. The cost of constructing the necessary irrigation works at this point would be greater than above the mouth of the Uinta, but still not beyond the ability of a colony. Green River flowed in Gunison Valley in September, 1877, 4,400 cubic feet of water per second, enough to irrigate at the standard adopted 860 square miles. There seems to be no arable land to which it is possible to take this great surplus, and probably for many years to come it will be suffered to flow "unvexed to the sea."

The area colored on the map is much greater than above indicated. The selections of irrigable lands will be made on either side of the river, in patches, within the colored district.

THE GRAND RIVER

The Grand River has but a small amount of arable land along its course in Utah, and flows for most of the distance in a close cañon. The volume of the stream, about 40 miles above its junction with the Green, was measured in September, 1877, and found to be 4,860 feet per second. It is probable that selections can be made to the extent of 40 square miles from the areas colored on the map.

THE SAN JUAN RIVER

But little is known concerning the arable lands or volume of water in the valley of the San Juan. It flows for the most of its course through Utah in a cañon, and all the arable land is thought to be so much subject to overflow that cultivation is impracticable.

OTHER STREAMS

A few smaller streams are also tributary to the Colorado and Green within the Territory of Utah, but they mostly flow in deep cañons, are often dry in some portion of their course during every year, have at best only a few acres of arable land anywhere along their courses, and have been omitted in this report.

The following table gives a summary of the facts relating to the flow of the several streams and the amount of arable and irrigable lands in the districts described above:

Name of stream			Estimated volume of flow during irrigating season (Feet per second)	Square miles of irrigable land	Acres of irrigable land
Virgin River			...	30	19,200
Kanab Creek			15	2½	1,600
Paria River			40	6	3,840
Escalante River			...	6	3,840
Fremont River			269	38	24,320
San Rafael River			1,118	175	112,000
Price River			189	11	7,040
Minnie Maud Creek			16	3	1,920
Uinta River			1,825	285	182,400
Ashley Fork			...	25	16,000
Henrys Fork			...	10	6,400
White River			1,468	75	48,000
Browns Park	}	Green River {	...	10	6,400
Below Split Mountain Cañon	}	Green River {	4,400	50	32,000
Gunnison Valley	}	Green River {	...	25	16,000
Grand River			4,860	40	25,000
Total			...	791½	506,560

CHAPTER X

LAND GRANTS IN AID OF INTERNAL IMPROVEMENTS

By Willis Drummond, Jr.

The land grant system in favor of internal improvements has become a well settled policy of this Government, and has attained not only a social but a political importance.

Like other American institutions its growth has been rapid, and donations of that character now cover millions of acres of the public domain. Of grants for railroads, wagon roads, and canals alone, however, will this chapter treat, and no reference other than necessary to a proper examination of the question will be made to concessions whose terms place the lands under specific disposal by the States, such as those for the establishment of schools, reclamation of swamp lands, etc.

The majority of grants, therefore, coming within our notice will be those in aid of railroads, though many have been made in favor of wagon roads and canals. The latter have, however, almost become things of the past, and are rapidly being superseded by the railway. More than one canal has given way to the more popular and general means of transportation, and it is safe to say that no further donations for canal purposes will be made, unless the circumstances should be such as to absolutely demand that means of conveyance. At any rate, they will not be made for purposes of general improvement.

The object of this chapter is to point out the origin, growth, character, and extent of these concessions.[1] It is therefore necessary to inquire into the early donations for various purposes.

[1] The map published with the *Arid Region* report, showing land grants in aid of railroads, wagon roads, and canals, is somewhat misleading, since it does not anywhere on its face indicate that the grants shown were generally alternate sections, and thus the total acreage granted was actually half what the map appears to show.

The first act making a donation in favor of internal improvements was approved on the 30th of April, 1802, and was entitled "An act to enable the people of the eastern division of the territory northwest of the river Ohio to form a constitution and State government, and for the admission of such State into the Union on an equal footing with the original States, and for other purposes."

By the third proviso to the seventh section of that statute, "one-twentieth part of the net proceeds of the lands lying within the said State sold by Congress, from and after the thirtieth day of June next, after deducting all expenses incident to the same," was granted and given to the said State (Ohio), and was to be applied to the laying out and making of public roads leading to the Ohio River, to the said State, and through the same, from the navigable waters emptying into the Atlantic. Such roads were to be laid out under the authority of Congress, with the consent of the several States through which they passed.

By an act approved March 3, 1803, the Secretary of the Treasury was directed to pay, to such persons as the legislature of the State of Ohio should designate, 3 per cent of the net proceeds, as above, which sums were to be applied to laying out, opening, and making roads within said State.

These acts, I believe, are the first two touching public improvements through congressional aid. Of course there had previously been many donations of land in favor of various persons, but they were for services rendered the Government, or special preëmption privileges.

Legislation similar to the acts above referred to, was enacted until the year 1824, varying only in the extent of the proceeds granted.

By an act approved May 26, 1824, the State of Indiana was authorized to open and build a canal, and the right of way with 90 feet of land on each side thereof, was granted, subject to use and occupancy for the purposes specified. Nothing, however, was done under that act by the State; and on the 2d of March, 1827, it was superseded by an act of greater extent. On that day two acts were passed giving to Indiana and Illinois, respectively, certain lands in aid of the construction of canals, the first to connect the navigation of the Wabash River with the waters of Lake

Erie, and the second to connect the waters of the Illinois River with those of Lake Michigan. A quantity of land, equal to one-half of five sections in width on each side of said canals, was granted, reserving to the United States each alternate section. The canals were to remain public highways for the use of the Government, free from toll or other charge whatever; were to be commenced in five years, and completed in twenty years, or the States were bound to pay to the United States "the amount of any lands previously sold," and the titles of the purchasers under the States were to be valid.

As soon as the lines of the canals were fixed and the selections of land were made, the States had power to sell, and give fee simple title to the whole or any part of the lands.

These may, properly, be considered the initiatory concessions of lands in favor of internal improvements.

As stated, a grant for right of way had been made, but that right was solely one of use and occupancy. In this case the right of the States to sell became absolute upon the selection of the lands. To be sure, they were liable to repay the Government the price received by the sale of any of the lands, but the titles of their purchasers were to be in "fee;" and by such right of disposal they were enabled to realize at once on their grant, and thereby secure a speedier construction of the canals.

On the same day (March 2) there was also granted to Indiana a certain strip of land formerly held by the Pottawatamie Indians, or the proceeds from the sale thereof, to be applied in building a road from Lake Michigan, via Indianapolis, to some convenient point on the Ohio River.

On the next day (March 3) an act was approved granting to Ohio one-half of two sections along the entire line of a road to be constructed from Sandusky to Columbus.

By an act approved May 23, 1828, a grant of 400,000 acres of "the relinquished lands" in certain counties in Alabama was made in aid of the improvement of the Tennessee and other rivers in that State; and in case that amount of "said relinquished lands" could not be found unappropriated, the necessary quantity could be selected from another section of the State. Provision was made for the sale of the lands, at the minimum price, but in case said lands or the proceeds thereof were applied to any purposes other than that for which they were granted, the grant was to become null and void.

In this grant we find the first provisions for indemnity if the grant was not full by reason of prior sales or disposals by the Government. There, if the lands were not to be found "in place," selections "in lieu" could be made from another county.

Grants like the one just referred to were made from time to time, differing but little in their character and extent.

By an act approved March 2, 1833, the State of Illinois was authorized to apply the lands granted by the act of March 2, 1827, for canal purposes, to the construction of a railroad instead; and the same restrictive impositions were continued.

This is the first act looking to the construction of a railroad through the assistance of land donations.

The railroad system was then but in its infancy, and the few miles built had been constructed by private means.

It is proper to add, however, that the State did not avail itself of the privilege granted, for it subsequently built a canal.

An act approved March 3, 1835, granted, for the purpose of aiding in the construction of a railroad by a corporation organized in Florida, the right of way through the public lands over which it might pass, thirty feet of land on each side of its line, and the right to take and use the timber for "one hundred yards" on each side for the construction and repair of said road; it was also granted "ten acres of land at the junction of the St. Mark's and Waculla Rivers," the point where said road terminated. This was the first right of way grant in favor of railroads, the previous grant having been for a canal.

Following this came an act approved July 2, 1836, granting the right of way "through such portion of the public lands as remain unsold," not to exceed 80 feet in width, to the New Orleans and Nashville Railroad Company. The first section of that statute required that a description of the route and surveys should be filed in the General Land Office within sixty days after the survey. The second section granted for depots, watering-places, and workshops, essential to the convenient use of the road, certain plats of land, not exceeding five acres in any one spot, nor nearer than fifteen miles to each other.

The third section gave the company the right to take from the public lands earth, stone, or timber necessary for the construction of the road; and provided that unless the work was commenced within two years after the approval of the act, and completed within eight years thereafter, the grant should "cease and determine." It provided, moreover, that if the road should be abandoned or discontinued, even after its completion, the grant was to "cease and determine."

So far as can be learned, this road was never completed. It is inserted so fully for the purpose of showing the gradual growth of the system.

Next to this came a grant to the East Florida and other railroads, similar in general terms to those previously referred to. It required, however, the companies to file, with the Commissioner of the General Land Office, maps showing the location of their roads. This was to be done within six months after such locations. I am unable to find that any of those roads were ever constructed. Certainly, no evidence thereof was ever furnished the General Land Office.

A grant similar to the one to the New Orleans and Nashville company was made by act of March 3, 1837, to the Atchafalaya Railroad and Banking Company in Louisiana.

Many grants of like character and extent were made from time to time, as also donations in favor of various other internal improvements. The greatest of these latter, however, were the grants in aid of improving the navigation of the Des Moines River in Iowa, and the Fox and Wisconsin Rivers in Wisconsin, which were approved August 8, 1846.

The first of these made a grant to the then Territory of Iowa, for the purpose of improving "the navigation of the Des Moines River from its mouth to the Raccoon Fork (so called), in said Territory," of "one equal moiety, in alternate sections, of the public lands (remaining unsold, and not otherwise disposed of, encumbered, or appropriated), in a strip five miles in width on each side of said river, to be selected within said Territory by an agent or agents to be appointed by the governor thereof, subject to the approval of the Secretary of the Treasury of the United States." The second section provided that "the lands hereby granted shall not be conveyed or disposed of by said Territory, nor by any State to be formed out of the same, except as said improvements shall progress; that is, the said Territory or State may sell so much of said lands as shall produce the sum of thirty thousand dollars, and then the sales shall cease until the governor of said Territory or State shall certify the fact to the President of the United States that one-half of said sum has been expended upon said improvement, when the said Territory or State may sell and convey a quantity of the residue of said lands sufficient to replace the amount expended, and thus the sales shall progress as the proceeds thereof shall be expended, and the fact of such expenditure shall be certified as aforesaid."

Section 3 declared that the river should forever remain a public highway for the use of the Government, free from toll or other charge whatever; and provided that the Territory or State should not dispose of the lands at a price less than the minimum price of public lands.

The grant to Wisconsin for the improvement of the Fox and Wisconsin Rivers, though approved the same day, was somewhat different from the Des Moines grant. It provided that "there be, and hereby is, granted to the State of Wisconsin," upon the admission of Wisconsin as a State (which, by the way, had been provided for by an act approved two days before), "for the purpose of improving the navigation of the Fox and Wisconsin Rivers in the Territory of Wisconsin, and of constructing the canal to unite the said rivers, at or near the portage, a quantity of land, equal to one-half of three sections in width on each side of said Fox River, and the lakes through which it passes from its mouth to the point where the portage canal shall enter the same, and on each side of said canal from one stream to the other, reserving the alternate sections to the United States, to be selected under the direction of the governor of said State, and such selection to be approved by the President of the United States." The rivers, when improved, were to remain forever public highways for the use of the Government, free from toll; and the sections reserved to the United States were not to be sold for less than $2.50 per acre.

By the second section, the legislature of the State was to accept the grant and fix the price at which the lands were to be sold (at not less than $1.25 per acre), and adopt such kind and plan of improvement as was for the best interests of the State.

The provisions for the sale of the lands were the same as in the

Iowa grant, except that the sum to be realized by such sales was fixed at $20,000.

Section 3 required the work to be commenced within three years after the admission of the State, and to be completed within twenty years, or the United States was to be entitled to receive the amount for which any of the lands may have been sold; the titles in the purchasers from the State were, however, to be valid.

The language employed in this statute was more definite than that used in the Des Moines grant, and in it is to be found the first provisions respecting the increase in price of the reserved sections.

Probably no grant of this character has received such widespread notoriety as the one for the improvement of the Des Moines River. It is owing, no doubt, in a great degree to the numerous conflicting decisions by the Executive Departments touching the extent of the grant. The Hon. R. J. Walker, Secretary of the Treasury [2] (under whose supervision the Land Office then came), decided on the 2d of March, 1849, that the grant extended above the tributary of the Des Moines River commonly known as the Raccoon Fork. The Land Office soon thereafter passed from the jurisdiction of the Treasury Department, and was placed as one of the bureaus of the Home or Interior Department. The Secretary of this lately established branch of the Government (Hon. Thomas Ewing) [3] decided on the 6th of April, 1850, that the grant did not extend above the Raccoon Fork. From that decision the State of Iowa appealed to the President, who laid the matter before the Attorney-General. That officer (Hon. Reverdy Johnson),[4] on July 19, 1850, expressed an opinion confirmatory of the decision of Secretary Walker. The Secretary of the Interior, however, being determined in his views, did not adopt the opinion of the Attorney-General, and the Commissioner of the General Land Office wrote, under date of 26th September, 1850, to the President, reviewing and objecting to the opinion of Mr. Johnson. The President, having been again applied to by the

[2] Robert John Walker (1801–1869) held this office in the Polk administration (1844–1849).

[3] Ewing (1789–1876) became Secretary of the new Department of the Interior in 1849 by appointment of President Zachary Taylor.

[4] Johnson (1796–1876) served in the Senate 1845–1849 before becoming Attorney-General under President Taylor.

State of Iowa to determine the matter, referred the whole question to the Attorney-General (then Hon. J. J. Crittenden).[5] That officer, without delivering an opinion on the merits of the case, expressed the belief that the President ought not to interfere, but should leave such questions to the proper officers. The then Secretary of the Interior (Hon. A. H. H. Stuart) [6] thereupon decided that the grant did not extend above the fork, but subsequently decided to approve the selections for lands above the fork. Attorney-General Cushing,[7] on the 29th of May, 1856, expressed the belief that on the merits of the case the grant was limited to the Raccoon Fork, but as Secretary Stuart had approved selections above that point, such practical enforcement of the grant had better be continued. The view of Mr. Cushing was subsequently maintained by the Supreme Court of the United States in Railroad Company vs. Litchfield (23 Howard, page 66). By the act of Congress approved July 12, 1862, the grant was extended to the northern boundary of the State, so as to include the alternate odd numbered sections lying within five miles of said river, upon the following conditions: The lands were to be held and applied in accordance with the provisions of the original grant, except that the consent of Congress was given to the application of a "a portion thereof" to aid in the construction of the Keokuk, Fort Des Moines and Minnesota Railroad, in accordance with the provisions of an act of the general assembly of the State approved March 22, 1858.

It is well to state that the work of improving the river was abandoned, and the railroad was constructed instead.

Without examining the numerous right of way and other lesser grants, I desire to direct attention to what is generally considered the *first* railroad grant. Reference is made to the donation by the act of September 20, 1850.

By that statute a grant was made to the State of Illinois of "every alternate section of land designated by even numbers, for six sections in width on each side of" the road and branches

---

[5] John Jordan Crittenden (1787–1863) was appointed Attorney-General by President Fillmore (1850–1853).

[6] Alexander Hugh Holmes Stuart (1807–1891) was President Fillmore's Secretary of the Interior (1850–1853).

[7] Caleb Cushing (1800–1879) was Attorney-General in the Pierce administration (1852–1856).

therein provided for. The road to be built was from the southern terminus of the Illinois and Michigan Canal to a point at or near the junction of the Ohio and Mississippi Rivers, with a branch of the same to Chicago, and another via the town of Galena, in Illinois, to the town of Dubuque, in Iowa.

The second section provided that should it appear that the United States had, when the lines of said road and branches were definitely fixed, sold any part of any section thereby granted, or that the right of preëmption had attached to the same, it should be lawful for any agent or agents (to be appointed by the governor of the State) to select so much land as would be equal to the tracts lost within the granted limits. This "indemnity" was to be selected within fifteen miles of the road and branches.

The third section provided that the sections and parts of sections which by the operation of the grant remained to the United States within six miles on each side of said road and branches, should not be sold for less than the double minimum price when sold.

Section 4 provided for the disposal of the lands, and declared that the road should remain a public highway for the use of the Government free from toll or other charge.

The fifth section declared within what period the roads should be completed, and provided that in the event of a failure on the part of the State to comply with the conditions of the grant, it was "bound to pay to the United States the amount which may be received upon the sale of any part of said lands by said State." The title of the purchasers was to be valid, but the tracts not sold were to revert and revest in the United States.

Section 6 said that the mails were to be transported at all times at such price as Congress might direct.

By the seventh section the grant was extended, on the same terms and conditions, to the States of Alabama and Mississippi, for the purpose of aiding in the construction of a road from Mobile to connect with the first above named road.

While this was not the first concession of lands in favor of railroads, it may properly be considered the initiatory measure of the present system. It granted specific sections instead of one-half of a certain number of sections; provided in positive terms for "indemnity" for lands lost to the grant; designated the manner in which the lands should be disposed of; increased the price of the reserved sections within the "granted" limits; provided for reversion in case of default, and virtually established a form of grant which was differed from but little in succeeding donations. It was the first railroad grant that became effective, for of all previous ones none appear to have been developed. The roads are now known as the Illinois Central and branches, and the Mobile and Ohio.

For the following two years no grants of importance were made, until by an act approved June 10, 1852, a donation was made to the State of Missouri for the construction of certain roads therein, now known as the Hannibal and Saint Joseph, and the Missouri Pacific, Southwest Branch. This grant was similar in character and extent to that to Illinois, save two sections — one providing for the disposal of the lands, and the other directing the Secretary of the Interior to offer at public sale, from time to time, at the increased price, the "reserved" or Government sections. The section respecting the disposal of the lands is as follows: "That the lands hereby granted to said State shall be disposed of by said State in manner following, that is to say: that a quantity of land, not exceeding one hundred and twenty sections on each road, and included within a continuous length of twenty miles of said road, may be sold; and when the governor of said State shall certify to the Secretary of the Interior that said twenty miles of road is completed, then another like quantity of land, hereby granted, may be sold; and so from time to time until said road is completed; and if said road be not completed within ten years, no further sales shall be made, and the lands unsold shall revert to the United States."

With the exceptions stated, and the omission of the clause requiring the State to reimburse the Government for lands sold, the grants are identical.

That act was followed by an act approved February 9, 1853, making, under like conditions and impositions, a similar grant to Arkansas, in aid of certain roads in that State. In this, however, the clause or section directing the Secretary to "offer" the lands was omitted.

For the next three years Congress seems to have been quite as liberal in donations for other purposes, but no grants were made in aid of railroads, unless note be made of a grant to Minnesota by act of June 29, 1854, which was repealed in August following.

By that act there was granted to the Territory of Minnesota, for the purpose of aiding in the construction of a railroad from the southern line of said Territory, via Saint Paul, to the eastern line of the Territory in the direction of Lake Superior, "every alternate section of land designated by odd numbers for six sections in width on each side of said road within said Territory;" but in case it should appear that the United States had, when the line of the road was definitely fixed, sold any section or any part thereof granted, or that the right of preëmption had attached to the same, then it should be lawful for any agent or agents to be appointed by the governor of said Territory, subject to the approval of the Secretary of the Interior, to select lands from alternate sections within fifteen miles of the road to make up the deficiency. The lands granted were to be applied to the construction of the road only. Section 2 increased the price of the "reserved" tracts.

Section 3 provided that the lands should be disposed of by the legislature for the purposes aforesaid and were not to inure to the benefit of any company then constituted or organized. The road was to remain a highway, as in previous grants; and the lands could not be sold until they had first been "offered" at the increased price.

By section 4 no title was to vest in said Territory or patent issue for any part of the lands until a continuous length of twenty miles of said road had been completed; and when the Secretary of the Interior was satisfied that any twenty continuous miles of said road had been completed, then patent was to issue for a quantity not exceeding one hundred and twenty sections of land; and so on from time to time until the road was completed. If the road was not completed within ten years no further sales could be made, and the lands remaining unsold were to revert.

By an act approved August 4, 1854, the act of June 29, 1854, was repealed; and although four grants have been declared forfeited, for failure of the grantees to perform the required conditions, this is the only one which Congress has in terms repealed.

It is to be regretted that subsequent legislation was not as devoid of ambiguity. Had it been, much embarrassment might have been saved the Government. I refer particularly to that clause or section respecting the vesting of title and the manner in which the State was to acquire rights under the grant. By the terms thereof no patents were to issue except as the work of building the road progressed.

By the omission of such language from the grants subsequently made from time to time to as late as 1862, the Department of the Interior believed that the duty of "disposal" was properly in the States charged with executing the trusts; and in all the earlier grants, immediately upon the location of the roads and determination of the limits of the grants, certified, in whole, the lands to which the companies would ultimately have been entitled had the roads been completed as required. At that time there was but little doubt that all of the roads would be rapidly constructed; but the civil conflict very naturally put a stop to such extended improvements, and to-day about twenty railroads remain uncompleted, and the lands certified to the States for their use and benefit exceed by 1,058,295.86 acres the lands actually earned by the portions of the several roads constructed.

Out of the act of June 29, 1854, and the repealing statute a very interesting question arose, which received, ultimately, the consideration of the Supreme Court. A suit was brought in trespass by Edmund Rice against the Minnesota and Northwestern Railroad Company, for cutting timber on a tract of land in Minnesota. The company, in its defense, set up title under the granting act aforesaid; to which plaintiff replied, reciting the repealing statute. On demurrer by the company, the question as to whether an interest had vested under said grant was thus fairly presented to the Supreme Court. That body decided, after elaborate review of the whole case, that the act of August 4 was "a valid law," and that no interest, beneficiary or otherwise, had vested under the said grant.

In 1856, at different times, various grants were made to the States of Iowa, Florida, Alabama, Louisiana, Michigan, Wisconsin, and Mississippi, and on the 3d of March, 1857, to Minnesota.

An examination of these grants — say the one to Iowa, it being first of the series — shows that, with the exception of the fact that the sections granted were designated by *odd* instead of *even* numbers, they were similar to the Missouri grant of 1852. The change there inaugurated was owing to the fact that certain even sections in each township had been previously given to the several States for school purposes, and in a grant embracing a large territory the difference to the railroad grants caused thereby would be considerable. From 1857 until 1862 Congress seems to have been otherwise engaged, for I am unable to find that any acts were passed during that period touching railroad grants.

By an act approved July 1, 1862, a new departure was taken. Certain persons were created into a body corporate under the title and name of the "Union Pacific Railroad Company." The object thereof was the construction and maintenance of a railroad and telegraph line from the Missouri River to the Pacific Ocean.

They were granted the right of way through the public lands to the extent of two hundred feet in width on each side of the line of road, together with the necessary grounds for stations, buildings, workshops, etc. They were also granted in aid of the construction of the road "every alternate section of public land," designated by odd numbers, to the amount of five alternate sections per mile, on each side of the road; and all lands which had been disposed of or reserved, and mineral lands, were excepted.

Sections 5 and 11 of the act related to the issuance of bonds by the United States. Section 7 required the company to file a map of its general route, and directed the Secretary of the Interior to thereupon withdraw the lands within fifteen miles of such line.

Various other roads were provided for upon the same conditions, now known as the Central Pacific, Central Branch of the Union Pacific, Kansas Pacific, and Sioux City and Pacific.

As it is not the purpose of this inquiry to look into any provisions except such as relate to *land* donations, I will not pursue the sections respecting the issuance of bonds, payment of interest, etc. But, before proceeding further, it is proper to notice the changes inaugurated by that act.

In the first place, the grant was to a corporation direct, and not to a State in trust for one.

Second. It was not confined to any particular State or section, but was transcontinental in character, extending in this case more than half across our country.

Third. It was a grant ten miles in width on each side, instead of six, as in previous grants, and no provision was made for indemnity.

Fourth. It provided for the filing by the company of a map of its general or designated route (before definite location of its line); and upon the filing thereof the lands became legislatively reserved or withdrawn.

By an act approved July 2, 1864, this act was amended in several particulars, and instead of "five" sections "ten" were granted, thereby increasing the limits from ten to twenty miles on each side of the roads. The term "mineral land" was construed not to include "coal and iron land."

By section 19 of this latter act a grant was made to the Burlington and Missouri River Railroad Company, for the construction of a road from the Missouri River to some point not farther west than the one hundredth meridian of west longitude to connect with the Union Pacific road, of ten alternate sections per mile on each side of its line of road. It has been decided that this company was not confined to any limit, but could go far enough to secure the quantity granted, and it is the only railroad whose grant is not confined to lateral limits. By a proviso to the twentieth section, however, the company received no bonds.

The rapidity with which the Union Pacific road was constructed was surprising, and the whole progress of the work displayed a spirit of energy seldom seen in an undertaking of that character. The most positive achievements, however, were those of the Central Pacific Company. The construction of that road over the Sierras is considered by professional authorities as one of the greatest results of engineering. It crossed the maximum summit, of 7,042 feet above the sea, within one hundred miles of the Pacific tide waters, requiring a distribution of ascent really scientific to render it practicable, and, by using a minimum radius of 573 feet, secured, comparatively speaking, a direct alignment.

The two roads were completed and a junction effected May 10, 1869, and the initial transcontinental line was thereby finished.

By an act approved March 3, 1863, there was a grant made to

the State of Kansas to aid in constructing certain railroads therein, now known as the Atchison, Topeka and Santa Fé; Leavenworth, Lawrence and Galveston, and Missouri, Kansas and Texas. It was of every alternate section of land designated by odd numbers for ten sections in width on each side of said roads. Indemnity was provided in ten additional miles and, except as to extent, it was not unlike the Iowa grant.

On the 5th of May, 1864, similar grants were made to the States of Minnesota and Wisconsin, and on the 12th of May to the State of Iowa. Various other grants followed of like character, differing only in few respects, to Arkansas, Alabama, Missouri, Iowa, Michigan, Minnesota, and Kansas; as also grants for wagon roads. The latter were similar in terms to the railroad grants, save that three sections on either side of the roads were given instead of six or ten. The Northern Pacific was created July 1, 1864, and was very much like the Union Pacific grant, except in extent, being double the quantity through the Territories, with provision for "indemnity." The Atlantic and Pacific and Southern Pacific grants were made by act of July 27, 1866; the Denver Pacific by act of March 3, 1869; the Southern Pacific (branch line) and Texas and Pacific by act of March 3, 1871.

Many of the grants made in early years were enlarged, and the time for their completion extended; but thus far only four grants have been declared forfeited. At present, however, about twenty grants have "lapsed" by reason of non-compliance with the terms of the granting acts, requiring completion within prescribed periods, and recommendations have been made urging proper legislation.

Neither time nor space permit an extended examination of every grant, but sufficient has been considered to point out the origin and growth of the system.

We have seen that the first donation was one-twentieth part of certain proceeds derived from the sale of lands; then ninety feet of land, followed soon by one-half of five sections per mile on each side; then by six sections; then by ten, and finally by twenty sections per mile on each side of the road.

If the lands granted, or in other words embraced within the limits of the grants, could be found available, the companies, not including those for canals or wagon roads, would receive, provided each built its road and complied with the laws, more than two hundred and fifteen million acres. That quantity if embraced in one compact body, would form an area of more than three hundred and thirty-five thousand square miles, or a tract of land more than seven times as large as the State of Pennsylvania, and only about six thousand miles less than the area of the thirteen original States. But, in fact, the grants will not realize near that quantity, and the estimate, as made by the Land Department, is only about one hundred and eighty-seven million acres.

By the aid of those grants, however, about fifteen thousand miles of road have been constructed. Those roads have been the means of developing vast fields of magnificent territory, and securing to the people many lesser lines built by private capital.

The various grants have been the subject of much explanatory, amendatory, and confirmatory legislation, and have also received numerous interpretations by the different courts. Of the latter, I deem it proper to refer only to the more important rulings of the Supreme Court which bear upon the fundamental principles underlying the whole system.

In nearly all grants, except the Pacific, provision has been made for indemnity in case it appeared, when the lines of the roads had been definitely fixed, that the United States had sold, disposed of, or reserved any of the sections or parts of sections contained within the grants. The theory has heretofore existed that "indemnity" was allowed for all tracts which might not be found subject to the operation of the grant; and selections have been permitted in lieu of such disposed of or reserved tracts.

A recent decision, however, casts some doubt upon the correctness of this theory. The question came up in a case from Kansas, under the act of March 3, 1863, and the court declared:

"We have before said that the grant itself was in præsenti, and covered all the odd sections which should appear, on the location of the road, to have been within the grant when it was made. The right to them did not, however, depend on such location, but attached at once on the making of the grant. It is true they could not be identified until the line of the road was marked out on the ground, but as soon as this was done it was easy to find them. If the company did not obtain all of them within the original limit, by reason of the power of sale or reservation retained by the United States, it was to be compensated by an equal amount of substituted lands. The latter could not, on any contingency, be selected within that limit. * * * It would be strange, indeed, if the [indemnity] clause had been intended to perform the office of making a new grant within the ten mile limit, or enlarging the one already made. Instead of this, the words employed show clearly that its only purpose is to give sections beyond that limit for those lost within it by the action of the government between the date of the grant and the location of the road. This construction gives effect to the whole statute, and makes each part consistent with the other."

If it be thought, however, that such was not the intention of the legislators who framed the statutes, consolation can be found in the construction given to the clause inserted in every grant, substantially as follows: "And the said road shall remain a public highway for the use of the Government, free from toll or other charge upon the transportation of troops or other property of the United States."

It is declared by the Supreme Court that the purpose of that clause was to allow the Government the right to place its locomotive engines and cars upon the railroad tracks, and to use such tracks as a public highway. The court says: "We are of opinion that the reservation in question secures to the Government only a free use of the railroads concerned; and that it does not entitle the Government to have troops or property transported by the companies over their respective roads free of charge for transporting the same."

The section providing for the disposal of the lands, recited in full in the Missouri grant of 1852, has been construed as vesting in the State the right to sell one hundred and twenty sections of land, contained within a continuous length of twenty miles at any place along the grant, even though the road contemplated was never built; and the title acquired by purchase from the State is valid. And the clause with which the section referred to ends, to the effect that if the road be not completed within a certain time the lands shall revert to the United States, has been declared inoperative without further action by the Government, either legislative or judicial, looking to an enforcement of the reserved right.

Fears have been awakened as to the power to ultimately control these corporations, on account of the enormous extent to which they have expanded; but, as has been said by an able writer, "this evil, however, if it be such, will probably work its own cure."

Be that as it may, their influences have been felt by all, and their benefits have extended to the remotest sections of our country. They have proved a bond between the eastern and western States — anxiously sought for by Washington when the lateral limits of the United States were less than half what they are at this time. They have united the Pacific with the Atlantic, and the Rocky Mountains of the west with the Alleghanies of the east. They have dispelled all ideas looking to the removal of the seat of Government, for they have put in direct communication the people of Oregon with the people of Maine. From ocean to ocean requires but days, where only a few years ago it required weeks.

In the past, long lines of moving wagons groaned beneath their loads of adventurous families, who at night, within the corral, seated themselves around the blazing camp fire, fearful of the dangers to which they were exposed. But the present has forgotten them. In their stead the ponderous wheels of frequent trains, moving with a speed surpassing that of the deer, traversing the valley and mountain, carry forward their loads of living freight; and, in place of dangerous encampments, provide means of sleep and refreshment, and afford the comforts of luxurious homes. The railway has brought to our doors the harvest of our fields; handed to our mints the vast resources of our mines, and opened to us direct communication with the older worlds. Its arms have extended into a hundred vales and over a hundred mountains, grasping in their embrace manifold evidence of civilization and prosperity.

INDEX

Abbott, 74
Abies amabilis, 116
Abies Canadensis, 114
Abies concolor, 114, 115
Abies Douglasii, 114, 115
Abies Engelmanni, 114, 115, 116
Abies grandis, 116
Abies Menziesii, 115, 116
Abies subalpina, 116
Acer grandidentata, 117
Agricultural land defined, 131
Agricultural resources: Bear River drainage basin, 133; Jordan River drainage basin, 135–138; Weber River drainage basin, 133–135
Agriculture: amount of rainfall necessary, 12, 13; communal institutions in Utah, 103; importance of Sevier River Valley, 142; influence of temperature, 12; land values dependent on water, 53; suitability of soils, 20; in Utah, dependent upon irrigation, 16, 17; utilization of small streams, 18; without irrigation, 13, 15, 61
Aira coespitosa, 123
Alabama, land grants, 180, 189, 192
Alkaline salts, 159, 160, 161
Antelope Island, 75–76, 81
Antelope Island Bar, 75–76, 81
Arid Region: boundaries, 11; extent, 15, 19; increase in water supply, 103–106; land system need, 36ff.; mining industries, 102; physical characteristics, 10; seasonal precipitation, 60
Arizona and New Mexico, seasonal precipitation, 67
Arkansas, land grants, 187, 192
Artemisia, 123, 155
Ashley Fork, 118, 163; irrigable lands, 174
Atchafalaya Railroad and Banking Company, land grant, 182
Atchison, Topeka and Santa Fe Railroad, land grant, 192
Atlantic and Pacific Railroad Company, land grant, 192

Barfoot, J. L., 71
Barton, 127
Bear River, 86, 131; irrigation by, 131, 132; mean flow, 86

Bear River Bay, 81
Bear River "City," 92
Bear River drainage basin, agricultural resources, 133
Beaver dams, effect of cutting, 88
Betula occidentalis, 117
Black Rock Bench, 74
Black Rock Pillar, 71, 72, 76
Blue Creek, 86
Bonneville Lake, 110
Book Cliffs, orographic structure, 112
Bouteloua oligostachya, 122
Bromus, 123
Brown Cliffs, orographic structure, 112
Brown's Park, irrigable lands, 175
Burlington and Missouri River Railroad Company, land grants, 191

Cache Valley, amount of irrigable land, 132
Canals, land grants for, 179, 180
Cañon Lands of Utah, 108, 119; coal lands, 120; description, 119; irrigable lands, 119–120; rivers, 108, 119
Carex Jamesii, 123
Carrington Island, 75
Castle Valley, 119
Celtis occidentalis, 117
Central Branch of Union Pacific Railroad Company, land grants, 190
Central Pacific Railroad Company, land grants, 190
Cercocarpus parvifolius, 124
Circle Valley, 143; amount of irrigable land, 150, 151, 152; physical characteristics, 150, 151
City Creek, measurement, 134
Coal, abundance of, 30
Coal lands, in Cañon Lands, 120; disposal of, 57; only easily accessible lands so classified, 57
Colony system, 40, 41
Colorado Basin, climate, 164; elevation, 164; irrigable lands, 165, 177; irrigation essential, 164; orographic structure, 109; precipitation, 164; source of water supply, 165; temperature, 164; volume of flow of streams, 177
Colorado River, principal tributaries, 163